Not White Enough, Not Black Enough

D1566931

This series of publications on Africa, Latin America, Southeast Asia, and Global and Comparative Studies is designed to present significant research, translation, and opinion to area specialists and to a wide community of persons interested in world affairs. The editor seeks manuscripts of quality on any subject and can usually make a decision regarding publication within three months of receipt of the original work. Production methods generally permit a work to appear within one year of acceptance. The editor works closely with authors to produce a high-quality book. The series appears in a paperback format and is distributed worldwide. For more information, contact the executive editor at Ohio University Press, The Ridges, 19 Circle Drive, Athens, Ohio 45701.

Executive editor: Gillian Berchowitz
AREA CONSULTANTS
Africa: Diane M. Ciekawy
Latin America: Thomas Walker
Southeast Asia: William H. Frederick
Global and Comparative Studies: Ann R. Tickamyer

The Ohio University Research in International Studies series is published for the Center for International Studies by Ohio University Press. The views expressed in individual volumes are those of the authors and should not be considered to represent the policies or beliefs of the Center for International Studies, Ohio University Press, or Ohio University.

Not White Enough, Not Black Enough

RACIAL IDENTITY IN THE SOUTH AFRICAN COLOURED COMMUNITY

Mohamed Adhikari

Ohio University Research in International Studies
Africa Series No. 83
Ohio University Press
Athens

Double Storey Books
Cape Town

14 13 12 11 10 09 08 07 06 05   5 4 3 2 1

The books in the Ohio University Research in International Studies Series
are printed on acid-free paper ⊗ ™

Published 2006 in Southern Africa by Double Storey Books,
a division of Juta & Co. Ltd, Mercury Crescent, Wetton, Cape Town, South Africa

ISBN 1 77013 002 0 (Double Storey)

Library of Congress Cataloging-in-Publication Data

Adhikari, Mohamed.
  Not white enough, not black enough : racial identity in the South African
coloured community / Mohamed Adhikari.
    p. cm. — (Ohio University research in international studies. Africa series ;
no. 83)
  Includes bibliographical references and index.
  ISBN 0-89680-244-2 (pbk. : alk. paper)
  1. Colored people (South Africa)—Race identity. 2. South Africa—Race relations.
I. Title. II. Research in international studies. Africa series ; no. 83.
  DT1768.C65A34 2006
  305.800968—dc22

                                                                    2005025268

For Rafiq and Zaheer

Contents

Acknowledgments

The long-germinating seed for this book and, more generally, my interest in the nature of Coloured identity was planted sometime in March or April 1979 when, as a second-year history student at the University of Cape Town, I went on one of my periodic visits to Marie Maud's office. Marie was a lecturer in the History Department, a colorful if somewhat eccentric figure. She was an inspired teacher who took a personal interest in her students and befriended many of them. Her office served as a congregating point for students where one could engage in discussion over a wide range of topics, particularly issues relating to contemporary politics in South Africa, over a cup of tea and a cigarette. By this time Marie had become a firm friend and a mentor despite my Non-European Unity Movement background teaching me to despise weak-kneed liberals. Marie might have been a self-proclaimed liberal but was not weak-kneed and did more than her share to undermine the apartheid system. On that late-afternoon excursion I encountered a forty-something first-year history student I had known for some weeks, in her office. He was a school principal from the tiny, conservative, northern Cape town of Keimoes who had taken a year's leave to complete his Bachelor of Arts degree at UCT. With his very fair skin and red hair he was obvioiusly white. After chatting for a while the principal from Keimoes left, whereupon Marie, in characteristically melodramatic fashion, said, "Mohamed, I feel so sorry for that poor man!" Immediately there flashed through my mind images of him being diagnosed with a dreaded disease, being informed that his wife had suddenly died or that one of his children had been run over by a bus. Upon inquiring what the matter was, Marie replied, "That poor man is Coloured. Can you imagine what it must be like for him living in Keimoes?" Marie had inadvertently provided future direction to my research, for in subsequent years, pondering the vagaries of life for a pale-skinned, red-haired, Coloured person in conservative Keimoes played an important part in my choice of research topics as a postgraduate student.

I would like to thank Richard Mendelsohn for his unflagging support, his wise counsel, and his incisive reading, as supervisor, of the doctoral thesis on which this book is based. On numerous occasions, I have drawn on the specialist knowledge of colleagues, and I have a memory of pestering Chris Saunders, Bill Nasson, Neville Alexander, and Satyendra Peerthum with esoteric questions. To these and others who have been willing to help, I am grateful. Special thanks are due to Robin Kayser and Shaheen Ariefdien for sharing with me their source material and research findings. I would also like to thank Colleen Petersen for her efficient and congenial help with a range of tasks. I am particularly indebted to her for being prepared to sacrifice time over a weekend to help me recover from a computer-related mishap. Many people, too numerous to mention here, have provided support and encouragement over the years. They have my undying gratitude. The efficient and courteous service of staff members at the African Studies Library at the University of Cape Town and the Cape Town branch of the National Library of South Africa is also greatly appreciated. I would, in addition, like to acknowledge research funding over several years from the University of Cape Town's University Research Committee. Funding from the National Research Foundation also helped ease the financial burden. Finally, the love and warmth of my sons, Rafiq and Zaheer, and a host of dear friends—including Shadow, Peggy, Ratso, Prince, Lady, Edgar, Oscar, and Junior (and hopefully Skipper will do his bit in the future)—have made the very rewarding task of producing this manuscript all the more enjoyable.

Introduction

The nature of Coloured identity, its history, and the implications it holds for South African society have evoked considerable interest in recent times. Debates around these issues have generated much controversy, yet there has been no systematic study of Coloured identity. At best, the current literature offers superficial attempts at analyzing its character or the social and political dynamic that informed Coloured exclusivism.

More recent studies on the history of the Coloured community focus narrowly on the racial oppression Coloured people suffered under white supremacy and on Coloured protest politics.[1] They largely ignore crucial questions relating to the nature of Coloured identity and the way in which it operated as a social identity. By either taking Coloured identity for granted—as something inherent that needs no explanation because it is the automatic product of miscegenation—or by portraying it as a false identity imposed on weak and vulnerable people by the ruling white minority, the existing literature minimizes the role that Coloured people played in the making of their own identity and presents an oversimplified image of the phenomenon. The most recent scholarly volume on the subject, a collection of essays edited by Zimitri Erasmus, a sociologist at the University of Cape Town, breaks with this pattern in that parts of it attempt an analysis of aspects of Coloured identity; further, it does not suffer the usual coyness about broaching sensitive issues such as racial hostility toward Africans within the Coloured community or the sense of shame that suffuses the identity. This work, however, consists of tightly focused contributions that collectively fail to provide a sustained narrative or consistent interpretation of the history or character of Coloured identity.[2]

This book aims to redress these imbalances and to contribute to a more nuanced understanding of the manner in which Colouredness functioned as a social identity from the time the South African state was formed in 1910 to the present. It analyzes the fundamental social and political impulses behind the assertion of a separate Coloured identity and explains processes of continuity and change in its expression throughout that period. This is achieved through close analysis of a range of key texts written by Coloured people in which they give expression to their identity as Coloured and reflect on the nature of their community, its past, and its place in the broader society. In addition to broad thematic analyses of Coloured identity, a series of chronologically arranged case studies are used to demonstrate the book's thesis.

The central argument of this study is that Coloured identity is better understood not as having undergone a process of continuous transformation during the era of white rule, as conventional historical thinking would have it, but as having remained essentially stable throughout that period. This is not to contend that Coloured identity was static or that it lacked fluidity but that the continuities during the period were more fundamental to the way in which it operated as a social identity and a more consistent part of its functioning than the changes it experienced. I argue that this stability was derived from a central core of enduring characteristics rooted in the historical experience and social situation of the Coloured community that regulated the way in which Colouredness functioned as a social identity under white domination. The principal constituents of this stable core are the Coloured people's assimilationism, which spurred hopes of future acceptance into the dominant society; their intermediate status in the racial hierarchy, which generated fears that they might lose their position of relative privilege and be relegated to the status of Africans; the negative connotations with which Coloured identity was imbued, especially the shame attached to their supposed racial hybridity; and finally, the marginality of the Coloured people, which caused them a great deal of frustration. Their marginality is the most important of these attributes, as it placed severe limitations on possibilities for social and political action. That marginality also put members of the Coloured community at the mercy of a ruling establishment that was generally unsympathetic to their needs and aspirations and that usually acted in prejudicial and sometimes even malicious ways toward them. The marked creativity in the way the identity is finding expression in the postapartheid environment accentuates its relative stability in the preceding period.

My initial intent was to provide a history of Coloured identity through the twentieth century and to show how it changed and developed during that period. The original assumption was that after its late nineteenth-century genesis, Coloured identity continually evolved through the twentieth century, with new departures such as the rise of the radical movement in the 1930s, the emergence of Black Consciousness thinking in the 1970s, and Coloured rejectionism in the 1980s representing periods of accelerated transformation. Faced with the empirical evidence and the actual task of explaining the evolution of Coloured identity, I was instead struck by how stable that identity had been throughout the era of white domination and how superficial the influences of earlier radical politics, Black Consciousness, and the rejectionist movement were. With the evidence failing to confirm my initial hypotheses, based on orthodox approaches within the discipline and assumptions in existing writing on the subject, a reconceptualization of Coloured identity and its history was clearly necessary. The result is a counterintuitive argument that through the era of white supremacy, Coloured identity is better understood as having been stable rather than as continually changing.[3]

Although it is recognized that broad parameters for the production and reproduction of Coloured identity were set by an authoritarian, white ruling establishment in control of an increasingly prescriptive state and that Coloured perceptions of the world were framed within a hegemonic racist ideology, this study is emphatic about Coloured identity being primarily and in the first instance a product of its bearers. The analysis focuses mainly on the manner in which processes of Coloured self-definition were influenced by the marginality of the Coloured people, their intermediate status in the South African racial hierarchy, class differences, ideological and political conflict, cultural affinities, and popular stereotyping. It is argued that their marginality was central to the relative stability of Coloured identity because of the limitations it placed on their possibilities for independent action. Their status of relative privilege was also critical in maintaining this equilibrium because it rewarded Coloured exclusivism and conformity with white racist expectations while discouraging alternative strategies, particularly association with a broader black identity. Their resultant assimilationism and fear of being cast down to the status of Africans were further incentives for maintaining the status quo. By concentrating on the role that Coloured people themselves played in the making of their identity and by exploring the ways in which ambiguities and contradictions within their group identity shaped their consciousness, this volume seeks to elucidate complexities in Coloured social experience hitherto neglected by historians and social scientists.

My main criticism of nearly all of the extant literature centers on its effective denial or underplaying of the role Coloured people have had in making their own identity, and in the pages ahead, I attempt to redress that shortcoming. Prominence is thus given to the utterances, actions, and writings of Coloured people in which they evince their primary social identity. The inquiry is anchored in analyses of key texts produced by some of the most prominent organic intellectuals in the community, in which they give expression to their identity as Coloured people and reflect on its essence, qualities, and history. Emphasis is placed on serial publications, especially newspapers, written by Coloured people for a largely Coloured readership. The great advantage of this type of source material is that it addresses a specific constituency and needs to communicate in language that is broadly accessible and through ideas that resonate with its intended readers. Serial publications also allow one to track changing manifestations of the identity within a specific sector of the population over time.

A word about the terminology used in this study is necessary. For want of better alternatives and for the sake of adding some variety to the text, I use the terms *petite bourgeoisie* and *elite* interchangeably when referring to the upper strata of the Coloured community. Though the individuals in these strata did not comprise a petite bourgeoisie or an elite as conventionally understood, they can nevertheless be distinguished from the Coloured proletariat by their relative affluence, literacy, and adherence to the norms and values of white middle-class respectability. A general consciousness of their superior status within the Coloured community also set them apart from the Coloured laboring poor. Having an elite status only within the context of the Coloured community, this group in reality consisted of a combination of petite bourgeois and "respectable" working-class elements and would perhaps be more accurately referred to as an emergent petite bourgeoisie for much of the twentieth century. It is only toward the close of the period under discussion that a substantive petite bourgeoisie in the usual sense of the term can be observed within the Coloured community.[4]

The advent of the new South Africa has complicated the use of racial terminology, as both the racist and the politically correct conventions of the apartheid era break down. Old terms have taken on new meanings and are invested with changing values as people have greater freedom to give expression to social identities and ethnopolitical preferences. Thus, for example, it has become much more fashionable for whites to identify as African, if not de rigueur for those with high public profiles, and the term *Coloured* has been rehabilitated in public discourse since the rejectionist tide receded after 1990. In this study, the term *black* is used in its inclusive sense to refer to Coloured, Indian, and African people collectively, and *African* is used to refer to the indigenous Bantu-speaking peoples of South Africa. The use of the term *Coloured* is still complicated by a residual politically correct lobby that rejects this practice and argues for a broader black or South African identity.[5] The emergence of a rejectionist voice within the Khoisan revivalist movement indicates that negative associations attached to Coloured identity still rankle with many. Given these and other sensitivities around the issue, I am driven to the tautology of stating that in this study, the term *Coloured* is used to refer to those people who regard themselves as Coloured. And wherever it is necessary to mention people who are generally regarded as being Coloured but who are known to reject the identity, this is indicated by placing the word between quotation marks if this is not apparent from the context of the discussion.

During the apartheid period and after, some scholars, myself included, refused to capitalize the first letter of the term *Coloured* in order to indicate both opposition to the enforced classification of people into racial and ethnic categories and distaste for ethnocentric values. The practice was further justified by the assertion that since the word was not derived from a proper noun, there was no need to capitalize it. In this study, however, I resort to the more normal practice of capitalizing the "C word," except for quotations using the lower case. This is partly a response to the gradual normalization of South African society in the postapartheid period and partly in recognition of a growing grass-roots sentiment neatly expressed by journalist Paul Stober: "As a distinct ethnic group with over three million members, we deserve a capital letter."[6] It is also an indication of the rapid change the identity is experiencing in the postapartheid environment, as old sensitivities die down and as new concerns and agendas impinge on people's consciousness.

Abbreviations

AAC	All African Convention
ANB	Afrikaanse Nasionale Bond
ANC	African National Congress
APO	African Political Organization
BLAC	Black Literature, Art and Culture
CAC	Coloured Advisory Council
CAD	Coloured Affairs Department
CATA	Cape African Teachers' Association
CPC	Coloured People's Congress
CPNU	Coloured People's National Union
CPSA	Communist Party of South Africa
CRC	Coloured Representative Council
FIOSA	Fourth International Organization of South Africa
ICU	Industrial and Commercial Workers' Union
NEUF	Non-European United Front
NEUM	Non-European Unity Movement
NLL	National Liberation League
SACPO	South African Coloured People's Organization
SAIC	South African Indian Congress
TARC	Train Apartheid Resistance Committee
TLSA	Teachers' League of South Africa
UCCA	Union Council of Coloured Affairs
UDF	United Democratic Front
UMSA	Unity Movement of South Africa

1

Continuity and Context

An Overview of Coloured Identity in White Supremacist South Africa

There is a general lack of familiarity with the history of the Coloured community of South Africa, except perhaps for an awareness that it has generally been a story of racial oppression and that for nearly the whole of the twentieth century, it followed a discernible trend of intensifying segregationism and a continual erosion of Coloured people's civil rights. This blind spot in South African historical knowledge, which is elaborated on in the next chapter, is a direct consequence of the marginality of the Coloured people. As one Coloured commentator put it, "We don't know our own history and out there in the community and schools there is no information about it because we are not empowered."[1]

A contexualizing opening chapter that sketches the social and historical background is thus a particular necessity. First, a thumbnail sketch of the history of the Coloured community is presented. This is followed by an elaboration of the core attributes that defined the manner in which Coloured identity operated in South African society during the era of white rule. The analysis here seeks to identify the fundamental impulses behind the assertion of a separate Coloured identity and to explain continuity and change in processes of Coloured self-definition. The overview is rounded off by a discussion of the popular stereotyping of Coloured people by dissecting a well-worn joke about their origin. This section demonstrates how a range of pejorative connotations coalesce in the stereotyping of Coloured people in the popular mind.

From Slavery to Khoisan Revivalism:
A Synopsis of Coloured History

In South Africa, contrary to international usage, the term *Coloured* does not refer to black people in general. It instead alludes to a phenotypically varied social group of highly diverse cultural and geographic origins. Novelist, academic, and literary critic Kole Omotoso aptly described Coloured people's skin color, the most important of these phenotypical features, as varying "from charcoal black to breadcrust brown, sallow yellow and finally off-white cream that wants to pass for white."[2] The Coloured people were descended largely from Cape slaves,[3] the indigenous Khoisan population, and other black people who had been assimilated to Cape colonial society by the late nineteenth century. Since they are also partly descended from European settlers, Coloureds are popularly regarded as being of "mixed race" and have held an intermediate status in the South African racial hierarchy, distinct from the historically dominant white minority and the numerically preponderant African population.

There are approximately three and a half million Coloured people in South Africa today.[4] Constituting no more than 9 percent of the population throughout the twentieth century and lacking significant political or economic power, Coloured people have always formed a marginal group in South African society. There has, moreover, been a marked regional concentration of Coloured people: approximately 90 percent of them live within the western third of the country, with more than two-thirds residing in the Western Cape[5] and over 40 percent in the greater Cape Town area.[6] The Coloured category has also generally been taken to include a number of distinct subgroups, such as Malays, Griquas, Namas, and Basters.

Although Coloured identity crystallized in the late nineteenth century, the process of social amalgamation within the colonial black population at the Cape that gave rise to Coloured group consciousness dates back to the period of Dutch colonial rule. However, it was in the decades after the emancipation of the Khoisan in 1828 and slaves in 1838 that various components of the heterogeneous black laboring class in the Cape Colony started integrating more rapidly and developing an incipient shared identity. This identity was based on a common socioeconomic status and a shared culture derived from their incorporation into the lower ranks of Cape colonial society.[7] The emergence of a full-fledged Coloured identity as we know it today was precipitated in the late nineteenth century by the sweeping social changes that came in the wake of the mineral revolution. The introduction of large-scale mining after the discovery of diamonds in 1867 and gold in 1886, being South Africa's equivalent of the industrial revolution, had a transformative impact on the social and economic landscape of the subcontinent. Significant numbers of Africans started going to the western Cape from the 1870s onward, and assimilated colonial blacks and a wide variety of African people who had recently been incorporated into the capitalist economy were thrust together in the highly competitive environment of the newly established mining towns. These developments drove acculturated colonial blacks to assert a separate identity as Coloured people, in order to claim a position of relative privilege in relation to Africans on the basis of their closer assimilation to Western culture and being partly descended from European colonists.[8]

Because of the marginality of the Coloured people and the determination with which the state implemented white supremacist policies, the story of Coloured political organization has largely been one of compromise, retreat, and failure. The most consistent feature of Coloured political history until the latter phases of apartheid was the continual erosion of the civil rights first bestowed on blacks in the Cape Colony by the British administration in the mid-nineteenth century.

The process of attrition started with the franchise restrictions imposed by the Parliamentary Registration Act of 1887 and the Franchise and Ballot Act of 1892.[9] A spate of racially discriminatory measures in the first decade of the twentieth century further compromised the civil rights of Coloured people. The most significant were the exclusion of Coloured people from the franchise in the former Boer republics after the Anglo-Boer War; the promulgation of the School Board Act of 1905, which segregated the Cape's education system by providing compulsory public schooling for white children only; and the denial of the right of Coloured people to be elected to parliament with the creation of the South African state in 1910.[10] The subsequent implementation of a policy of segregation progressively entrenched white privilege and Coloured disadvantage before even more draconian measures were introduced with the coming of apartheid in 1948.

In the 1920s and 1930s, the economic advancement of the Coloured community was undermined by the civilized labor policy,[11] as well as a number of laws designed to favor whites over blacks in the competition for employment. For example, the 1921 Juvenile Affairs Act set up mechanisms for placing those who left white schools into suitable employment. Also, the Apprenticeship Act of 1922 put apprenticeships beyond the reach of most Coloured youths by stipulating educational entry levels that very few Coloured schools met but that fell within the minimum educational standard set for white schools. The 1925 Wage Act subverted the ability of Coloured labor to undercut white wage demands by setting high minimum-wage levels in key industries. Furthermore, in 1930, the influence of the Coloured vote was more than halved by the enfranchisement of white women only.[12]

It was during the apartheid era, however, that Coloured people suffered the most severe violations of their civil rights. Their forced classification under the Population Registration Act of 1950, which categorized all South Africans according to race, made the implementation of rigid segregation possible. The Prohibition of Mixed Marriages Act of 1949 and the Immorality Amendment Act of 1950 outlawed marriage and sex across the color line, respectively. Under the Group Areas Act of 1950, over half a million Coloured people were forcibly relocated to residential and business areas, usually on the periphery of cities and towns. The Group Areas Act was probably the most hated of the apartheid measures among Coloureds because property owners were meagerly compensated, long-standing communities were broken up, and alternative accommodation was inadequate. The 1953 Separate Amenities Act, which introduced "petty apartheid" by segregating virtually all public facilities, also created deep resentment. In 1956, moreover, after a protracted legal and constitutional battle, the National Party succeeded in removing Coloured people from the common voters' roll.[13]

Because their primary objective was to assimilate into the dominant society, politicized Coloured people initially avoided forming separate political organizations. By the early twentieth century, however, intensifying segregation forced them to mobilize politically in defense of their rights. Although the earliest Coloured political organizations date back to the 1880s, the first substantive Coloured political body, the African Political Organization (APO), was established in Cape Town in 1902.[14] Under the leadership of the charismatic Abdullah Abdurahman, who served as president from 1905 until his death in 1940, the APO dominated Coloured protest politics for nearly four decades. It became the main vehicle for expressing this community's assimilationist aspirations as well as its fears at the rising tide of segregationism until its demise in the mid-1940s. A number of ephemeral political organizations such as the United Afrikaner League of the late 1910s and the Afrikaanse Nasionale Bond (ANB) of the latter half of the 1920s—bodies that were promoted by Cape National Party politicians hoping to win Coloured electoral support—failed to subvert the dominance of the APO.[15]

Intensifying segregation and the failure of the APO's moderate approach contributed to the emergence of a radical movement inspired by Marxist ideology within the better-educated, urbanized sector of the Coloured community during the 1930s. The National Liberation League (NLL), founded in 1935, and the Non-European Unity Movement (NEUM), established in 1943, were the most important of these radical organizations. Prone to fissure and unable to bridge the racial divisions within the society, the radical movement failed in its quest to unite blacks in the struggle against segregation.[16] The South African Coloured People's Organization (SACPO),[17] which was founded in 1953 and affiliated with the Congress Alliance, led by the African National Congress (ANC), also organized protests and demonstrations, especially against the removal of Coloured people from the voters' roll.[18] Organized opposition to apartheid from within the Coloured community was effectively quelled by state repression following the Sharpeville shooting of March 1960. The Sharpeville massacre, in which 69 unarmed anti-pass protestors were killed and 180 injured by police, represents a dramatic turning point in South Africa's history and resulted in a harsh crackdown on the extraparliamentary opposition by the apartheid state. Organized Coloured resistance reemerged only in the wake of the Soweto uprising of 1976. A few scantily supported political organizations that were prepared to work within apartheid structures, such as the Labour Party of South Africa and the Federal Coloured People's Party, were, however, sanctioned during the heyday of apartheid.

From the latter half of the 1970s onward, starting with the popularization of Black Consciousness ideology within the Coloured community,[19] the nature of Coloured identity became an extremely contentious issue, for growing numbers of educated and politicized people who had been classified "Coloured" under the Population Registration Act rejected the identity. The Soweto revolt, which started as a protest by schoolchildren in June 1976 and soon spread to other parts of the country, including Coloured communities of the western Cape, greatly accelerated this trend because it fomented a climate of open resistance to apartheid and fostered a far stronger sense of black solidarity than had existed before. Colouredness increasingly came to be viewed as an artificial categorization imposed on the society by the ruling minority as part of its divide-and-rule strategies. The burgeoning of the mass, nonracial democratic movement in the 1980s under the leadership of the United Democratic Front (UDF), founded in 1983, fed Coloured rejectionism. Controversy over the participation of some Coloured leaders in the Tricameral Parliament of the P. W. Botha government from 1984 onward further inflamed rejectionist passions.[20] With the western Cape an epicenter of resistance to apartheid, Coloured identity became a highly charged issue, and within the antiapartheid movement, any recognition of Coloured identity was repudiated as a concession to apartheid thinking.[21]

In spite of this, the salience of Coloured identity has endured. During the four-year transition to democratic rule under president F. W. de Klerk, political parties across the ideological spectrum made ever more strident appeals to Coloured identity for support. Once again, it became politically acceptable to espouse a Coloured identity; moreover, postapartheid South Africa has witnessed a rapid retreat of Coloured rejectionism and a concomitant Coloured assertiveness. This has been due partly to a desire to project a positive self-image in the face of the pervasive negative racial stereotyping of Coloured people and partly to attempts at ethnic mobilization to take advantage of the newly democratic political environment. The resurgence of Colouredism has, to a significant extent, also been motivated by a fear of African majority rule and the perception that, as in the old order, Coloureds were once again being marginalized. Though far from allayed, these anxieties have, in recent years, been alleviated by the fading influence of *swart gevaar* (black peril) tactics in South African politics and by the acclimatization of people to the new political order.

Hope, Fear, Shame, Frustration: The Dynamic of Coloured Exclusivism

The central contention of this section—and of the book as a whole—is that Coloured identity is better understood not as having undergone a series of transformations during the era of white rule but rather as having maintained a high degree of stability despite obvious changes to the identity. This is not to imply that Coloured identity was in any way fixed or that it was not pliable but that it operated within a range of fairly predictable parameters. The changes that it did experience during that time did not fundamentally alter the way in which it functioned as an identity. These changes were more in the nature of the accretion and sloughing off of elements around a core of enduring characteristics, adding further complexity and subtlety to the way the identity found expression, rather than the evolution of the identity itself. Thus, viewed on the eve of the transition to democracy in 1994, Coloured identity was very much the same phenomenon it was at the inauguration of Union in 1910 despite radical changes in the social and political landscape and within the Coloured community itself.

Besides the conventional expression of Coloured identity derived from its stable core, it is possible to identify a number of developments during the twentieth century that influenced processes of Coloured self-perception. The emergence of a radical movement in Coloured politics from the second half of the 1930s, though limited in its impact, was significant because it introduced the idea that black unity or a class-based identity was possible and because it initiated some impetus in this direction within the Coloured petite bourgeoisie. From midcentury onward, apartheid thinking and the implementation of apartheid social engineering had the countervailing effect of reifying Coloured identity as never before. The latter phases of the apartheid era witnessed a reaction to this tendency with the growing rejection of Coloured identity within sections of the community. Coloured rejectionism was fostered by the revival of mass protest against apartheid after the Soweto revolt and by an intensifying disapproval of any form of racial thinking within the antiapartheid movement. As mentioned earlier, during the transition to democratic rule in the first half of the 1990s, insecurity at the prospect of majority rule and new opportunities for ethnic mobilization saw a resurgence of Coloured exclusivism.[22] Finally, since the mid-1990s, there have been initiatives to reinvent Coloured identity, largely in the form of attempts to stimulate Coloured people's pride in their Khoisan and slave pasts.

Nevertheless, until the late 1970s, there was a high degree of consensus both within the Coloured community and among outsiders about who the Coloured people were and what the concept of Colouredness embodied. The conventional wisdom—that Coloured people constituted a distinct racial group with its own historical trajectory and destiny—was first challenged in the 1930s when radical intellectuals rejected Coloured separatism as playing into the hands of the ruling classes who sought to divide the black majority and split the proletariat. The emphasis on non-European unity among Coloured radicals during the middle decades of the twentieth century was not so much a rejection of Coloured identity as an assertion that racial differences were not in any way intrinsic and that Coloured particularism undermined the freedom struggle. From the early 1960s, however, there was an explicit rejection of Coloured identity within NEUM circles. This incipient rejectionism remained extremely limited in its impact, in that it did not penetrate much beyond a section of the tiny intelligentsia within the Coloured elite. It was only toward the latter half of the 1970s, when Black Consciousness ideology took hold in significant sectors of the Coloured community, that the rejection of Coloured identity found popular support, growing to its zenith in the nonracial democratic movement during the late 1980s and early 1990s. Even at its height the rejection of Coloured identity was limited to a relatively small minority of better-educated and more highly politicized people associated with the antiapartheid movement.[23]

What is the essence of the stable core at the heart of Coloured identity, and how does one explain the continuities in that identity and the way in which it operated through the period of white domination? This chapter identifies four key characteristics that formed the foundation of Coloured identity.

One of these essential features was the desire to assimilate into the dominant society. This assimilationism was less an impulse for acculturation than a striving on the part of Coloured people for acknowledgment of their worth as individuals and citizens and acceptance as equals or partners by whites. Throughout the twentieth century, gaining such affirmation was one of the strongest imperatives within the Coloured community, especially among the petite bourgeois elite. The late nineteenth-century genesis of Coloured identity emanated from a worldview and a political strategy that was profoundly assimilationist. And during the twentieth century, despite criticism of the racist order, all that the Coloured political leadership and the petite bourgeoisie it represented really wanted was for Coloured people to be accepted into the dominant society and share in the benefits of citizenship on the basis of individual merit.[24] Though the majority of the Coloured elite aspired to acceptance into English-speaking, middle-class culture, there was also a significant movement within the Coloured community for accommodation within the fold of Afrikanerdom.[25] Despite occasional warnings that the continued oppression of Coloured people could have dire consequences for the society as a whole, the Coloured political leadership had no interest in overthrowing the system or changing South African society fundamentally, except for eliminating institutionalized racial discrimination. As is so often the case in any discussion of Coloured politics after the mid-1930s, the exception represented by a small minority of radicals needs to be noted here.

This assimilationism, which in more recent times has often been misunderstood and denounced by radicals as mere rationalizations of self-serving sycophants and collaborationists, was rooted in a worldview informed by nineteenth-century Cape liberal values. For much of the twentieth century, moderate Coloured political opinion still clung to a weltanschauung reminiscent of mid-nineteenth century progressionism. The first key assumption of this utopian outlook was that humanity was on a path of inevitable progress toward the ultimate attainment of an elysian future of social harmony and prosperity. The second assumption was that all people, no matter what their current condition, were capable of self-improvement and the acquisition of "civilization," which equated to Western bourgeois culture in the minds of the Coloured elite. These assumptions were reinforced by deeply held religious beliefs that not only posited the equality of all humans in the eyes of God but also fed the progressionist vision with ideas about the ultimate redemption of humankind and the notion that its destiny was directed by the guiding hand of a just God.[26]

These assimilationist hopes were remarkably resilient and underlay the longer-term vision of the Coloured communal leadership regarding the future of the Coloured people and the destiny of humanity in general. The Coloured elite continued to nurture hopes of being accepted into the dominant society even as new obstacles were placed in their way and as the prospect of realizing these aspirations deteriorated with the continued tightening of segregationist measures through most of the twentieth century. Though the elite were disconcerted by each new discriminatory regulation and alarmed by the more draconian developments, setbacks were usually rationalized as temporary reversals, and acceptance into white middle-class society was often seen as something that Coloured people still needed to earn—something that would only be attained after a struggle worthy of the prize.[27] Indeed, this notion often served as justification for clinging to their assimilationist hopes in the face of intensifying segregation. Not even the utter rejection of any form of assimilation with the implementation of apartheid policies entirely extinguished these dreams. The desire for acceptance into the dominant society was evident in its most acute form among those individuals willing to disown their identity as Coloured; turn their backs on friends, family, and former lives; and take the considerable risk of exposure by attempting to pass for white.[28] To a significant degree, the durability of these yearnings for acceptance explain the eager response of so many Coloured people to the National Party's overtures in the 1994 general election campaign.

With the benefit of hindsight, it is clear that these dreams of assimilation were badly misplaced and out of step with the social and political realities of white supremacist South Africa. Such optimism might have had a degree of compatibility with nineteenth-century Cape liberalism or have resonated with Western liberal or Left opinion in the twentieth century. And in the first decade of the century, though the prospects were increasingly remote, it was not entirely unrealistic to hope that individual Coloured people would be accepted into white middle-class society on the basis of personal merit and that the community as a whole might, in time, assimilate into the mainstream of Cape society. These desires were, however, completely out of place in the unified South African state, whose policies were increasingly informed by social Darwinist and segregationist assumptions.

Yet the Coloured elite and the political leadership could not avoid coming to terms in some way with the reality of intensifying segregationism that confronted them. Because they were denied their first choice of assimilation into the dominant society, politicized Coloureds had little alternative but to mobilize along racial lines to defend their rights and promote their interests as a group. This brings to the fore a second fundamental attribute of Coloured identity in South Africa, namely, its intermediate status in the South African racial hierarchy.

Coloured people experienced the South African racial hierarchy as a three-tiered system in which Coloureds held an intermediate position between the dominant white minority and the large African majority. As sociologist Zimitri Erasmus put it, "For me, growing up coloured meant knowing that I was *not only* not white, but *less than white: not only* not black but *better than black* (as we referred to African people)."[29] Similarly, in 1943, radical activist Ben Kies criticized the self-segregationist ethos of the Teachers' League: "For thirty years they accepted the idea that their children were not fit to be taught with white children and were too good to be taught with African children."[30]

The symbolism of referring to Coloured people as "brown" neatly captures this intermediate status. The equation of Coloured people with the color brown is even more entrenched in the Afrikaans language, in which words such as *bruinman* (brown man) and *bruinmens* (brown person) are translated as "(Cape) Coloured man" and "(Cape) Coloured person."[31] Indeed, writing in 1960, leading Afrikaner literary figure N. P. van Wyk Louw declared the conventional Afrikaans term for Coloured, *Kleurling*, to be a nauseating word, stating that he preferred *bruinmens*.[32] That Coloured people have, on the whole, accepted this description of themselves is indicated by the fact that Coloured intellectual Christian Ziervogel entitled his late-1930s book on the Coloured people *Brown South Africa* and Coloured poet and educator S. V. Petersen, in a 1956 address to the Stellenbosch Afrikaanse Studentebond, protested he was not a "*kleurling*" but a "*bruinman*"; similarly, in the mid-1990s, Coloured politician Peter Marais described himself as a "*bruin Afrikaner*" (brown Afrikaner). In additon, this particular usage is common in Cape Vernacular Afrikaans.[33]

Because their assimilationist aspirations were thwarted and their intermediate position gave Coloured people significant privileges relative to Africans, the basic dynamic behind the assertion of Coloured identity and the main thrust of mobilizing politically as Coloured people was to defend this position of relative privilege. Their minority status and political powerlessness as well as intensifying segregationism engendered fears that Coloureds might end up being relegated to the status of Africans and lose their position of relative privilege. These concerns reinforced Coloured exclusivity and encouraged a separatist strategy with respect to Africans within the Coloured political leadership.[34] Only a tiny minority of Coloured people chose the alternatives of communism or black unity or some combination of the two.

Their assimilationism, together with the insecurities engendered by their intermediate status, meant that in daily life the most consistent—and insistent—element in the expression of Coloured identity was an association with whiteness and a concomitant distancing from Africanness, whether in the value placed on fair skin and straight hair, in the prizing of white ancestors in the family lineage, or in taking pride in the degree to which they were able to conform to the standards of Western bourgeois culture. This "white-mindedness," as one commentator referred to it,[35] could give rise to a sense of shame with regard to any personal associations with blackness or an aggressive bigotry toward Africans. The former is illustrated by the ludicrous yet poignant example of Betty Theys, who was considerably darker than her light-skinned father. Throughout her life, she felt inadequate, and considered herself a disappointment to him. She finally felt vindicated when she gave birth to her fair-complexioned daughter and immediately sent her father the message, "Your black hen has laid a white egg."[36] The latter is demonstrated by a 1993 interview, in which a working-class Coloured woman, identified as Mrs. D. E., gave voice to the racist chauvinism that often resulted from this affiliation with whiteness: "And a kaffir, even if he wears a golden ring, still remains an ape. . . . They have nothing, they say they have a culture, they don't have a culture, they're raw. They say we brown people are mixed masala, but we brown people are closer to white people, than they are to white people. Because our culture and the white people's culture are the same."[37] Colloquially, this deference to whiteness is often referred to as the Coloured or slave mentality.

In spite of the racially egalitarian rhetoric that characterized so much of the discourse of Coloured protest politics, it has to be recognized that Coloured political organizations were, on the whole, racially exclusive and strove to entrench the relative privilege Coloured people enjoyed. If the ultimate aim of much of Coloured political organization was acceptance into the dominant society, then most of its day-to-day politicking was a narrow concern with the advancement of Coloured interests. Thus, though there was an assertion of nonracial values and protest against discrimination, there was also an accommodation with the racist order and an attempt to manipulate it in favor of Coloured people.[38]

That members of the Coloured community, especially within the petite bourgeoisie, were ambivalent about their identity should not come as a great surprise. Even as their assimilationism tended to dampen separatist tendencies from whites, their desire to protect their status of relative privilege pushed Coloured people into asserting a separate identity with respect to Africans. And although being the victims of racial discrimination promoted the principle of non-racism, political realities forced them to organize on a racial basis. The attempt to exploit segregationism to their own advantage confirms John Cell's observation that though "force lay behind segregation . . . most of the time segregation was self-enforcing."[39] The structurally ambiguous position of the Coloured community within the South African racial hierarchy thus played an important part in reinforcing and reproducing the identity.

The intermediate status of the Coloured grouping contributed in two ways to a third key characteristic of Coloured identity, namely, that it was largely the bearer of a range of negative and derogatory connotations. First, because of their lack of political and economic clout and because they formed a relatively small stratum within the racial hierarchy, the Coloured people tended to be perceived in terms of the larger groups. This was most notable in official definitions of the term *Coloured*, in which the category was usually described as consisting of those people who were neither white nor African.[40] Consequently, the Coloured community was usually not identified in a positive manner, as social groups typically are, in terms of a set of distinctive characteristics but was instead conceived in a negative fashion with reference to other groups, in terms of what it was not—as Erasmus put it, "in terms of 'lack' or taint, or in terms of 'remainder' or excess which does not fit a classificatory scheme."[41]

This was one of the more subtle ways in which negative associations came to be attached to the concept of Colouredness. It reinforced ideas that the Coloured people were not of the same standing as other groups, that their claims to autonomous group status—usually articulated in terms of "nation," "people," or "race"—were deficient or lacked a degree of authenticity. The ultimate expression of this belief came from none other than former first lady of South Africa, Marike de Klerk, who, in a 1983 interview, declared that Coloureds "are a negative group. The definition of a coloured in the population register is someone that is not black, and is not white and is also not an Indian, in other words a no-person. They are the leftovers. They are the people that were left after the nations were sorted out. They are the rest."[42] Such ideas were often internalized by Coloured people, for, as one working-class Coloured informant in the early 1990s put it to me, "We Coloured people are not a proper nation, we don't have our own culture or land that we can say is our own. The Coloured people is like a mixed *bredie* [stew] made up of all different kinds of people."[43] Comparing the Coloured people to a mixed *bredie* is a common colloquialism used to emphasize their racial and cultural hybridity.[44] The perception that the Coloured community lacked cultural distinctiveness and full status as an ethnic group reinforced not only their marginality but also the idea that Coloured people, being the product of miscegenation, were misfits and somehow inherently deficient. Charles Sebe, at the time director of state security in the Ciskei, the eastern Cape bantustan, exemplified these attitudes in his rejection of miscegenation during a speech reported by Joseph Lelyveld, a *New York Times* journalist: "'What will you get from [black/white] *in-ter-mar-riage?*

You get a Coloured.' The word was pronounced with contempt. 'You don't get a white person, you don't get a black person, but a frustated child which does not belong anywhere.'"[45]

A second way in which the intermediate status of the Coloured people contributed to these negative perceptions is that it served as a residual category into which smaller groups that did not fit into either the white or the African categories were placed. This, again, was very much apparent in official practice, where, for example in census figures or in the compilation of statistics in official publications, those groups who were not manifestly white or African were lumped with the Coloured category. Thus, groups such as Malays, Griquas, Rehoboth Basters, Namas, and even Indians were sometimes treated as distinct groups and at other times included under the rubric of Coloured.[46] The Population Registration Act went to the ridiculous length of creating a category labeled "Other Coloured" for those people who did not fit into any of the other six subcategories into which it divided those classified as Coloured.[47]

Because of negative associations attached to it, Colouredness was not enthusiastically embraced as an affirmation of self and group identity except in relatively rare or transient instances. The derogations were far too many and deeply entrenched—among both outsiders, especially whites, and, more important, many Coloured people themselves—for the identity to function in a positive, affirmative fashion. Coloured identity instead tended to be accepted with resignation and often with a sense of shame by its bearers, as a bad draw in the lottery of life.[48]

Erasmus listed some of the negative associations attached to Coloured identity as "immorality, sexual promiscuity, illegitimacy, impurity and untrustworthiness."[49] One could add other attributes to the list, as well, such as supposed propensities for criminality, gangsterism, drug and alcohol abuse, and vulgar behaviour. The most pervasive of the negative characteristics attached to Colouredness, however, and one that is usually seen as the source of other weaknesses was the idea that it was a product of miscegenation. For a popular mind-set suffused with social Darwinist assumptions, the implications of this notion were that Coloured people were therefore deficient in positive qualities associated with racial purity and handicapped by negative ones derived from racial mixture. Having internalized the racist values of the dominant society and having accepted racial mixture as the defining characteristic of their identity, Coloured people by and large viewed their community as indelibly stigmatized by their supposed condition of racial hybridity. This has been an extremely onerous burden, especially for the Coloured petite bourgeoisie, in a society obsessed with racial purity and the dangers of "mongrelization." Reflecting on her own upbringing in a "respectable" Coloured family, Zimitri Erasmus commented, "I can see how respectablity and shame are key defining terms of middle class coloured experience."[50]

In this regard, the Coloured community was trapped in a catch-22 situation that was partly of its own making. In order to distance themselves from Africans and protect their status of relative privilege, Coloureds emphasized their partial descent from European colonists. But it was precisely this claim that encumbered them with the stigma of racial hybridity. The import of white supremacist discourse about the origins of the Coloured people was that they were the unwanted and unfortunate consequence of the colonization of southern Africa.[51] The Coloured people were thus a source of embarrassment to the white supremacist establishment as reminders of past lapses in morality. As the Reverend Allan Boesak inimitably put it, "We were there looking them in the eye and saying to them, 'Well here we are. So what about your pure race theory and what about your chosen-people-of-God theory?' We were the living proof that [they were] not really able to lock up every human emotion."[52] To white racists, Coloured people also presented the danger of an ongoing infiltration of white society by light-skinned Coloureds and raised the specter of racial degeneration. This prompted fears that, in the long run, white supremacy and the very survival of Western civilization in southern Africa were at stake. One of South Africa's most popular authors in the first half of the twentieth century who wrote extensively on the theme of race from a racist perspective, Sarah Gertrude Millin, quoted Prime Minister Jan Smuts as cautioning that "white South Africans (must) have a care lest one day . . . 'little brown children play among the ruins of the Union Government Buildings.'"[53] The promulgation of the Immorality and Mixed Marriages Acts confirms just how seriously these threats were taken.

A concomitant problem was the inability of organic intellectuals within the community to delineate a positive set of symbols, a distinctive culture, or an acceptable myth of origin around which those who regarded themselves as Coloured could cohere with a sense of pride. Their slave past and Khoisan heritage were generally treated as embarrassments requiring a tactful silence rather than as affirmations of group identity. Although their assimilation to Western culture was emphasized because of their determination to distance themselves from Africans, organic intellectuals within the group were sensitive to the general perception that the Coloured people did not have a distinctive culture. This was illustrated by the emotional response of a prominent Coloured politician from the Western Cape on visiting the museum at the Genadendal mission station. Asked afterward why he had been visibly moved by the experience, the politician replied that he had always been under the impression that Coloured people did not have a culture but that the history of Genadendal had proved otherwise to him.[54]

What is more, those cultural features commonly accepted as distinctively Coloured have generally been denigrated and accorded low status in South African society. The Afrikaans vernacular distinctive to the Coloured community and variously referred to as *Capey, Gamtaal* (language of Ham), or *kombuis* (kitchen) Afrikaans has, for example, customarily been stigmatized as a mark of social inferiority. Until relatively recently, before the argument for Afrikaans being a creole language gained popularity, there was widespread acceptance within the Coloured community of white and especially Afrikaner denigration of *kombuis* Afrikaans as a vulgar patois. By way of example, a middle-class Coloured informant in the mid-1990s told me that although *kombuis* Afrikaans was his home language, he felt ashamed of using it when speaking to whites or "respectable people," as it would mark him as "low class."[55] An Afrikaner school inspector in the mid-1970s exemplified white attitudes toward the dialect when, on hearing me speak the vernacular to some of my high school students, he admonished me, in a gentle but paternalistic tone, for using *"daardie gebasterde taal"* (that bastardized language) and perpetuating uncultured practices among my students.[56] The Coon Carnival, a celebration of the new year particular to the Coloured community—though embraced by most working-class Coloured people as their own and more recently touted as an example of colorful Cape culture to promote tourism—was similarly stigmatized among whites and middle-class Coloureds as boorish, disreputable, and even depraved.[57]

The lack of positive identification with Colouredness meant that much of the social mobilization and political activity conducted in the name of the Coloured people was in reaction to white racism rather than a proactive marshaling of ethnic resources. Throughout the era of white domination, anger, anxiety, and fear engendered by the social

injustices they suffered rather than a positive identification with Colouredness proved to be the more potent means for mobilizing people
on the basis of their identity as Coloured. Coping with white racism
rather than affirming Colouredness motivated a great deal of these
separatist agendas. Virtually all Coloured communal organizations,
whether cultural, professional, or political, either were formed because
Coloured people were excluded from the corresponding white bodies
or were established in response to one or another segregationist development. Coloured responses to segregationism, which, with the exception of the radical movement, generally sought to protect Coloureds'
position of relative privilege, thus tended to reinforce existing racial
boundaries despite the nonracial rhetoric that usually accompanied
them. The pervasiveness of racial identifications was such that even in
the most obvious exception to this pattern, the Non-European Unity
Movement, the outcome of fifteen years of endeavor was a split largely
along racial lines in 1958.[58]

The essentially opportunistic nature of Coloured identity politics,
especially in response to segregationism, points to the marginality of
the Coloured people. This, the fourth of the key attributes of Coloured
identity, was the most important core element because it dominated
the day-to-day conditions under which the identity operated. The
Coloured community's response to its predicament of marginality
was central to the manner in which the identity manifested itself socially and politically. The marginality of the Coloured people goes a
long way toward explaining how they perceived themselves as a social group; it also helps explain the contradictions and ambiguities
within the identity and the changes it experienced through the twentieth century. Further, that marginality was the source of a great deal
of frustration and anger, as well as a degree of fatalism within the
Coloured community.[59]

The Coloured people comprised a marginal group in that they
never formed more than about 9 percent of the South African population throughout the twentieth century.[60] Although it constituted a
significant minority, the Coloured community did not enjoy anything
near a commensurate level of influence or power under white supremacy. A heritage of slavery, dispossession, and racial oppression
ensured that Coloured people lacked any significant economic or political power as a group and that by far the greater majority consisted
of a downtrodden proletariat. Under white minority rule, the Coloured community had no meaningful leverage to bring about change

in the society or to reform or influence the way in which it was governed. Indeed, Coloured communal and political leaders had great difficulty drawing attention to their standpoint and having their protestations taken seriously by the ruling authorities. Coloured political organizations were doomed to be bit players on the political stage, and Coloured protest politics was little more than a sideshow in the national arena. Even in the western Cape, where two-thirds of Coloured people were concentrated and formed a majority of the population,[61] their political influence progressively declined through the greater part of the century. This impotence was highlighted early on by the APO's protest campaign against the Act of Union. Despite being remarkably successful in mobilizing Coloured opinion behind the campaign, the APO was unable to change a single clause in the draft South Africa Act.[62] And in subsequent decades, Coloured protest politics was unable to boast a single clear-cut victory in the battle against white supremacism. The clearest demonstration of the community's powerlessness came with the removal of Coloured people from the common voters' roll in 1956, notwithstanding mass protests and substantial support from liberal whites.

The marginality of the Coloured community meant that it had little choice in the matter of accepting an inferior social status to whites or the second-class citizenship imposed on it by the state. To a large extent, this marginality accounted for the pragmatism and opportunism of much of Coloured protest politics, as well as the incrementalism that characterized its strategies. Grappling with this predicament of marginality also goes some way toward explaining key developments in the history of the Coloured community, such as the emergence of a radical movement in the mid-1930s, the rejection of Coloured identity from the late 1970s onward, and the resurgence of Colouredism at the end of the twentieth century. Whatever else may have gone into their making, frustration engendered by impotence played a part in the adoption of new political strategies.

Trapped by their condition of marginality, Coloureds found their options for social and political action severely constrained. With their assimilationist overtures spurned by whites and with joint organization with the African majority either impractical or unattractive, they were left isolated and powerless. To the majority of the political and communal leaders, the only realistic option open to them was to bow to white power and work toward an incremental improvement in conditions for their constituency. Consequently, they adopted an outlook

that was highly opportunistic, taking advantage of every chance to reinforce Coloureds' status of relative privilege.[63]

The various radical movements were too narrowly based and
ephemeral to have broken this isolation decisively. It was only relatively late in the twentieth century, when a significant sector within the
Coloured community broke categorically with the separatist agenda
and embraced nonracialism as part of a populist strategy, that individuals from within its ranks such as Allan Boesak, Trevor Manuel,
and Patricia de Lille started having a significant impact on national
politics and the broader society. Even then, however, the majority of
Coloured people in the 1990s felt vulnerable and alienated from the
African majority, preferring to ally themselves with their former oppressors. Their insecurity is captured in the colloquial expression
"We are the jam," which likens Coloured people to the thin layer of
jam squeezed between two slices of bread. The metaphor gives expression to both their marginality as well as their intermediate status.
This expression, usually uttered in a resigned tone of voice and used
to express alienation and political apathy or to justify support of the
National Party, became especially popular during the uncertain times
facing the Coloured community in the mid-1990s.[64]

The dynamic behind the assertion of a separate Coloured identity
and the continuities in its expression identified here have been reinforced by the popular stereotyping of Coloured people. This stereotyping has played an important part in the social construction of Coloured
identity within the Coloured community and especially within the
dominant society. Because of their marginality, Coloured people have
been more vulnerable than most to this form of prejudice. The stereotyping of Coloured people in the popular mind will be explored
through the analysis of a well-known joke from the apartheid era that
has been making the rounds in South Africa for several decades.

God, Jan van Riebeeck, and the Coloured People: The Anatomy of a South African Joke

The joke in question hinges on the audience's awareness of the status
of Jan van Riebeeck, the commander of the first Dutch settlement established at the Cape in 1652, as the "founding father" of white South
Africa. One of the most basic "facts" drummed into children in school
history lessons in apartheid South Africa was that van Riebeeck's landing marked the start of South African history proper and of civilized

life in the subcontinent.[65] Elaborate state-sponsored celebrations of
the tercentenary of his arrival at the Cape to establish a victualing station for the Dutch East India Company ensured van Riebeeck a prominent place in apartheid propaganda from the early days of National
Party rule.[66] The presence of van Riebeeck became even more ubiqui-
tous when his image appeared on the obverse side of the currency
after South Africa became a republic in 1961. Van Riebeeck was thus
not only an icon of white supremacism in South Africa but also an important element in the mythmaking and ideological manipulation used
to justify apartheid ideology.

The joke begins by describing a scenario that provokes a Coloured
person into hurling racial insults at an African and repudiating him as
an inferior being. A typical setting for the joke would be an apartheid-
era situation in which an African person tries to gain entrance to some
facility, such as a movie theater or a public conveyance reserved for
Coloured people. In a fashion all too familiar in the apartheid experience, the Coloured protagonist expels the African from the facility
and ends a racist diatribe by exclaiming, "No Kaffirs are allowed here!"[67]
The African then counters this tirade with the punch line: "God made
the white man, God made the black man, God made the Indian, the
Chinese and the Jew—but Jan van Riebeeck, he made the Coloured
man."[68]

This joke, which has taken on a variety of forms, became a well-
established means of teasing or deriding Coloured people, and the
premises on which it is based are understood over a broad spectrum
of South African society. Although typical of the apartheid era, the assumptions, images, and values that underlie the joke would nevertheless have resonated with South Africans from all walks of life from at
least the late nineteenth century onward. In my experience, it was a
very common joke often openly told to and by Coloured people during
the apartheid period. Though never acceptable in politically progressive circles, the coming of the "new" South Africa, with its heightened
sensitivity to anything that might be deemed racially offensive, has
caused the joke to lose much of its appeal; where still in evidence, the
joke is mainly restricted to private discourse among people who share
a high degree of personal trust.

The van Riebeeck joke harnesses several key features of the racial
stereotyping of Coloured people in apartheid South Africa and, indeed, reveals much about the popular concept of Colouredness. The
punch line makes sense only if both teller and audience share particu-

lar assumptions about Coloured people or, at the very least, acknowledge the existence of a popular image of Coloured people that embodies these characteristics. The joke's broad appeal is apparent from a local entrepeneur who arranged tours of Cape Town's black townships for foreign visitors in the late 1980s, kicking off these tours with a version of this story "about old Jan van Riebeeck and his comrades frolicking with the local maidens . . . giving birth to the 'colourful folk.'"[69] Clearly, these assumptions about Coloured people were shared widely enough that even foreigners were able to get the joke.

The exchange of insults between the Coloured and African protagonists in the van Riebeeck joke is set within the context of the racial hierarchy of white supremacist South Africa. The conventional perception of this racial stratification has the ruling white minority on top, the African majority at the bottom, and the Coloured people in between. It is evident from the treatment of the African protagonist that the Coloured person in the joke shares this perception of the social order. In terms of the value system in which the joke operates, Coloured people are accorded a superior status to Africans within the racial hierarchy because they can claim to be partly descended from whites and more closely assimilated to Western bourgeois culture. As the riposte from the African demonstrates, however, the conventional perception of the social order was open to dispute. Although the punch line does not necessarily challenge the dominant status of whites, the African rejects the relatively privileged status of Coloureds by asserting that racial purity trumps genetic proximity to whiteness or assimilation to Western culture.

The punch line of the van Riebeeck joke invokes the most salient characteristic associated with Colouredness in the popular mind, namely, racial hybridity. Through hybridity, the closely allied attributes of racial inferiority and illegitimacy are also assigned to Coloured people as a group. The joke turns on a shared perception between teller and audience of the pejorativeness of racial hybridity and illegitimate conception. Without these associations, the joke would hardly be considered funny.

The attribute of racial hybridity is virtually inherent to the concept of Colouredness in the popular mind and is the most prominent of the array of negative qualities associated with it. Coloured people are generally considered to be of "mixed race" or, less flatteringly, to be a "half-caste" or even a "bastard" people, with racial mixture viewed as their defining characteristic. The idea of racial hybridity has been so intrinsic to the concept of Colouredness that even an ultra-left-wing Coloured intellectual such as Kenny Jordaan, a leading member of the Trotskyist Fourth International Organization of South Africa, writing in 1952, accepted that Jan van Riebeeck was the "father of the Cape Coloured people."[70] The *Torch*, the mouthpiece of the Non-European Unity Movement—the most prominent of the Marxist liberation organizations to gain support within the Coloured community—also accepted that the Coloured people "arose as a result of the glandular carelessness of van Riebeeck and his men."[71] For evidence that the perception of Colouredness as the automatic product of miscegenation has survived into the "new" South Africa among people regarded as politically progressive, one could point to Tokyo Sexwale, the former Gauteng premier who is married to a white woman and has described his children as Coloured;[72] similarly, the novelist Achmat Dangor declared that "in my own case, I'm so bastardized I can only call myself Coloured."[73]

If racial hybridity is the defining attribute associated with Colouredness in the popular mind, then the idea that Colouredness is an inherent racial condition that results automatically from miscegenation between black and white people is the fundamental misconception associated with the identity. In popular thinking, Colouredness is not treated as a social identity but tends to be reified into a cluster of innate qualities that spontaneously and inexorably are assumed to manifest themselves in the offspring of black-white sexual intercourse. As with another version of the joke, which dates the genesis of the Coloured people at nine months after the landing of van Riebeeck's party,[74] the popular mind looks back to primal acts of interracial sex rather than processes of social interaction and identity formation in nineteenth-century southern African society for the making of Coloured identity. Thus, no matter how "respectable" a Coloured person may have become or what his or her level of personal achievement is, the taint of that original sin has persisted in racial thinking that remains entrenched in the broader South African society.

Indeed, the risqué element of the van Riebeeck joke is derived from the image of the Coloured people having been conceived through illicit sexual intercourse immediately on the landing of the first Dutch colonists. Implicit in most people's understanding of the joke is what "Coloured" novelist Zoë Wicomb referred to as "the nasty, unspoken question of concupiscence that haunts coloured identity."[75] This racially attributed trait is not nearly as unmentionable as Wicomb's comment might suggest—except perhaps in genteel company, especially within "respectable" sectors of the Coloured community itself—as the widely recognized stereotype of the *goffel* confirms. *Goffel* is a highly pejorative term that generally refers to working-class Coloured women and characterizes them as socially inferior, usually physically unattractive, but sexually available.[76] Zimitri Erasmus attested that for her, "being Coloured is about living an identity that is clouded in sexualized shame."[77] There can be little doubt that for most people, the van Riebeeck joke is enhanced by tacit assumptions about Coloured females' lasciviousness or the ease with which they may be sexually exploited.

Throughout Western society and probably more so in South Africa, racial hybridity has carried a heavy stigma, with ideas of miscegenation and "mixed blood" conjuring up a host of repugnant connotations for most people. Negative attitudes toward "hybridization" as opposed to "purity of breed" are well entrenched in modern popular culture, whether applied to livestock, household pets, or humans.[78] Writing at the end of the 1930s, historian J. S. Marais confirmed that "this philosophy of blood and race . . . leads to a passionate aversion to miscegenation . . . which is the primary article of faith of the South African nation."[79] In South Africa, these attitudes found concrete expression in the notorious Mixed Marriages and Immorality Acts.[80] This kind of prejudice was still very much in evidence in the latter phases of white rule. Take, for example, the way Maria van Niekerk, a conservative white South African woman, expressed her horror at the repeal of the Mixed Marriages Act in 1985. Van Niekerk claimed that she "did not stand for bastardizing our land" and that she wanted South Africa "to be pure white, pure Indian, pure blacks [*sic*] and the Coloureds must be proud of what they are now."[81] This repugnance is a product of the commonly held belief that miscegenation of necessity pollutes the resulting offspring and renders them inferior. Although archconservative Andries Treurnicht's claim that "Coloureds are our 12-year-old children and must remain under our guardianship" is at the extreme end of the spectrum of racist opinion,[82] there was a general acceptance among whites that Coloured people were intellectually and morally inferior, to varying degrees, as a result of their miscegenated origins.[83]

As the van Riebeeck joke illustrates, Africans broadly shared these negative perceptions of racial hybridity and therefore of Coloured people. The Xhosa-derived Afrikaans colloquialism *malau*, a pejorative reference to Coloured people signifying a supposed lack of cultural or racial integrity and suggesting that they are thus rootless and uncouth, is a clear indication of this.[84] Sol Plaatje, in a telling if exaggerated example, gave expression to these negative perceptions of racial hybridity among Africans in his novel *Mhudi*, which had been written between 1917 and 1920 but was published only in 1930 and is generally accepted as the first South African novel in English by an African writer. In a speech to rally the defeated and dispirited Ndebele people, Mzilikazi is made to denounce the alliance between Bechuana and Boer ranged against him. He predicts that after betraying and subjugating the Bechuana, the Boers "shall take Bechuana women to wife and, with them, breed a race half man and half goblin, and . . . these Bechuana will waste away in helpless fury till the gnome offspring of such miscegenation rise up against their cruel sires."[85] The poignant story of Thuli Nhlapo, who endured a life of ridicule and rejection by both her family and the wider community that taunted her as *"boesman"* (bushman) and "this yellow thing" because she was the "love child" of an African mother and a white father, provides an intimate insight into the torment that can result from the odium that is often attached to racial hybridity in African society.[86] "Coloured" academic Roy du Pre summed up a common attitude among Africans toward Coloured people: "Africans despise Coloured people in general. They [look] upon them as 'mixed-breeds' with no nationhood, no identity, no land, no culture. The African, on the other hand, is a proud, full-blooded, 'pure-breed' with a history, culture and identity going back centuries."[87]

In keeping with the social Darwinist and eugenicist assumptions that have thoroughly permeated South African racial thinking at the popular level, it has generally been assumed that miscegenation breeds weakness. This was predicated on the notion that the progeny of racially mixed sexual unions tend to exhibit the combined or even exaggerated weaknesses of their progenitors and for the positive qualities to be diluted or lost altogether. Indeed, many of the racial traits attributed to Coloured people have often been explained in terms of the deleterious effects of racial mixture. Allegedly inherent characteristics of Coloured people—such as being physically stunted, lacking in endurance, and naturally prone to dishonesty, licentiousness, and drink—have often been explained or justified in terms of the effects of racial mixture or of *gebastenheid* (bastardization), resulting in physical and moral weakness.[88] In my experience, it was not uncommon to find both serious and tongue-in-cheek explanations suggesting that Coloured people are morally weak, confused, and vacillating by nature because their white "blood" pulls them in one direction and their black "blood" pulls them in another.[89]

Popular assumptions about the racial hybridity of the Coloured community are based on the premise that miscegenation gives rise to offspring that are related but nevertheless racially distinct from their parents.[90] In this way, from the very start of Dutch colonization, sexual relations between European male settlers, on the one hand, and Khoi and slave women, on the other, were thought to have given birth to a distinct racial entity, the Coloured people. This much is apparent from the way the joke employs Jan van Riebeeck as the symbolic father of the Coloured people and the alternative version of the joke dates the origin of the Coloured people at nine months after the landing of van Riebeeck.[91] The common characterization of Coloured people as "mixed-race"—which presupposes the prior existence of "pure races" and their "mixture" to be unnatural and undesirable or even pathological—demonstrates an unreflective popular acceptance of Coloured people as both different and inferior.[92]

In popular thinking and in a great deal of academic writing as well,[93] there is very little if any recognition of the necessary historical reality that Coloured identity arose as a result of social change and human agency rather than simply being an automatic product of miscegenation. Indeed, the assertion of a separate Coloured identity in the late nineteenth century proved to be a highly successful strategy precisely because it utilized those very ideas and assumptions of racial difference and hybridity on which the doctrine of white supremacy rested. The key assumption in this respect was that humanity consisted of a hierarchy of races in which status was determined by the degree to which a particular group conformed to the somatic and cultural norms of Western Europe.[94] Being able to assert partial descent from European settlers was thus essential to Coloureds being able to justify, and receiving, favored treatment relative to Africans.

The claim to kinship with whites was, as noted before, a double-edged sword for members of the Coloured community. Although it allowed them to argue for a status of relative privilege, it also meant accepting racial hybridity as an integral part of their being. For the white establishment, there was, of course, no question that such kinship could be the basis for a claim to equality. For some, however, kinship underpinned attitudes of paternalism. For example, Jan Boland

Coetzee, a former rugby hero who gained a reputation for progressive labor practices on his farm in the 1980s, believed that his "Coloured labourers were like children . . . didn't know what was good for them, only wanted their daily *dop* (tot) of wine."[95] But when asked whether Afrikaners were different from Coloureds, he replied, "We made them," evading the question but acknowledging paternity as well as a degree of responsibility toward Coloured people.[96] For others, the claim to kinship was embarrassing and even threatening, as demonstrated by the story of Mrs. C. S., a Coloured woman who was born on a farm in Swellendam in 1922 and lived in a Windermere squatter camp on the outskirts of Cape Town in the 1950s. Employed on a white-owned farm as a young girl, she rejected the claim of the farmer and his wife that Coloureds were different from and inferior to whites. Resorting to the van Riebeeck mythology, she countered, "The blood is then the same, there is not a white blood or a black blood or a brown blood . . . from Jan van Riebeeck's time he mated with the brown people and the whites with the brown people." Both as a form of denial and as a reinforcement of master-servant relationships, the farmer dragged her into his garage and gave her a thrashing for her insolence.[97]

It is through the misconception about their racial hybridity that the stigma of illegitimacy has also been imputed to Coloured people. In terms of popular thinking, Coloured people originated largely from black-white sexual unions outside of wedlock. There is an enduring myth that they resulted from prostitution and casual sex between slave and Khoisan women and passing soldiers, sailors, and white riffraff.[98] Cedric Dover's memorable description of the "half-caste" in Western literature—"His father is a blackguard, his mother is a whore"—suggests that it is not a peculiarly South African perception that miscegenation tends to be a failing of the lowest elements of society.[99] These associations have contributed to the perception that Coloured people lack a proper heritage or pedigree, for, as Hombi Ntshoko, an African woman from Langa, maintained, "Coloureds don't know where they come from. We know where we come from. Whites know where they come from."[100] Winnie Mandela's comment in 1991 that the Coloured people came about as a result of white men raping black women demonstrates that the idea that the Coloured community originated from extramarital unions across the color line is not only current among white racists but also broadly accepted in South African society.[101] Despite coming from an ideological position diametrically opposed to that of white racism and meant as a rebuke to white maledom, Mandela's remark reveals a similar misunderstanding regarding the nature and origin of Coloured identity.

Perceived to have originated largely from illicit sexual relations, the Coloured community as a whole has also been indelibly stained by the mark of illegitimacy. The idea that at their very genesis, the Coloured people had been conceived in "sin" contributes to the notion among racists that Coloureds are somehow defective and form a special breed of lesser beings—God's stepchildren, as Sarah Gertrude Millin vividly put it.[102] This is also apparent from the way the punch line of the van Riebeeck joke sets Coloured people apart from the rest of humanity. This outlook is, furthermore, reflected in jokes that depict Coloured people as the unintended consequence of the devil's hapless attempts at imitating God's creation of humanity. In these jokes, the devil's creations turn out to be brown and not white, and when placed on earth, they walk off singing, dancing, and drinking wine.[103] A variant on this joke has God baking figures of clay that come to life when placed on earth. Every now and then, God is heard to exclaim in frustration, "Damn, I burnt another one!" before tossing the figure into Africa. Depending on the degree of scorching, the damaged figures would turn out to be either Coloured or African and exhibit behavior appropriate to their respective racial stereotypes.

To evoke laughter, the punch line of the van Riebeeck joke draws mainly on a shared perception between teller and audience that both racial hybridity and illegitimacy are humiliating and shameful. It is clear that for people to react spontaneously to this joke, the images, values, and assumptions about Colouredness that are evoked have to be part and parcel of their waking consciousness and instantaneously accessible to their minds, given the appropriate cues. The joke, however, goes beyond the imputed traits of hybridization and illegitimacy and draws on other aspects of Coloured stereotyping for embellishment.

Although not raised directly by the joke, the implicit question of who van Riebeeck and his merry band's sexual partners were evokes the popular association of Coloured people with the Khoisan and hence with a "savage" past. Whereas the Coloured protagonist in the van Riebeeck joke might put much store by his or her partial European descent and assimilation to Western culture, both teller and audience are nevertheless likely to be mindful of the Khoisan heritage associated with Colouredness.

In the popular mind, the association is an extremely derogatory one. This much is evident from the terms *Boesman* (Bushman or San) and *Hotnot* (Hottentot or Khoikhoi) being among the most opprobrious of racial slurs that can be hurled at Coloured people. The contractions *Hottie, Bushy,* or *Boesie* are also sometimes used.[104] The extreme derogation of these words lies in the images of physical ugliness, repulsive social practices, and mental and social inferiority they conjure up. In 1919, a correspondent to the *S. A. Clarion,* a newspaper aimed at a Coloured readership, remarked that "one would have a quarrel on one's hands if one addressed a coloured in a Cape Town street as Hotnot even if that person had three-quarters Hotnot blood in his veins."[105] Gerald Stone's description of the meaning of *Boesman* in the lexicon of working-class Coloured people more than half a century later is "a seriously insulting reference to coloured person, denoting putatively San features: sparse peppercorn hair, flat nose, wizened face, dry yellow skin, steatopygic posture, small stature: connoting insignificance, ugliness, poverty, vagrancy, treachery."[106] From my experience of the way in which the term has been used by out-groups to describe Coloured people, moral and intellectual inferiority should be added to this list. Generations of South Africans, both black and white, have had negative stereotypes of "Bushmen" and "Hottentots" instilled into them, especially during school history lessons.[107] Indicative of the deep opprobrium and emotive associations attached to these terms, a riot was sparked in the sleepy west coast town of Laaiplek in 1987 when a local white resident called one of the Coloured townsmen a "Hotnot."[108]

In popular discourse, the Khoisan origins of Coloured people are often used to explain racial traits ascribed to them. Negative characteristics attributed to the Khoisan have thus been projected onto the Coloured grouping as a whole, invoking images of inveterate laziness, irresponsibility, dirtiness, and a penchant for thievery, all of which are often assumed to have been inherited by Coloured people from their Khoisan ancestors. This much is apparent from another popular joke that sometimes also served as an utterance of frustration, especially among employers, at the alleged waywardness of Coloured employees—"You can take the Coloured out of the bush but you cannot take the bush out of the Coloured"—or alternatively and more to the point— "You can take the Coloured out of the bush, man, but you cannot take the Bushman out of the Coloured."[109]

It is worth noting that although Coloured people have been strongly associated with their Khoisan progenitors, the identification with a slave heritage has been tenuous. There are two basic reasons for this. First, the Cape Colony, unlike most New World slave societies, did not develop a vigorous slave culture, largely because of the atomized pattern of slaveholding, the extreme ethnic diversity of the slave population, and the high death rate among importees.[110] Since slaves were thus, by and large, not able to transmit a coherent body of learned behavior and communal experience from one generation to the next, an identifiably slave culture remained weak and attenuated at the Cape.[111] Therefore, the conscious identification with a slave past did not survive much beyond the lives of the freed slaves themselves. Second, because slaves were defined in terms of their legal status, their descendants were able to escape the stigma of slave ancestry fairly easily after emancipation. In popular consciousness, vague connotations of a servile past have been attached to Coloured identity, for example, through the annual reminder of the Coon Carnival and the use of the pejorative label *Gam* (Ham) to describe working-class Coloured people.[112]

Coloured people, however, could not so easily avoid being associated with the Khoisan because the defining characteristics, in this instance, were racially attributed and genetically transmitted physical traits. Many Coloured people have had little choice but to live with physical traits that have served as markers of the Khoisan physical type, as indicated by the colloquialisms *boesman korrels* (Bushman corns or tufts) and *Hotnot holle*, vernacular Afrikaans for steatopygia. The nicknames *Boesman* or *Hotnot* for people who display what are taken to be typical Khoisan physical features have also been fairly common within the Coloured working class.[113] Although these nicknames could signify endearment or be ironic and self-deprecating,[114] they are generally derogatory and are an indication that white racist values have, to a considerable degree, been internalized by those Coloured people who use them.

The van Riebeeck joke also draws on the marginality of the Coloured community for heightened effect. Whites are represented by a proactive and familiar figure symbolic of white supremacy, but in the supposed making of the Coloured people, their black ancestors remain essentially faceless and passive. There has been an abiding perception that Coloured people played little or no constructive part in the making of South African society and thus do not deserve the recognition of historical personalities beyond what is necessary for whites to make sense of their own history. This is very much part of the depersonalization that is almost universally present in the way that dominant groups perceive those whom they dominate.

Coloured marginality is evoked in a second and more subtle way by the joke. In human interaction, one of the psychosocial functions of humor is to demonstrate and affirm power. Jokes therefore often seek to humiliate and demean or depend on vituperation to raise a laugh, as the international examples of "Paddy" jokes or blonde jokes and local examples of "Gammatjie and Abdoltjie" or "Raj" jokes demonstrate.[115] Thus, those who considered themselves superior to Coloureds were likely to have found the joke all the funnier because it reinforced their conceit that they were able to laugh at Coloured people with impunity. However, Coloured people who laughed at it—and in my experience, many more Coloured people laughed at the joke than took offense—confirmed their marginality by acquiescing in their own denigration.

Yet the targets of demeaning humor are not entirely powerless because humor can, of course, also be harnessed for retaliation. This would explain the immense popularity of "van der Merwe" jokes among Coloured people during the apartheid era. The "stupid and uncultured Afrikaner" stereotype represented by van der Merwe provided the perfect foil for Coloured people to assert their worth as human beings and to hit back at those whom they regarded as the most rabidly racist and their main oppressors.

The popularity of the van Riebeeck joke has waned in recent years. The amelioration of interblack political divisions in the post-1976 environment, the growth of a mass, nonracial democratic movement during the 1980s, and the dawning of the "new South Africa" have progressively made the values and sentiments embodied in the joke less acceptable in public discourse. The growing rejection of Coloured identity by politicized Coloureds from the mid-1970s onward meant that crude racist thinking of the sort embodied in this joke became unacceptable to a widening constituency of people. By the late 1980s, even the likes of the Reverend Allan Hendrickse, the leader of the collaborationist Labour Party, at times rejected Coloured identity. In a heated moment in parliament, for example, he lashed out at the National Party: "God made me a man, the National Party made me a Coloured man."[116]

Although the image of van Riebeeck is far less pervasive than it was in the "old South Africa," it has nevertheless remained a powerful symbol of white supremacism in the new millennium.[117] Bizarre confirmation of this occurred at a formal dinner on 31 October 2000, organized by a local black economic empowerment company to celebrate Cape Town's cultural diversity and to promote racial tolerance. At the dinner, held in the banquet hall of the Castle in Cape Town, one of the guests, Priscilla De Wet-Fox, who claims to be the headperson of the Chainnoquia Khoi-Khoi tribe of the Oudtshoorn region, heckled speakers and subjected the gathering to a tirade about the colonial oppression of the Khoi. On being escorted out of the function, she attacked a bronze bust of van Riebeeck in the foyer, damaging it and causing its eyes to pop out when she pushed it off its pedestal. De Wet-Fox later justified her actions by saying that "van Riebeeck lied to my ancestors" and that he was a symbol of European colonialism that had made her feel "ashamed of being me, of looking like me."[118]

Humor is intrinsic to human interaction and forms an integral part of popular culture. For these reasons, jokes disclose much about the societies and communities in which they become current. Because people reveal their values, aspirations, fears, hatreds, and most other aspects of their social experience through humor, jokes—especially the more enduring and popular ones—are authentic reflections of the perceptions, attitudes, and mores of the societies in which they circulate and are often more reliable indicators of popular thinking than the conventional sources used by historians and social analysts.[119] This authenticity is guaranteed to the extent that jokes not only have to resonate with the values, sensibilities, and experiences of their target audiences to survive but also have to make sense instantaneously to elicit the appropriate response.

The van Riebeeck joke, by any yardstick, provides an accurate and dependable gauge of popular attitudes toward Coloured people during the apartheid era. At the core of its success and longevity as a joke lie the popular assumptions that Colouredness is an automatic product of miscegenation and that racial hybridity, together with its associations of illegitimacy and racial inferiority, are shameful and therefore open to ridicule. The joke also indirectly draws on a wide range of derogatory imagery about the Khoisan, the marginality of the Coloured people, and the racially attributed trait of their profligacy for embellishment. That most Coloured poeple were able to laugh at this ribbing and accept Jan van Riebeeck as the "father" of the Coloured people is a measure of just how hegemonic the racist ideas and assumptions behind the joke were in apartheid South Africa. The evidence indicates that this mindset has been slow to change in the postapartheid period, despite the dictates of political correctness that now govern South African public life.

This overview of Coloured identity and the history of the Coloured people in white-ruled South Africa has provided insight into the way Coloureds viewed themselves, their community, and its place in the broader society. It has elucidated the dynamic behind the expression of a separate Coloured identity, highlighting continuities in processes of Coloured self-definition. This analysis has identified their assimilationism, their intermediate status in the racial hierarchy, the negative associations attached to the identity, and their marginality as core elements of Coloured identity and demonstrated how they meshed to reproduce and stabilize that identity through the twentieth century. In addition, the role of popular stereotyping in the social construction of Coloured identity has been explored, explaining how associations of hybridity, illegitimacy, Khoisan primitiveness, and marginality converged in reinforcing and reproducing the racial typecasting of Coloured people. These themes are elaborated on in the following chapter, which investigates the ways in which Coloured people viewed their history and how interpretations of this history changed over time.

2

History from the Margins

Changing Perceptions of Its Past
within the Coloured Community

The marginality of the Coloured community is reflected in South African historiography in that relatively little has been written on the history of this social group and much of what has been written is polemical, speculative, poorly researched, or heavily biased. In many general histories, Coloured people have effectively been written out of the narrative and marginalized to a few throwaway comments scattered through the text.[1] In addition, only a handful of works on the subject have been written by Coloured people themselves. As early as 1913, Harold Cressy, a Coloured educator and school principal, decried this state of affairs when he urged the Coloured teaching profession to help build self-confidence and pride in the community by dispelling the myth that Coloured people played little part in the history of their country.[2] Les Switzer, historian and professor of communication at the University of Houston, summed up the situation eloquently in 1995 when he wrote that "South Africa's coloured community has remained a marginalized community—marginalized by history and even historians."[3]

This chapter charts changing approaches to Coloured identity and the history of the Coloured people within that community itself by analyzing popular perceptions of this past as well as the writing of Coloured intellectuals on the subject. Both popular beliefs and intellectual discourse about the nature of Colouredness and its history played an important part in defining the identity and creating a sense

of community among its bearers. In addition to epitomizing the thinking within sectors of the community, the texts chosen for analysis also
reflect the social and political currents of the time. Importantly, they
lay bare ideological contestation around the meaning of Colouredness
and strategies for social and political action.

Contending Historiographical Paradigms

Historical writing on the Coloured community, both that of a popular
nature and that emanating from the academy in the era of white supremacy, can be divided into three broad classes. The first, which may
be termed the essentialist school, is by far the most common approach
and coincides with the popular view of Coloured identity as a product
of miscegenation going back to the earliest days of European settlement at the Cape. According to this approach, racial hybridity is considered the essence of Colouredness. For essentialists, there is usually
no need to explain the nature or existence of Coloured identity because it is part of an assumed reality that sees South African society
as consisting of distinct races, of which the Coloured people is one.
The existence of Coloured identity poses no analytical problem because it is regarded as having developed naturally and self-evidently
as a result of miscegenation.[4] This approach is inherently racialized
because it assigns racial origins and racial characteristics to the concept of Colouredness, though it has to be recognized that not all writing within this category is necessarily racist. Indeed, a good deal of it,
including some of the best writing in this genre, was intended to help
break down racial barriers and expose the injustices suffered by Coloured people under the South African racial system.[5] Because the
essentialist approach embodies the conventional wisdom about Coloured identity, virtually all of the popular writing and most of the
older and more conservative academic works are cast in this mold.[6]

A second approach to the history of the Coloured people emerged
in the 1980s in reaction to the prejudicial assumptions of the traditional mode of analysis and a desire among scholars within the "liberal"
and "radical" paradigms of South African history to distance themselves from any form of racist thinking. This school, whose adherents
will be referred to as the instrumentalists, regarded Coloured identity
as an artificial concept imposed by the white supremacist state and
ruling groups on a weak and vulnerable sector of the population.[7] Positions in this respect range from seeing Coloured identity simply as

a device for excluding people of mixed race from the dominant society to viewing it as a product of deliberate divide-and-rule strategies by the ruling white minority to prevent black South Africans from forming a united front against racism and exploitation.[8] The instrumentalist approach was grounded in the growing rejection of Coloured identity that gained impetus from the latter half of the 1970s onward and was buttressed by the nonracism of the mass democratic movement of the 1980s. This approach represented the politically correct view of the post-Soweto era and stemmed from a refusal to give credence to apartheid thinking or, in the case of the expedient, from a fear of being accused of doing so.[9]

A third paradigm, to which this study subscribes and which may be dubbed social constructionism, emerged from the latter half of the 1980s in response to the inadequacies of both the essentialist and instrumentalist approaches. It criticizes both those approaches for their tendency to accept Coloured identity as given and to portray it as fixed. Their reification of the identity, it is argued, fails to recognize fluidities in processes of Coloured self-identification or ambiguities in the expression of the identity. In essentialist histories, this is a product of a profoundly Eurocentric perspective and a reliance on the simplistic formulations of popular racialized conceptions of Coloured identity. The problem in instrumentalist writing partly stems from a narrow focus on Coloured protest politics and the social injustices suffered by the community, which has had the effect of exaggerating the resistance of Coloured people to white supremacism and playing down their accommodation with the South African racial system. The overall result has been an oversimplification of the phenomenon in this literature.[10]

The cardinal sin of both these schools, however, is their condescension in denying Coloured people a significant role in the making of their own identity. Essentialist interpretations do this by assuming Colouredness to be an inbred quality that arises automatically from miscegenation. Instrumentalists share the essentialist premise that Coloured identity is something negative and undesirable, but they try to blame it on the racism of the ruling white minority. Though they may have had the laudable intention of countering the racism of essentialist accounts, instrumentalist histories have nevertheless contributed to the marginalization of the Coloured people by denying them their role in the basic cognitive function of creating and reproducing their own social identities. Even the best of these histories, Gavin

Lewis's *Between the Wire and the Wall,* despite its firm focus on the Coloured people themselves and its stress on their agency in the political arena, is nevertheless condescending by suggesting that "the solution to this dilemma [of defining Coloured identity] is to accept Coloured identity as a white-imposed categorization."[11] Both approaches treat Coloured identity as something exceptional, failing to recognize it for what it is—a historically specific social construction, like any other social identity. In this respect, both schools reflect the undue influence of contemporary ideological and political considerations.

The main concerns of the social constructionist approach have therefore been to demonstrate the complexity of Coloured identity and, most important, to stress the agency of Coloured people in the making of their own identity. Emphasis has also been placed on the ways in which ambiguities in Coloureds' identity and their marginality influenced their social experience and political consciousness. This approach also seeks to demonstrate that far from being the anonymous, inert entities of the essentialist school or the righteous resisters of instrumentalist histories, Coloured people exhibited a much more complex reaction to white supremacism that encompassed resistance as well as collaboration, protest as well as accommodation. By its very nature, social identity is largely and in the first instance the product of its bearers and can no more be imposed on people by the state or ruling groups than it can spring automatically from miscegenation or their racial constitution. Social identity is cultural in nature in that it is part of learned behavior and is molded by social experience and social interaction. At most, social identities can be manipulated by outsiders—but even then, only to the extent that it resonates strongly with the bearers' image of themselves and their social group as a whole.

Up from Servitude and Savagery: Earlier Perspectives on Coloured History

Within the broader category of essentialist writing, it is possible to distinguish three further divisions. First, there are those I refer to as traditionalists, who analyze Coloured identity and history in terms of the racist values and assumptions prevalent in white supremacist thinking. Second, there are the liberal essentialists, who dissent from the dominant racist view and seek to demonstrate that cooperation and interdependence rather than racial antagonism marked historical interaction between South Africa's various peoples.[12] The third distinct strand within the essentialist school might be termed the progressionist interpretation of Coloured history, and for the greater part of the twentieth century, this interpretation represented the conventional view of members of the Coloured community regarding their own history. Until challenged by ideas emanating from a Marxist-inspired radical movement during the 1940s and 1950s, the progressionist version reigned supreme within the better-educated and politicized sector of this group. This approach was progressionist in that it was based on the assumption that human society and, with it, the Coloured people were on a path of inevitable progress to a future of peace, prosperity, and social harmony.[13]

In essence, the progressionist perspective wove together an affirmative view of Coloured history with key elements from the traditionalist and liberal strands. This interpretation thus accepted the racist view that Coloured people formed a separate "race" and were socially and culturally "backward" by Western standards but stressed their common history and cultural affinities with whites while strongly emphasizing that theirs was a history that demonstrated a hunger for personal development and the achievement of social advancement against enormous odds. The progressionist interpretation was not so much an alternative to the white supremacist version as an acceptance of it in broad outline but with major qualifications. It reinterpreted crucial aspects of the dominant society's version to give it a positive spin and an optimistic outlook for the future. For the Coloured people themselves, the critical difference between their progressionist visions of their history and those of the traditional genre of white South Africa was that, even though they admitted they were "backward," they did not accept their inferiority as permanent or inherent. Combining an environmentalist concept of racial difference with liberal values of personal freedom, equality in the eyes of the law, interracial cooperation, and status based on individual merit, progressionists argued that the history of the Coloured people demonstrated that they were well advanced in the process of becoming as fully "civilized" as whites and thus deserved to be accepted into the dominant society. Espoused publicly by organic intellectuals and political leaders within the Coloured community, this interpretation was usually coupled with a plea for fair treatment or the preservation of their status of relative privilege within the South African racial hierarchy.

Although there was no attempt from members of the Coloured community to produce any formal or systematic account of their history until the latter half of the 1930s, educated and politicized Coloured people nevertheless exhibited a clear sense of the trajectory of their history as a community. This much is evident from Harold Cressy's 1913 exhortation to his colleagues to raise the profile of the community's history. During the earlier part of the twentieth century, this historical consciousness, though it had not yet been formalized as written history, was implicit in discourse about Coloured people as a community, including their political ideals and social aspirations. This consciousness, usually expressed in terms of a common oppression dating back to slavery and the dispossession of the Khoisan, informed the endeavors of Coloured communal organizations and can be deduced piecemeal from a range of evidence in which Coloured people reflected on their community and its place in South African society. This sense of shared history was expressed not so much as an interest in the past for its own sake but as a means to justify social and political demands and support strategies for communal advancement. Abdullah Abdurahman's presidential addresses to the 1909, 1923, and 1939 APO conferences are good examples of the progressionist interpretation of Coloured history harnessed to support particular social or political agendas.[14]

This popular perception of Coloured history looked back to the period of Dutch colonial rule as a dark night of slavery, savagery, and serfdom during which the Coloured people came into being as a result of miscegenation. In 1923, Abdurahman described the Dutch policy of *conciliatie* (conciliation) as having "always meant, for the Coloured races, the acceptance of servitude." It was the introduction of liberal policies under British rule and the endeavors of missionaries on their behalf that was seen to mark the start of the Coloured people's ascent from servile and brutish origins into the light of civilization. The 1828 repeal of the vagrancy laws that had enserfed the Khoisan and the emancipation of slaves in 1834 were regarded together as the main watershed in the history of the Coloured people because these acts gave them personal freedom and the opportunity to cultivate a communal life. The establishment of the principle of equality in the eyes of the law and the introduction of a nonracial franchise in 1853 were viewed as the other key developments because they bestowed citizenship rights on Coloured people and provided a means for their integration into the mainstream of Cape colonial society. In the words of Abdurahman during his 1939 presidential address to the APO, "The Ordinance [50 of 1828] was the real foundation of the broad political framework of 1852 [*sic*] within which White and Coloured were joined together by a bond of loyalty as free and equal citizens." The Coloureds' assimilation to Western culture and their acquisition of education were presented as proof of their ongoing integration into the civic life of the Cape Colony until unification in 1910, which allowed the triumph of northern racism over southern liberalism, reversed this process. Abdurahman summed up the course of this history in his 1923 presidential address: "Since van Riebeeck's day there was a period of bitter struggle, then followed a period of comparative tranquility and hopefulness in the Cape . . . from 1854 to 1910 during which years the Non-European races enjoyed political privileges." After that, however, "the policy of van Riebeeck has been steadily, vigorously, and relentlessly followed."[15]

The earliest known attempt from within the Coloured community itself to provide an account of the history of the Coloured people is found in a history textbook entitled *The Student Teacher's History Course: For the Use in Coloured Training Colleges*, which was published in Paarl by Huguenot Press in 1936 by two relatively junior members of the Coloured teaching profession, Dorothy Hendricks and Christian Viljoen. Hendricks was the daughter of Teachers' League of South Africa (TLSA) stalwart Fred Hendricks and lectured at the Zonnebloem Training College. The twenty-six-year-old Viljoen, who taught at the Athlone Institute, a Coloured teachers' training college in Paarl, was to become a leading member of the Teachers' League, serving on its executive committee in the late 1930s and elected president in 1941.[16] Hendricks, who had bachelor of arts and bachelor of education degrees, and Viljoen, with master of arts and bachelor of education degrees, not only were very highly qualified by the standards of their community at the time but also held some of the most prestigious teaching posts to which Coloured people could aspire.

The textbook followed the history syllabus for training Coloured primary school teachers and provided a broad outline of modern European, British imperial, and South African history from 1652 to the 1930s. Interspersed in the section on the history of South Africa are short subsections on Coloured history, which, if stitched together, would provide a coherent sketch of the history of the Coloured people.[17] Hendricks and Viljoen's rendition of South African history conformed to white settler views, as one would expect of a textbook diligently following the syllabus set out by the Cape Education Department. Accordingly, the writing on the history of the Coloured community was suffused with the phraseology and assumptions of white supremacist discourse.

The authors largely accepted settler stereotyping of the indigenous peoples, in that they present the "Bushmen" as primitive, dangerous, and essentially unassimilable whereas the "Hottentots" were described as an incorrigibly lazy and thieving people. Slaves were depicted as having adapted well to civilized life under the paternalistic care of colonists and the relatively benign conditions prevalent at the Cape. Hendricks and Viljoen followed the customary line that miscegenation and a limited degree of interracial marriage early on in the life of the Cape Colony gave rise to a "half-breed" population that formed the nucleus of "a new race that was emerging." They claimed that "this hybrid race, together with pure-blooded slaves and detribalized Hottentots, became known as the Cape Coloured people and gradually developed more and more homogeneity as they became subjected to positive and constructive forces of European society." According to Hendricks and Viljoen, the emergent Coloured race benefited not only from the civilizing efforts of the colonists but also from "the unconscious influence of example and suggestion which acted with peculiar power upon an imitative and susceptible race."[18]

The authors asserted that with the emancipation of the Khoi in 1828 and then of slaves in 1834, the Coloured people "entered a new era of development . . . to work out their own salvation, to rise as a class or revert to barbarism." By 1834, the Coloured people were seen to have come into existence as an identifiable race, for "when emancipation took place they had already developed the physical and psychological characteristics which they today exhibit." Not able to adapt well to the competitive environment engendered by the mineral revolution, the Coloured people "remained hewers of wood and drawers of water." Hendricks and Viljoen concluded that they then "gradually began to develop into a distinct community and withdraw to the slums and locations [where] the church continued to take care of them."[19]

In part, this abject complicity in the denigration of their own community was clearly the result of the authors' need to comply with the syllabus in order for their text to be accepted as a course reader. Although there was only the slightest trace of the progressionist vision in their interpretation, there can be little doubt that Hendricks and Viljoen, being typical members of the moderate faction within Coloured politics, subscribed to this view but were prepared to suppress it for the sake of having the volume approved as a textbook. Their meek conformity with the expectations of the Education Department was also an indication of Coloured marginality, as negotiation with its officials or any form of protest or assertive action on their part would have been futile.[20] The only alternative was not to publish at all.

That Hendricks and Viljoen, in line with the progressionist vision, would presumably have believed that the Coloured people were indeed "backward" and had relatively recently emerged from a barbarous past probably helped make their distasteful task a little easier. And at the very least in the case of Hendricks, a personal identification with whiteness and a dissociation from Colouredness played a role. Ralph Bunche, an African American professor of political science at Howard University who spent three months traveling through South Africa toward the end of 1937, reported that the "very fair" Hendricks, "though known to staff [at Zonnebloem] as coloured, has nothing to do with coloured people."[21] Although it is not known whether Hendricks and Viljoen's volume was approved as a textbook or how widely it was used, it is clear that their version of Coloured history was representative of what Coloured teacher trainees were fed and in turn passed on to their pupils.[22]

The "Benefit of Their White Blood": A Late 1930s Progressionist Interpretation

Given the schematic nature of Hendricks and Viljoen's outline history and the constraint of having to conform to the syllabus, Christian Ziervogel's *Brown South Africa*, a slim volume that appeared a mere two years later, deserves recognition as the first history of the Coloured people to have been written by a Coloured person. An autodidact who had worked his way up from humble origins, Ziervogel devoted his energies to the spiritual, cultural, and socioeconomic uplifting of the Coloured community, particularly in District Six, a depressed inner-city area of Cape Town, where he lived. Ziervogel, a noted bibliophile and librarian, had a reputation as one of the leading Coloured intellectuals in the 1930s and 1940s and was nicknamed "the Professor of District Six."[23] In this book, he wrote self-consciously as a Coloured intellectual deliberating on the history and current condition of his community.

Ziervogel was an enigmatic and contradictory figure. On the one hand, he was active in left-wing circles, supporting the National Liberation League and contributing to its journal, *The Liberator*.[24] He confided to Ralph Bunche that he not only had "'left' inclinations" but also "hates white people and can't help it."[25] Yet *Brown South Africa* as well as his other publications were politically conservative, racist in outlook, and, although critical of white supremacism, nevertheless deferential toward white authority. His work, moreover, contained not the slightest trace of class analysis or radical rhetoric of the sort that would ordinarily have been expected from someone with left-wing sympathies. In tone and content, the book was typical of moderate, assimilationist discourse within the Coloured elite. And in keeping with the moderate political agenda, a key objective of the book was to plead with whites for fair treatment of the Coloured people and to aid their social advancement.

Ziervogel's use of the term *brown* in the title signaled his acceptance of popular racialized perceptions of Colouredness. Indeed, he regarded the term *coloured* to be inaccurate and preferred *brown hybrid*. His interpretation differed little from white supremacist versions of Coloured history in broad principle except that he wove a strongly progressionist strand into his narrative, arguing that in the case of Coloured people, racial differences should not lead to their exclusion from the dominant society. The contorted logic and profoundly racist assumptions that at times informed Ziervogel's tract can be gauged from his explanation of why various sections of the Coloured community could be expected to develop at different rates:

> The hybrids of South Africa, the coloured people, are in many cases partly descended from English people, and must of necessity have inherited some of the virtues of that race. Hence, though they are comparatively backward at the present time, it is reasonable to suppose that it will not take them nine centuries to reach their ancestors' high standard of development. Those descended from Asiatics will naturally develop in accordance with the stage of development previously reached by their ancestral race. That is, the people of Indian descent will develop more rapidly than those of Javanese descent, since the former come from a stock where there has been greater enlightenment. On the other hand, the hybrids of Bantu origin cannot be expected to develop as rapidly as others, since the degree of development reached by the Bantu is not equal to that of the Europeans or the Asiatics.

All this was offered despite the author's declared standpoint that "humanity is greater than race," that "'pure races' are hypothetical . . . and have no present existence," and that he rejected the "Nordic Myth" of Aryan superiority.[26]

Ziervogel's interpretation of the history of the Coloured people not only typified the progessionist vision but was also the most comprehensive and fully developed example of this paradigm. Its appearance was conveniently timed, coming as it did just as Marxist-inspired views of this history were about to challenge the conventional wisdom. The unifying thread of his none-too-coherent and often rather vague narrative was the persistent struggle of the Coloured people to rise from a benighted past to ever higher levels of civilization, their distinctive characteristic as a people being that they were "constantly responsive" to the "progressive" influence of Western civilization.[27]

Brown South Africa followed the conventional pattern of having the Coloured people originate as a result of miscegenation during the Dutch colonial period, describing van Riebeeck's landing as "the beginning of White South Africa, and also of Brown South Africa." He regarded the emancipation of slaves as pivotal to the emergence of a specifically Coloured identity, although he gave no explanation of how Coloured identity came about; he offered no more than "before and after 1834, the half-castes, Hottentots and slaves were merged together as the Cape Coloured people." The real significance of emancipation for Ziervogel was that it "released coloured energies for self-improvement and ambition up to then repressed by social injustices." Their newfound freedom gave the people the incentive to profit from their own efforts and aroused a quest "for education, the acquiring of property and the cultivation of the mind." And although "mental and spiritual progress" was slow at first, the Coloured people, with the help of sympathetic whites, always managed to find ways to overcome obstacles—not least of which were the legal impediments raised by the colonial government—to their "upward course in the common life of South Africa."[28]

Ziervogel depicted Coloured people as well on their way to being integrated into the dominant society on an equal footing with colonists by the mid-nineteenth century, when the "strong rush of the Bantu peoples sweeping downwards from the north, and the European advance upward from the south, meant that the two virile forces came face to face." The ensuing struggle for supremacy and the growing incorporation of Africans into the South African economy after the discovery of minerals instilled a "fear complex in whites." The

consequent hardening of racial prejudices not only put an end to Coloureds' integration into the dominant society but also reversed the
trend to the extent that in the twentieth century, they fell victim to
white South Africa's segregationist policies.[29]

The author accepted that the Coloured people were "comparatively
backward at the present time" but rejected the view of racists such as
Sarah Gertrude Millin who regarded this condition as permanent. He
asserted that during nearly three centuries of miscegenation and acculturation, "this half-caste type has evolved into something very like
the Southern Europeans." Despite huge impediments, the Coloured
people had made great strides in the last generation and were rapidly
catching up with whites. He viewed educated Coloureds as a dynamic,
modernizing group fully imbued with the "spirit of civilization" and
the most progressive elements of Western culture. He thus resented
white perceptions that "the coloured man is only fit to be a messenger
or a hawker" and the tendency not to judge Coloured people as individuals but to assume that they were "of an inferior race, whose most
striking characteristics are those of lower intelligence, lower knowledge and lower general constitution." Ziervogel was also frustrated
by the indifference of the state and whites in general to the plight of
the Coloured working classes living in squalor and the detrimental
effect that the civilized labor policy and other discriminatory measures
had on their progress as a people.[30]

Writing in a context of intensifying racial chauvinism internationally and tightening segregationism at home, Ziervogel feared that
Coloureds could suffer a fate similar to that of Africans, to the extent
of perhaps even finding themselves subject to territorial segregation.
He was thus at pains to stress the long history and cultural affinities
that Coloured people shared with whites. Although he did not broach
the issue directly in *Brown South Africa*, in his pamphlet *The Coloured
People and the Race Problem*, published two years earlier, he explicitly
raised a related question: "On which side of the dividing line is he (the
coloured man) to be placed?" Asserting that the two groups were so
closely related that it was often difficult to distinguish between Coloured and white individuals, he argued that Coloureds "have practi-
cally nothing in common with the Bantu. While the Native is one who
is at home in the countryside, has a language of his own, a culture of
his own, and lives in many cases under tribal law, the coloured people
came into being and live the whole of their lives in the midst of European civilization and culture."[31] On this basis, he invoked the call at-

tributed to Lord Selborne, high commissioner for South Africa from 1905 to 1910—"Give the coloured people the benefit of their white blood"—and appealed for "absorption" and not segregation as the solution to the "Coloured problem."[32]

"A Purposeful Social Instrument": Radical Counter-positions of the 1940s and 1950s

It was fully forty-three years after the publication of *Brown South Africa* that the next significant book on the history of the Coloured community by a "Coloured" author—Maurice Hommel's *Capricorn Blues*—appeared. Meanwhile, during the 1940s and 1950s, the radical movement in Coloured politics developed an interpretation of Coloured history that provided an alternative to the progressionist version.

The elaboration of a contending version of Coloured history was spearheaded by intellectuals within the Trotskyist tradition of radical politics, of which the Non-European Unity Movement and the Fourth International Organization of South Africa (FIOSA) were the main factions during the 1940s.[33] The rival radical tradition, allied to the Communist Party and later the Congress Movement, made little contribution to the fleshing out of this new interpretation. With its emphasis on political activism, the Communist Party faction appears to have been too caught up in the cut and thrust of day-to-day politicking to pay too much attention to polemics about the significance of history and debate over the implications of South Africa's past for current and future revolutionary strategy. Coloured political activists in the Trotskyist tradition were prone to a more cerebral and highly theorized approach and the precept expressed by FIOSA member Kenneth Jordaan: "In history [lies] the key to understanding the present which in turn is the indispensable guide to the future."[34]

Like its progressionist counterpart, the radical view of the trajectory of Coloured history was implicit in the ideology and aspirations of the left-wing movement as well as in its political strategy. In addition, this historical consciousness was sometimes invoked for political purposes, such as arguing that black unity was a prerequisite for overthrowing white rule in South Africa, or to score points off opponents in ideological infighting. The best example of such an exchange involving the history of the Coloured people is Kenny Jordaan's riposte to Willem van Schoor's history of segregation in South Africa.[35] Besides wanting to refine the relatively crude analysis of van Schoor,

Jordaan was also clearly engaged in a contest of one-upmanship between FIOSA and the NEUM, of which van Schoor, president of the TLSA for much of the 1950s, was a leading member.

This radical discourse, however, differed from the progressionist interpretation in that little attention was paid, directly or exclusively, to the history of the Coloured people per se, and it did not find expression in a focused history in the way the progressionist view was represented in *Brown South Africa*. Drawing on Marxist theory, radical historical analyses were usually situated within a framework of the development of international capitalism and the imperatives behind imperialism. In contrast to the more parochial concerns of the progressionist perspective, social issues tended to be viewed in the context of international relations and global history by radicals.[36] And given the radicals' explicit goal of fomenting social revolution, their reflections on South African society and its history by and large trancended narrower issues relating to localized identities, such as the specific role or significance of the Coloured people on any particular question. Their emphasis on black and working-class unity also discouraged separate consideration of the Coloured community. In the writings of radical Coloured intellectuals, issues relating specifically to the Coloured community were therefore either ignored, subsumed under a broader black rubric, or referred to obliquely or parenthetically. The collective radical perception of the history of the Coloured people thus needs to be unraveled and extracted by inference from broader analyses of the history of South Africa or of the "oppressed."

Although Coloured radical politics had always been rent by fierce ideological infighting and irreconcilable doctrinal splits, there was sufficient common ground for one to discern a generic radical notion of the history of the Coloured people. The spirit with which Coloured activists in the radical movement, especially the Trotskyist faction, approached history in general and the history of South Africa in particular is neatly summed up in the opening sentence of van Schoor's address on segregation to the Teachers' League of South Africa in October 1950 and repeated for emphasis as its closing sentence: "A people desiring to emancipate itself must understand the process of its enslavement." He went on to explain that "we who have thus far been the victims of South African history, will play the major role in the shaping of a new history. In order to make that history we must understand that history."[37] Radicals would also have shared Edgar Maurice's view that "the phenomenon of colour prejudice and the colour bar is largely one of capitalist exploitation of peoples . . . a purposeful social instrument, politically manufactured to serve certain ends."[38] Insofar as it referred to the Coloured people, radical historical writing was framed in these broad terms.

Historical analyses by radical Coloured intellectuals, though recognizing the existence of the Coloured people as a separate social entity, avoided treating them as an analytical category distinct from the African majority. Van Schoor's monograph on the origin and development of segregation in South Africa, for example, focused almost entirely on the African experience and hardly made any mention of Coloureds or Indians. It is noteworthy that in this review of South African history stretching back to the arrival of van Riebeeck, the first substantive comment by van Schoor on the Coloured people related to the establishment of the Coloured Advisory Council in 1943. He indirectly justified this approach by claiming that Africans formed a large majority of the oppressed and that exploitative measures had largely been directed at them.[39]

Jordaan criticized this tendency of "placing the Cape Coloured people in the same category as the Bantu" as ahistorical and a distortion of the past.[40] It should thus come as no surprise that it is in his writing that one finds the most explicit treatment of the history of the Coloured people in radical writing. But even he did not address the history of the Coloured people directly as an independent topic of inquiry. In his disquisition, "Jan van Riebeeck: His Place in South African History,"[41] Jordaan chalked out the barest outline of the history of the Coloured people as a by-product of his analysis of the "social systems" that have characterized South African history and a concomitant attempt to provide a rough periodization of the South African past.[42] Besides using his analysis to support the call for a boycott of the van Riebeeck tercentenary festival, one of Jordaan's aims was to correct ahistorical perceptions that the treatment of South African blacks through history could be explained in terms of an abstract, uniform white racism. He wanted to demonstrate that each social system had its own set of policies "toward the black and mixed people," grounded in their specific "living historical reality which grew out of a definitive stage in the productive process."[43] For all its sketchiness, Jordaan's text will have to serve as the model for the radical perception of Coloured history in the absence of any more explicit example.

Born in Cape Town in 1924 and a teacher by profession, Kenneth Jordaan was a prominent member of FIOSA in the latter half of the

1940s. Together with a small band of associates who declined to comply with the Fourth International's recommendation that FIOSA amalgamate with the rival Cape Town Trotskyist grouping, the Worker's Party of South Africa, Jordaan formed the Forum Club, an independent left-wing discussion group that met during the early 1950s. In the 1950s, Jordaan won broad respect in left-wing circles for a number of theoretical papers he wrote on the nature of South African society, its history, and the implications this held for revolutionary strategy.[44]

The first social system of South African history identified by Jordaan existed during the era of Company rule at the Cape, from 1652 to 1795. He claimed that because the Cape served mainly as a refreshment station and military outpost, the economy was not expansionist and there was no attempt to bring indigenous peoples under direct Dutch control. Because of the colony's simple social organization and its imperative of consolidating control over the southwestern tip of the continent, Jordaan asserted that "there was no colour policy" and that Cape colonial society "absorbed all mixed elements—the result of miscegenation between whites, blacks and imported slaves." Jordaan was emphatic about the miscegenated origins of the Coloured people, and he emphasized that they were an integral part of Dutch colonial society: "The father of the Cape Coloured people is therefore van Riebeeck. It is he who, by encouraging mixed unions, called them to life and it is he who, realizing their close affinity to the Dutch, made them an indissoluble and indistinguishable part of the European population." Although he indicated that substantial numbers of miscegenes passed into the settler community, he did not explain how and why the rest of this supposedly "indistinguishable part of the European population" nevertheless remained separate.[45]

According to Jordaan, the second stage of South Africa's development, which lasted from 1795 to 1872, was dominated by the ideology of British liberalism. Under this social system, the integration of Coloured people was taken further, in that "all the Coloureds and detribalized Hottentots were assimilated into European society on the basis of complete legal and political equality for all."[46] At the same time that black people were being integrated into Cape society, a third social system that implemented a rigid constitutional colour bar coexisted in the Boer republics. Jordaan characterized this system, which he saw as having lasted from 1836 until 1870, as consisting of isolated and isolationist peasant communities.

Then, from 1870, argued Jordaan, "the entire face of South Africa was radically transformed by the discovery of gold and diamonds which heralded the Industrial Revolution." With the introduction of wage labor and industrial methods of production, the relationship between white and black, employer and employee changed as all pre-existing social systems were rapidly eroded and the integration of Coloured people into the dominant society was reversed with the introduction of segregationist policies to facilitate the exploitation of black labor. Jordaan did not pursue this line of inquiry any further, making it clear that his concern in this essay was with preindustrial South African society.[47]

What is most striking when comparing progressionist and radical visions of Coloured history are the similarities they share despite the ideological gulf and a vitriolic mutual antagonism that separated them. First, both accepted the Coloured people as originating from miscegenation during the earliest days of Dutch rule, which is an indication of just how hegemonic white supremacist conceptions of Coloured identity were in South African society. Second, both saw the Coloured people as experiencing a long period of acculturation and incorporation into the dominant society followed by a sudden reversal, leading to twentieth-century segregationism. Though the reasons for, and timing of, the about-face differed, the pattern remained consistent. This period of incorporation was presumably necessary to support the perception that Coloured people were the product of miscegenation and to explain their assimilation to Western culture. Finally, the radical view was also progressionist and even more dogmatically so than its moderate counterpart, in that it followed Marxist doctrine that society would progress through a series of stages culminating in a socialist utopia—only the timing and method of its attainment were in question. Instead of the inner impulse for self-improvement posited by Ziervogel, it was the objective conditions of capitalist development that were seen by radical intellectuals to drive progress.[48]

"Contingent on the Liberation of the African People": A Novel Approach in the Early 1980s

The views of Jordaan and other radical theorists had a very limited impact on popular consciousness because their ideas were confined to a tiny set of intellectuals within the Coloured elite. But these ideas remained alive within this intelligentsia, even through the quiescent heyday of apartheid, and they were to feed into the climate of resistance that arose from the mid-1970s onward. The views of radical theorists, especially Jordaan's, would be extremely influential in the writing of Maurice Hommel, who took up their ideas and arguments—even verbatim chunks of their writing, some of it unacknowledged[49]—in *Capricorn Blues.*

Maurice Hommel was born in 1930 in Uitenhage, South Africa, where he worked as a teacher and journalist. Unable to find suitable employment because of his radical sympathies, he emigrated in 1964. Taking up residence first in Zambia and then in the United States and Canada, Hommel made a living as a journalist and writer, obtaining a doctoral degree in political science from York University, Toronto, in 1978.[50]

Capricorn Blues was based on Hommel's doctoral dissertation.[51] The book was not so much about "the struggle for human rights in South Africa," as the volume's subtitle claimed, but about "the organization and evolution of Coloured political movements," as its abstract and introduction admitted.[52] Hommel's study represented something of a landmark in the historiography of the Coloured community. Besides being the first book on Coloured history written by a Coloured person in over four decades, it was the first to deploy an instrumentalist argument and to assert that the Coloured people were an integral part of a wider black constituency. These were not original insights, as they were derived from the radical critique of Coloured exclusivism dating back to at least the 1920s.[53] But it was in *Capricorn Blues* that they first appeared in a formal history. The truly novel feature of the book, however, was that it was the first to switch the focus of Coloured history from narratives of miscegenation and acculturation in preindustrial South Africa to the evolution of Coloured protest politics in industrializing South Africa.[54]

Hommel was confused and confusing on exactly what the concept of Colouredness entailed. He denied that the Coloured people constituted "a cultural group distinct from the white community" and instead asserted that they were "best described in terms of their socio-economic characteristics." This did not make much sense because the Coloured community was far from homogeneous in its socioeconomic makeup, and how Coloured people were to be distinguished from others of similar socioeconomic status was left unexplained. Hommel skirted around racial definitions of Colouredness, it would appear, because of an emphatic rejection of apartheid ideology. He repudiated what he called "a genetic analysis" of the role of Coloured people in South African society "because it mystifie[d] relations between ethnic units in the State" and formed "part of the ideology of domination." The "genetic analysis" he referred to was the apartheid idea that "the Coloured people constitute a *'volk'* [people] in their own right, as a nascent nation in the making, requiring a separate and distinct orbit for socio-political development."[55]

The underlying tenet of Hommel's study, by contrast, was that the Coloured people "are politically and economically an integral part of the black base on which white domination and privilege rests" and that their liberation "is contingent on the liberation of the African people with whom their destiny is inextricably bound." It was around this axiom that Hommel interwove the two principal themes of the book. The first motif was that racial discrimination, especially from the early twentieth century onward, forced a separatist strategy onto the Coloured people and that this, in turn, facilitated the state's divide-and-rule strategies through "the imposition of the artificial ethnic State divisions."[56] The second motif was that a combination of deliberately divisive strategies by the state, assimilationist tendencies within the Coloured community, and weaknesses within the Coloured political leadership frustrated the fruition of a natural alliance between Coloured and African peoples against white domination. By far the greater emphasis of this study was on the Non-European Unity Movement, with nearly two-thirds of the book devoted to the two and a half decades from the founding of the NEUM in 1943 to the establishment of the "puppet" Coloured Representative Council by the National Party government in 1969. Although Hommel was critical of the NEUM, his political sympathies very clearly lay with the Trotskyist tradition in radical Coloured politics.

Hommel started off his account with a conventional line: "The arrival of the first white person from Europe was, in fact, the beginning of the evolution of the Coloured people"; he also referred to Jan van Riebeeck as the "father of the Coloured people."[57] The introductory chapter, which was heavily dependent on Jordaan's "van Riebeeck" treatise, covered the period from the landing of van Riebeeck through to the early twentieth century. It had very little to say about the origins and history of the Coloured people and instead sketched out the consolidation of white domination in South Africa. It was never made clear exactly how his claim that the Coloured people originated as a result of miscegenation in the mid-seventeenth century squared with his insistence that an "artificial" Coloured ethnicity was imposed on society by the white supremacist state in the twentieth century.

Where Hommel parted company with previous histories was by following Jordaan's insistence that a new set of socioeconomic conditions engendered by the mineral revolution, rather than a process of historical evolution dating from the first landing of the Dutch at the Cape, shaped twentieth-century racial antagonisms in South Africa. Since his focus was the evolution of Coloured political organization, Hommel's analysis proper started with the founding of the African Political Organization in 1902. He depicted the APO as vacillating between making common cause with Africans and the deluded idea that it could advance Coloured interests on its own. The political weakness of the APO and the flawed leadership of the charismatic but ambitious Abdurahman, according to Hommel, led the APO into political compromise and down the blind alley of reformist politics that failed to deliver any gains for the Coloured people. In the meantime, especially from the mid-1920s onward, a divisive tendency Hommel referred to as "Colouredism" arose as a result of false promises of Coloured assimilation into the white community made by J.B.M. Hertzog's Pact government. He then went on to assert that during the 1930s, the emergence of "a new radicalism on the part of the sons and daughters of the APO's founding fathers" polarized Coloured politics. This cleavage became particularly acute when the Smuts ministry announced the formation of the Coloured Advisory Council in 1943, which Hommel conspiratorially saw as a deliberate attempt to sap the strength of the liberation movement by smothering its most progressive element, the Coloured intelligentsia.[58]

On one side of this rift were the "conservative integrationists" represented by the Coloured People's National Union (CPNU), founded in 1944 in response to the radical takeover of the APO. The CPNU argued in favor of collaboration and using segregated institutions to advance the Coloured cause. On the other side was the NEUM, which rejected any form of collaboration with the ruling group and advocated a total boycott of all racially segregated bodies. The Achilles' heel of the NEUM, Hommel argued, was the predominance of teachers in its leadership corps. Intimidation by the state and fear that they would lose their jobs prevented NEUM leaders from translating their revolutionary program into political action. During the 1950s, fierce ideological disputes leading to schism within the radical Left, the removal of Coloureds from the common voters' roll in 1956, and intensified political repression emasculated Coloured resistance to apartheid even before the quelling of extraparliamentary opposition in the wake of the Sharpeville shooting. With the passing of the Prohibition of Political Interference Act of 1968, which outlawed formal interracial political cooperation, and with the inauguration of the "dummy" Coloured Advisory Council in 1969, the apartheid state was completely in the ascendent when Hommel drew his study to a close.[59]

Despite being based on a doctoral dissertation, Hommel's study has several serious flaws and can hardly be described as scholarly. There are substantial lacunae in his narrative of Coloured political history, particularly in the period prior to 1943, as a reading of Richard van der Ross or Gavin Lewis's studies will confirm.[60] The book is heavily reliant on a limited selection of secondary sources and contemporary political tracts, with works by Kenneth Jordaan, Jack and Ray Simons, and Isaac Tabata featuring prominently.[61] There are times when sizable sections of Hommel's writing do little more than summarize one or two of these secondary sources. Hommel's lack of primary research shows in his decidedly idiosyncratic interpretation of many aspects of Coloured political history, his analyses of both the APO and Afrikaanse Nasionale Bond (ANB) being cases in point. The book, moreover, is poorly structured and extremely repetitious. On occasion, however, Hommel makes good use of limited source material and produces some useful insights.[62] This is especially true of his discussion of the NEUM, in which he displays particular interest. Yet for much of the time, the analysis is decidedly amateurish.

The "Moral and Logical Undoing of Apartheid": A Liberal Essentialist Intervention in the Mid-1980s

Five years after the publication of *Capricorn Blues*, a history of Coloured politics written from an opposing ideological viewpoint made its appearance. Richard van der Ross's *The Rise and Decline of Apartheid*, a much more detailed and comprehensive work, fell squarely within the liberal essentialist approach to Coloured history. Indeed, van der Ross went so far as to present his work as a continuation of the narrative begun by J. S. Marais's *The Cape Coloured People*, picking up where Marais had left off in the early twentieth century.[63]

Van der Ross, the son of a leading Coloured teacher, was born in Cape Town in 1921. His long and varied career has included work as a teacher, educationist, journalist, politician, and, most recently, South Africa's ambassador to Spain. One of the more prominent and articulate representatives of the moderate faction within the Coloured petite bourgeoisie of the post–World War II era, van der Ross is recognized as a leading intellectual in his community.[64]

Contrary to the politically correct stance of the time, van der Ross embraced Coloured identity and did not shy away from using the term *Coloured* in his work. Rejecting the effete political correctness of the antiapartheid movement, his retort to those who found the word repugnant was, "I use the term as the most widely understood, if not universally accepted. 'A rose by any other name would smell as sweet.'"[65] Van der Ross was very clearly conscious that, as a leader and spokesman within his community, he was providing an insider's view of the history of the Coloured people in his book.[66]

Although its main title is misleading, the subtitle of the volume—*A Study of Political Movements among the Coloured People of South Africa, 1880–1985*—accurately describes its content. The book is a narrative and descriptive account of organized Coloured politics from the founding of what was purportedly the first Coloured political organization, the Afrikander League (Coloured), in Kimberley in 1883 through to the violence-wracked unraveling of apartheid in the mid-1980s. It focuses on the steady erosion of Coloured people's civil rights over this period of a century and their increasingly hostile reaction to the deterioration in their sociopolitical status. Van der Ross tries to distance himself from any high-flown intellectual pretensions or overt ideological bias by describing his book as "essentially a record" and noting that "it does not set out to interpret the course of events from the standpoint of a particular philosophy of history."[67] Despite these disclaimers, van der Ross's liberalism nevertheless shines through brightly, and his allegiance to the moderate faction within Coloured protest politics is never in doubt.

In line with the essentialist approach, van der Ross perceives South African society as consisting of distinct races and the Coloured people as a product of miscegenation.[68] Despite having previously written a polemical book on myths and fallacies about Coloured identity,[69] he takes the identity for granted and sees no need to analyze or explain the phenomenon. *The Rise and Decline of Apartheid* describes the emergence of the Coloured people as a gradual process of miscegenation, characterizing it as an "ever-continuing process."[70] Indeed, van der Ross claims that the "very existence of the Coloured people belies apartheid" and predicts that they "will prove to be the moral and logical undoing of apartheid."[71] After briefly reviewing the main milestones in the essentialist narrative of the making of Coloured identity, in particular Ordinance 50, slave emancipation, and the 1853 constitution, van der Ross takes the reader on a rather desultory tour of major developments in Coloured political history.

Van der Ross starts his analysis proper in the late nineteenth century by recounting the first tentative steps toward separate Coloured political organization, with the formation of the Afrikander League in 1883, the founding of the Coloured People's Association in 1892, and Ahmed Effendi's candidacy for the Cape parliament in 1894. From there, he moves on to the coming of the Anglo-Boer War and the formation of the APO in 1902 in response to growing racial discrimination at the turn of the century and Coloured people being barred from the franchise in the former Boer republics. Van der Ross successively describes the APO's subsequent domination of Coloured protest politics, the rise of the radical movement through the 1930s and 1940s, the trauma of the imposition of apartheid policies on the Coloured minority, and their response to the new political environment, which ranged from opportunistic collaboration to the revolt of township youths from the mid-1970s onward. Numerous related issues, such as the holding of the Stone meetings, the ANB challenge to the APO, developments on the trade union front in the 1920s, the Joint Council Movement, the Non-European Conferences, and the establishment of the Union Council of Coloured Affairs (UCCA) and the Coloured Representative Council (CRC), are worked into a rather disorganized narrative. His discussion of the apartheid period, moreover, draws extensively on his personal experience in the political arena.

Despite the author's reputation as an intellectual, his academic achievements, and his twelve-year stint as rector of the University of the Western Cape, *The Rise and Decline of Apartheid* cannot be regarded as a scholarly work. Van der Ross's history of Coloured politics is, for the most part, a bland chronicle of organizations being formed and fading from the scene; of racially discriminatory measures from the white supremacist state being piled one on top of another; and of leaders making speeches, conferences being organized, and protest meetings passing resolutions. The narrative is recounted, often in bewildering detail, in nearly four hundred pages of tightly packed print but within an oversimplified analytical and theoretical framework that has limited explanatory value. Throughout the book, lists of various sorts, lengthy quotations, and the wholesale reproduction of documentary material clutter the writing and substitute for analysis.[72]

Further, although van der Ross covers the broad sweep of Coloured political organization, his history is episodic and the inclusion of material indiscriminate in that he provides very uneven coverage of the subject. Some aspects are examined in exhaustive detail, others are cursorily passed over, and there are some omissions, such as the failure to deal with the United Afrikaner League of the late 1910s or the Cape Malay Association of the latter half of the 1920s. These weaknesses stem partly from the limited range of both primary and secondary source material consulted by van der Ross. The content of the book appears to have been determined more by his extensive personal collection of documents relating to Coloured politics than by a systematic research of source material available in libraries and archives.[73] A related flaw is that extended sections of writing draw on a single source.[74] In addition, despite a broadly chronological approach, the book is poorly structured, with frequent digressions and clumsy flash-forward and flash-back techniques disrupting the narrative flow. Repetitiousness is another symptom of the book's poor structure.

The approach of trying to provide an objective chronicle was doomed to failure from the start and is effectively abandoned halfway through the study. Although van der Ross remains reasonably detached during the first half of the book, he becomes much more subjective in dealing with the post–World War II period when he himself was politically active. For example, he tends to exaggerate the importance of organizations in which he played a leading role, most notably the Convention Movement, an early 1960s initiative by a small group of moderate Coloured leaders to form a nonracial front to petition the government to lift the color bar and other repressive measures.[75] Similarly, his onetime political ally George Golding, reviled among radicals as a government stooge, receives decidedly generous treatment. In contrast, the Non-European Unity Movement, the severest critic of his more accommodationist political philosophy, is subjected to close, fault-finding scrutiny not extended to other organizations.[76] The repeated description of the NEUM and its supporters as "virulent" and "vituperative" is an indication that van der Ross was still smarting from the scorn heaped on him and his political associates by the Unity Movement.[77]

Ironically, it is precisely in its subjectivity—as an informed and wide-ranging account of Coloured political history by a prominent member of the moderate faction of Coloured politics—that its value lies. Van der Ross was a participant in many of the events he describes, and in this way, he is able to provide firsthand information and interesting insights into aspects of Coloured politics. The latter half of the book thus reads more like a memoir than an impartial history. Although the book is a mine of information on Coloured politics, its superficial analysis does not do the complexity of its subject justice. One merit of van der Ross's study when it was published was that it provided an easily accessible body of knowledge—a framework of names, dates, events, and organizations relating to Coloured politics—at a time when that was not readily available to layperson, student, or researcher.

Of "Vengeful Afrikaners" and "Spineless English": An Angry Outburst on the Eve of Democracy

A highly eccentric work on the history of the Coloured people appeared at the very end of the apartheid era. The book in question, Roy du Pre's *Separate but Unequal*, is remarkable for the author's sustained and angry denunciation of whites, especially Afrikaners, for their oppression of Coloured people and his outraged rejection of the apartheid system that had forcibly classified him as Coloured.[78] The book is historiographically ambiguous because the author mixes up essentialist and instrumentalist views. The latter, though, is dominant and is his intended standpoint.

At the time of publication, du Pre, a former high school and college of education teacher, was lecturing in the History Department at the University of Transkei; he subsequently served as executive director of the Committee of Technikon Principals. In 1994, du Pre also completed a doctoral dissertation on the history of the Labour Party of South Africa.[79] It needs to be said at the outset that despite du Pre's academic credentials, *Separate but Unequal* is not a work of scholarship. It is, on the whole, poorly researched, openly biased, inadequately referenced, and simplistic in its formulations. The author does, however, acknowledge his lack of academic rigor by characterizing the book as a "polemical history" and trying to justify his approach by claiming that "it was written with the layman in mind." Indeed, du Pre freely admits to being "subjective in [his] analysis," confessing his "bias against whites, especially Afrikaners" and noting that he "makes no excuse for writing from the viewpoint of anger."[80]

The title of this book is misleading in that the work falls far short of a political history of the Coloured people. Neither can it be considered a study of Coloured social experience under apartheid, as the chapter headings collectively suggest. Although it does deal with aspects of these topics, it does not attempt to do so in any systematic way. It is also far too personal and circumscribed an account to be taken as representative of experience within the Coloured community as a whole. The book instead consists of a curious amalgam of the author's fulminations against "Afrikaner racism, English hypocrisy, National Party immorality and government brutality" for their role in the oppression of Coloured people, on the one hand,[81] and a fragmentary history of the Labour Party of South Africa, on the other. This odd combination comes about as a result of du Pre scrambling together an outpouring of bitterness at having been a victim of apartheid and research he did for his master's and doctoral theses.

The study is divided into four parts, of which the first and last are devoted primarily to du Pre's rant against apartheid. Part one takes the reader on a haphazard, sixty-page ramble through South African history from 1652 through to 1948. This section serves little more than as a vehicle for castigating whites for their maltreatment of Coloured people from the earliest days of Dutch settlement at the Cape. Part two deals with the imposition of apartheid on Coloureds, focusing in particular on issues of race classification, the Group Areas and Separate Amenities Acts, job reservation, "gutter" education, and disfranchisement. Part three, which is entitled "The Political Separation of the Coloured People, 1943–1993," is devoted mainly to aspects of the history of the Labour Party. Hardly any mention is made of the Non-European Unity Movement, the South African Coloured People's Organization, or the United Democratic Front, all key players in Coloured protest politics during that period. In the concluding section, du Pre redirects his full attention to upbraiding whites, this time under the guise of examining the consequences of racism and apartheid. He ends by offering gratuitous advice to Coloured people on moving from "second class citizen to first class human being," urging them to "stop thinking like 'Coloureds'" and to "hold their heads high and look the white man in the face."[82]

This brief outline gives a false sense of the coherence of the volume. The book is extremely poorly organized, both in the way chapters and themes fit together and in the manner in which paragraphs, ideas, and individual sentences mesh on the page. Tim Couzens, in his review of the book, graphically described the disorder that greets the reader: "Themes in this book jump around like fleas off a sinking dog . . . At one moment there will be a Jungian analysis on lightness and darkness and their correspondence to masculine rationality and female emotionality in the 17th century, the next, one will be pondering over the devastating blow to Afrikaner masculinity and superiority brought on by the loss to England in a rugby test."[83] This lack of organization is most evident in the extreme repetitiousness of the book, which also suffers from a number of other stylistic and technical shortcomings.[84]

What analysis du Pre does offer has little explanatory value and often accounts for apartheid and the oppression of Coloured people in terms of the "vengefulness" of the Afrikaner toward Coloureds or simply the "base naked racism" of the National Party.[85] Indeed, du Pre is of the opinion that "the Afrikaner has an over-developed sense of vengeance which he will carry into the next century" and that "it is the nature of Afrikaners to discriminate against people who are different to them and to practice segregation." Du Pre never fully explains his oft-leveled allegation that Afrikaners harbored deep-seated feelings of revenge against Coloureds. At one point, though, drawing on Carl Jung, he suggests that apartheid might have been due to displaced anger over the Afrikaners' maltreatment by the British, which they then projected onto black people in general. The irony is that, whatever the motives of Afrikanerdom may have been, du Pre is himself clearly driven by revenge. Although Afrikaners are by far the main target of his invective, he does enjoy the occasional swipe at the "spineless English."[86]

Seething with resentment at the injustices Coloured people suffered under apartheid, du Pre allows his emotions to get the better of his judgment. The author, who claims the moral high ground of nonracism for himself, has no compunction about using racist arguments to condemn Afrikaners. Du Pre recognizes the contradiction in his thinking but is so set on getting his own back that he, paradoxically, resorts to contorted reasoning that echoes the twisted logic of the system he rails against: "This book discusses Afrikaners as if they are a homogeneous group, which of course they are not. However, it is difficult for the layman to distinguish them in any other way, because Afrikaners have presented themselves as such. By setting themselves up as an exclusive people, a 'chosen' nation and 'die volk,' Afrikaners have created in the minds of others the idea that they are indeed a homogeneous group. They cannot now expect others to see them as anything else."[87] Du Pre's aversion to Afrikanerdom, it would appear, extends to the point where he has tried to disguise the Afrikaner origins of his own surname. Somewhere between 1987, when he completed his master's thesis, and 1990, when he published *The Making of Racial Conflict in South Africa,* du Pre dropped the last two letters of his surname, changing it from du Preez, a typically Afrikaner surname, to a name that sounds French.

This book, in the end, has little to say about Coloured people themselves because du Pre uses it primarily to vent his own anger and bitterness at the system of segregation that blighted his life. It would seem that the writing of this book was an emotional catharsis for the author.[88] Throughout the book, du Pre does not so much write about Coloured people as speak for them, substituting his voice for theirs and generalizing his opinions for theirs. At times, he does this literally, as, for example, when he writes, "Whites will therefore have to understand when Coloureds today say: 'We don't trust De Klerk; we intensely despise the Afrikaner; we hate the NP; we want to have nothing to do with whites.'"[89] If anything, he has an extraordinarily condescending attitude toward Coloured people, presenting them as faceless, voiceless victims of white aggression and not autonomous people with minds and wills of their own.[90]

Although du Pre claims to speak for all Coloured people, his book is written from the perspective of the Coloured petite bourgeoisie and focuses almost exclusively on the concerns of this social class. Hardly any mention is made of the impact of apartheid laws on the urban working class or the impoverished rural proletariat, who together make up a large majority of the Coloured population. The book, accordingly, is preoccupied with the sensibilities of the Coloured petite bourgeoisie, and disproportionate attention is paid to the humiliation that apartheid visited on them. For example, du Pre is incensed at the "odious practice" of building "'Coloured' slums next to middle and upper class 'Coloured' suburbs"; he sympathizes with "better class" Coloureds who were forced to travel in the same coaches as their poorer bethren, who themselves were "often under the influence of liquor"; and he complains that Coloured hotels were "grubby and surrounded by [Coloured] drunks using the bars and off-sales." At one point, he even appears to condone Coloured and Indian racism toward Africans:

Afrikaner officials made it a practice to book coloureds, Indians and Africans in the same compartments of 1st and 2nd class coaches. Coloureds from the Cape and Indians in general objected vehemently to sleeping with Africans as they never mixed with Africans on a personal level. Railway officials ignored all complaints by "Hotnots" and "Coolies" about sleeping with Africans in the same compartment. Afrikaner ticket examiners retorted that as far as they were concerned, all non-whites were the same, and therefore the [*sic*] could not understand what the objections were about.

The author appears oblivious of the irony in criticizing bigoted white officials for not being sensitive to the racist sentiments of Coloured and Indian passengers.[91]

In *Separate but Unequal*, intellectual coherence is sacrificed to du Pre's polemical purpose. This is most evident in his treatment of the origin and nature of Coloured identity, in which he repeats the essentialist and instrumentalist practice of presenting Coloured people as having had little or no part in the creation of their own identity. Much of the time, du Pre is content to have the powerful white establishment thrust on the diverse group of "mixed-race" people in South Africa the artificial identity of Colouredness. He presents Coloured people as having no will or creativity of their own, passively accepting a view of the world and of themselves imposed on them by whites. On occasion, however, du Pre feels the need to emphasize just how cunning and self-serving whites were in their dealings with Coloured people. He then presents Coloured identity as the clever invention of white supremacists, who use it to divide and rule the black majority. Coloureds then become nothing more than the dupes of a white ruling class that manipulates them at will to bolster white supremacy in South Africa.

Du Pre's deep confusion about the nature of Coloured identity is demonstrated by the conflicting timing he proposes for the emergence of that identity. In keeping with the politically correct view that prevailed within the radical Left during the latter stages of apartheid, du Pre, on several occasions, denies that Coloured identity ever existed except as an artificial category in apartheid legislation, which "created a new nation out of the leftovers of other nations." His claim that "the only glue which held the Coloured people together after 1950 was the law which classified them as such" is clearly untenable.[92] In some instances, however, he accepts the popular perception that

Coloured identity came into existence as a result of miscegenation from the mid-seventeenth century onward. To compound the confusion, du Pre, also accepts the idea that Coloured identity developed "in the early 1900s" as a result of growing racial discrimination at the turn of the century.[93] That these explanations entail assumptions and implications that are mutually exclusive seems to matter little to Du Pre. What is important is that he finds a stick with which to beat whites.

Perhaps the most significant feature of *Seperate but Unequal* is that it provides several sustained examples of a discourse that, in my experience, was fairly common within the private domain of Coloured middle-class life during the apartheid years but rarely surfaced in the public arena. I have often enough heard people privately express their rejection of apartheid in the vehement tone that du Pre uses in this book. Never have I seen it done with such lack of restraint in print, though. A good example comes from the appendix entitled "The Mark of Cain":[94]

> Slowly, but steadily, I developed a hatred of the Afrikaner. This hatred manifested itself mostly in an aversion to his language. Even today, I detest listening to any Afrikaans radio programmes and refuse to watch Afrikaans programmes on TV. . . . My special hate was the Afrikaans epilogue. When the pious and righteous-looking "dominees" appeared on the screen and began to pontificate in those dulcet "holy" tones, I almost wanted to puke. . . . I suddenly realized that I intensely hated the brutal Afrikaner; I despised the cowardly Englishman; I was disgusted with the pathetic Alan Hendrickse and the opportunistic Labour Party; I had nothing but contempt for the unprincipled members of the House of Representatives; and I loathed whites in general.[95]

This is not the tirade of a lone eccentric but a fairly representative example of the private rage with which many Coloured people, especially within the politicized petite bourgeoisie, expressed their visceral rejection of apartheid. If the unrelenting diatribe of *Separate but Unequal* has any value, it is that it sheds light on the private response of the Coloured petite bourgeoisie to a social system that frustrated their ambitions, stunted their lives, and humiliated them deeply.[96]

In writing this book, Du Pre was blinded by his anger to the extent that he was incapable of rational argument or cogent analysis. The long-winded tirade, though at times entertaining,[97] is sterile and does very little to advance one's understanding of the Coloured past. *Separate but Unequal* was fortunate to have appeared at a singular time in South African history that gave it a degree of relevance it would not otherwise have enjoyed. During the fluidity of the transition to democratic rule in the mid-1990s, when white guilt over apartheid was at its height and rainbowism at its most auspicious,[98] the impotent fury of a marginal man venting his anger did not appear quite as incongruous as it does today.

Coloured social experience in white-dominated South Africa is mirrored in the historiography of Coloureds' writing on their own history in a number of ways. Features of this historiography that stand out in this regard are its relatively poor quality, its paucity, and the high degree of confusion it reflects in terms of the nature of Coloured identity. There is also a tendency for opinions to be polarized, with Coloured identity either being taken for granted, as in the case of Ziervogel and van der Ross, or imbued with intense political significance and rejected with vehemence, as with Hommel and du Pre.

The poor quality and scantness of this historiography is, to a very large extent, a product of racial oppression and the marginalization of the Coloured community. Inferior education for the mass of Coloured people, restricted access to tertiary education for the small petite bourgeoisie, and a virtual absence of opportunities for training and employment as academics for much of the period under consideration meant that only a handful of professionally trained historians have come from within the ranks of the Coloured community—and then only toward the latter stages of the apartheid period.[99] The bulk of historical writing from within the Coloured community was thus produced by untrained amateurs, especially activists and organic intellectuals of various kinds. Professionally trained historians from within the Coloured community have tended to reject being labeled Coloured and to work on topics other than the history of the Coloured community.[100]

Confusion and controversy over Coloured identity in Coloured historical writing stems from more than one source, not least of which is the ambiguous status of Coloured people in the South African racial hierarchy. Given the subjective nature of historical inquiry as well as long-standing and highly politicized disputes over the nature of Coloured identity, it is not at all surprising that there is intense disagreement over Coloured identity within this historiography or that individual authors exhibit a degree of confusion over the issue. Thus, for example, Ziervogel and van der Ross accept Coloured identity as given and do not find it necessary to inquire into its nature, whereas Hommel and du Pre, for much of the time, deny that Coloured identity existed except as a state-enforced category but then proceed to write about it as if it were a social reality with its origins in the seventeenth century. The contradictions within Hommel and du Pre seem to emanate from the tension that existed between an impassioned rejection of apartheid thinking, on the one hand, and the need to come to terms with the reality of Coloured identity, on the other.

Historical writing on the Coloured community also reflects the hegemony of racist thinking with regard to Coloured identity. The idea that Colouredness was the product of miscegenation was so deeply entrenched in South African society that nearly all people, including academics and radical polemicists, accepted this assumption until the latter phases of the apartheid era. As pointed out earlier, even a hard-nosed Trotskyist intellectual such as Kenneth Jordaan could accept Jan van Riebeeck as the "father of the Cape Coloured people."[101] But once that leap of understanding was made—once people came to see that Coloured identity was not necessarily an automatic consequence of miscegenation or an inadvertent product of South Africa's colonial past but that it functioned as a tool of social control—the basis for the opposing instrumentalist approach was laid. The strong emotions that this could awaken are nowhere more evident than in du Pre's *Separate but Unequal*.

Another striking feature of this body of writing is that despite the controversial nature of Coloured identity, authors fail to engage with one another—or, for that matter, with other historians—on the issue. Instead, the pleas, polemics, accusations, and refutations are directed largely at the state and white South Africa.[102] Although this is due partly to inadequate research and poor conceptualization of the projects, it is also due to the emotion-laden response evoked by white supremacism and attempts to vindicate ideological positions taken up in relation to it. The emotional and politicized response also means that there is no clear trend in the historiography and no sense of a growing sophistication of analyses as authors build on work that has gone before.

This survey has covered the entire ideological spectrum of opinion within the Coloured community on the nature of Coloured identity, from the self-abasing interpretation of Hendricks and Viljoen, which mimicked white supremacist writing, to the ultra-Left theorizing of

Kenneth Jordaan. Although this historiography most clearly reflects the marginality of the Coloured community, it also corroborates other aspects of the analysis of Coloured identity outlined in the opening chapter. Thus, for example, Hendricks and Viljoen as well as Ziervogel confirm the internalization of the dominant society's racist values by many Coloured people; Abdurahman's and van der Ross's analyses attest to the assimilationism of the Coloured community; Jordaan's writing verifies the hegemony of ideas relating to the miscegenated origins of Coloured people; and du Pre's fulminations reflect the frustration and impotent rage that many Coloured people felt. The great value of the texts analyzed in this chapter is that they represent discourses on the nature of Coloured identity in which authors try to account for the prevailing status and condition of their community. Thus, although such writing is sparse and generally of poor academic quality, it nevertheless reveals a great deal about Coloured social experience. Not only do these discourses epitomize thinking within various sectors of the community about the essence of their social being and not only do they reflect the social and political currents of their time, they also played an important part in creating a sense of Colouredness.

The first two chapters of this study have explored general themes in the expression of Coloured identity, with the analysis traversing the entire period under consideration. The next three chapters will be devoted to a series of chronologically arranged case studies that individually corroborate aspects of this study and collectively confirm its contentions. The first set of case studies will focus on the official organs of the two most important Coloured communal organizations during the earlier decades of Union.

3

The Predicament of Marginality

Case Studies from the Earlier Period of White Rule

This chapter is based on two case studies of key texts produced within the Coloured community during the first three decades of the Union of South Africa. The first focuses on the *APO* newspaper, the mouthpiece of the African Political Organization, which was by far the most dominant Coloured political pressure group until it was challenged by an emergent radical movement in the late 1930s. The second examines the *Educational Journal*, the organ of the Teachers' League of South Africa, the largest professional organization within the Coloured community. Produced by the most prominent leaders and respected intellectuals within the community, these two publications were broadly representative of Coloured opinion on matters of politics, identity, and intercommunal relations. Together, they illustrate the impetus behind the expression of a separate Coloured identity and the ambiguities that arose from their exclusivist agenda.

Ambiguities in the Racial Perceptions of the *APO:* 1909–23

Founded in Cape Town in 1902 as a result of intensifying segregationism in the late nineteenth century and disappointment at Coloured people effectively being excluded from the franchise in the Transvaal and Orange Free State by the Treaty of Vereeniging,[1] the APO was the first substantive Coloured political association and would dominate Coloured protest politics for nearly thirty-five years. Spearheading the Coloured community's protests against segregationist measures in the run-up to unification, the organization grew rapidly in the first decade of its existence, especially after the energetic Abdullah Abdurahman became president in 1905. By the time of Union, the APO had grown into a national body with several thousand members in a countrywide network of branches, making it the largest black political organization of the time.[2]

At its seventh annual conference in April 1909, the APO decided to publish its own newspaper to help promote its protest campaign against those clauses of the draft South Africa Act that denied black people outside of the Cape Colony the franchise and deprived those within the Colony of the right to be elected to the new Union Parliament.[3] The newspaper was seen as an invaluable tool not only for addressing the immediate concern of mobilizing Coloured people in defense of their civil rights but also for educating the Coloured community politically and furthering the aims of the organization in general.[4] The first issue of the *APO*, which appeared on 24 May 1909, justified its existence on the grounds that the Coloured community needed a means with which to voice its opinions and advocate its cause. Claiming that no other newspaper dared to champion "our just claims to political equality with whites," it accused the existing press of promoting only the "rights of property for the few who have it, rather than the broad rights of humanity" and of acting "on the assumption that South Africa belongs to the whites . . . by right of conquest."[5]

A quarto-sized paper published on alternate Saturdays, the *APO* was bilingual, having an English section that took up at least three-quarters of the space and a Dutch section confined to the back pages. Editorials and the more important articles appeared in both languages. Over and above reports on social, sporting, and cultural events within the Coloured community, the *APO* news agenda concentrated mainly on local and national politics insofar as they affected Coloured people. It is also clear that Abdurahman had by far the greatest influence in shaping the political outlook of the newspaper, despite Matt Fredericks, the general secretary of the APO, being editor. Abdurahman was the preeminent leader of the organization and dominated it for the entire thirty-five years of his presidency, from 1905 to his death in 1940. He effectively decided editorial policy, and Fredericks was also his closest collaborator within the APO.[6]

Despite repeated claims of speaking for the Coloured people as a whole, the APO reflected the values and aspirations of the emergent

Coloured petite bourgeoisie, which formed the elite stratum within the Coloured community. This was especially true in the one and a half decades during which the *APO* was published because the Coloured petite bourgeoisie was never more united in its political aims and its social aspirations, with the APO completely dominating Coloured politics during those years. Other contemporary Coloured political movements, such as Francis Peregrino's Coloured People's Vigilance Committee, John Tobin's Stone meetings, the South African Coloured Union under the leadership of James Curry, and the United Afrikaner League of the late 1910s, drew negligible support.[7] It was only during the latter half of the 1920s, after the APO had ceased publishing its newspaper, that a serious rival emerged in the form of the Afrikaanse Nasionale Bond. The APO, however, remained far more popular than the ANB, which supported Hertzog's National Party and was formed partly at the instigation of leading Cape nationalists.[8] Eventually, toward the end of the 1930s, the APO was eclipsed by the National Liberation League, representing the radical political movement that had emerged within the Coloured community during that decade. Throughout its life, the *APO* newspaper proved to be as authentic a voice of the Coloured petite bourgeoisie as one could hope to find.

The Coloured elite, forming little more than 5 percent of the Coloured population,[9] consisted largely of artisans, small retail traders, clerks, clerics, teachers, and a handful of professionals in the earlier decades of the twentieth century. This nascent petite bourgeoisie was assimilated to Western bourgeois culture, on the whole sharing its values, aspirations, and social practices. Despite some rhetoric about the need to cultivate race pride among Coloured people, the ideals of the members of this social group were almost entirely assimilationist. They wanted little more than to be judged on merit, to exercise citizenship rights, and to win social acceptance within white middle-class society. The *APO* thus continually reiterated the sentiment that "it is not race or colour but civilization which is the test of man's capacity for political rights." Being marginal, acceptance into the dominant society on the basis of individual merit appeared to be the only viable means whereby the Coloured elite could prosper and provide the rest of their community with the opportunity for future advancement.[10]

Although the majority of the APO's membership was drawn from the Coloured elite, there was no great social distance between the Coloured petite bourgeoisie and the Coloured laboring poor during that period. The greater part of this elite had, as a result of the impact of the mineral revolution, graduated from poverty to respectability during the course of their lives or were in the process of doing so. Virtually all lived in or close to working-class neighborhoods and continued to socialize with friends and relatives from the humbler ranks of the community. Even the most anglicized members of the Coloured elite spoke Cape Vernacular Afrikaans, the language of the Coloured working classes.[11]

The most eminent member of the Coloured elite, Abdullah Abdurahman, was a case in point. Abdurahman's family was of humble origin, his grandparents having been slaves who had managed to buy their freedom. During the latter half of the nineteenth century, the Abdurahman family did well enough in the greengrocer's business they ran in Cape Town to be able to provide the precocious young Abdullah, who had been born in 1872, with a secondary education, something quite exceptional for people of their social status. Abdurahman went on to qualify as a medical doctor in Glasgow in 1893 and to become the first black person elected to the Cape Town City Council in 1904 and the Cape Provincial Council in 1914. Despite his social standing, Abdurahman had nevertheless remained acculturated to Coloured working-class life. He expressed, for example, a clear preference for the humble but flavorful fare of traditional Coloured working-class cooking and freely spoke vernacular Afrikaans in his day-to-day dealings with patients and political supporters. By retaining the common touch, he became immensely popular within the Coloured community and gained a reputation as a champion of the poor.[12]

Despite their strong ties to Coloured working-class life, this modernizing elite regarded English bourgeois culture as the apotheosis of "civilization." The predominance of English in the *APO* points both to the aspiration of the Coloured elite to conform to Western bourgeois norms and to the class attitudes prevalent within this social group. By far the greater majority of the Coloured population spoke the emergent Afrikaans language, or Cape Dutch, as it was often called, or one of its laboring-class variants, but the educated elite preferred English. In general, English enjoyed far greater prestige within the Coloured community because it was an international language with a rich literature and was identified as the language of "culture," "civilization," and "progress." Very importantly, there was a general perception that proficiency in English held the key to social and occupational advancement. Cape Dutch was derided as a "vulgar patois fit only for the kitchen" because it lacked a formal grammar or a significant literature. The *APO* therefore considered it "the height of impudence to claim for it the same rights as for the language of Shelley, Milton and Tennyson."[13] In contrast to English, which was associated with the liberalism and racial tolerance of British rule, Cape Dutch was identified with the racism and the boorishness of the Afrikaner.[14] Being the language of the Coloured laboring poor, Cape Dutch was also regarded as a badge of social inferiority. For this reason, most status-conscious Coloured people preferred English even though Cape Dutch may have been their mother tongue.

It was with these considerations in mind that an *APO* editorial advocated that Coloured people should: "endeavour to perfect themselves in English—the language which inspires the noblest thoughts of freedom and liberty, the language that has the finest literature on earth and is the most universally useful of all languages. Let everyone . . . drop the habit as far as possible, of expressing themselves in the barbarous Cape Dutch that is too often heard."[15] However, perceiving itself as representing the Coloured community as a whole and feeling the need to carry its message to its entire constituency, the APO published part of its newspaper in Dutch.[16] That only a quarter—or sometimes less—of the paper appeared in Dutch is a measure of the *APO*'s class bias and the degree to which it aspired to English middle-class norms.

Until mid-1910, protesting against the conditions of Union was decidedly the main focus of the *APO.* For the first year of its existence, the newspaper was largely devoted to campaigning against the draft South Africa Act, which it characterized as "The Great Betrayal," and pointing to the unfairness and the folly of Union on those terms.[17] In addition, much publicity was given to the joint Coloured and African delegation to petition the British government to modify the act. After the inauguration of Union on 30 May 1910, which it observed as a "day of mourning" for the Coloured people of South Africa,[18] a demoralized APO changed its strategy and, gradually, its political outlook as well—shifts that were clearly evident in its newspaper.

The organization was forced to reconsider its objectives and methods because the failure of its high-profile political campaigns in the decade prior to Union had brought home the extent of Coloured political impotence and the futility of these tactics. Coloured assimilationist aspirations were excited by the prospect that support for the British war effort during the Anglo-Boer War (1899–1902) would be rewarded with a broadening of civil liberties, especially the extension of the liberal Cape franchise to the Transvaal and Orange Free State after the British had secured victory. That these promises came from imperial officials as highly placed as Lord Milner and Joseph Chamberlain greatly encouraged these expectations.[19] Politicized Coloureds were therefore severely disappointed in May 1902 when the Treaty of Vereeniging effectively ruled out the enfranchisement of blacks in the former Boer republics by stipulating that the question of black voting rights would be settled only after the Transvaal and Orange Free State had attained self-government. It is thus not surprising that Britain's willingness to sacrifice black political rights to appease the Boers helped to precipitate the formation of the APO later that year.[20]

In 1905, the Coloured political leadership, together with a handful of white liberal allies, failed to have the provisions of the School Board Act extended to Coloured people despite the most spirited protest campaign yet launched in their name. This act introduced statutory segregation into the Cape school system by providing for compulsory public schooling for all white children up to standard IV (grade 6) or the age of fourteen and confining black children to the vastly inferior church schools.[21] This measure greatly angered the Coloured elite because it deprived them of what they believed to be a major opportunity for social advancement.[22] The following year, the APO sent a delegation to London to petition the British government to extend the franchise to Coloured males in the Transvaal and the Orange River Colony on their attainment of responsible government in 1907 and 1908, respectively.[23] The failure of this deputation was a severe setback to the Coloured elite and foreshadowed the "humiliation" of Union in 1910, the clearest demonstration yet of the political impotence of the Coloured community.

These reverses since the turn of the century had an important influence on the post-Union strategy of the APO and the outlook of its newspaper. The string of failures accentuated the political marginality of the Coloured community and the ineffectiveness of the APO's tactics. The *APO* newspaper thus came into being at a time when Coloured people were feeling particularly threatened by the erosion of their civil rights. And after Union, the APO faced a political environment far less sympathetic to Coloured aspirations than the old Cape colonial system had been. Union had the effect of further marginalizing Coloured political influence, as well as greatly diluting the clout of the Cape liberals, the APO's main political allies within the white establishment.[24]

In the face of this deteriorating political climate, the APO after Union progressively abandoned its activism of the previous decade in favor of a more pragmatic, incremental approach.[25] Mass protest meetings, high-profile deputations, and denunciatory speeches gave way to discreet lobbying, cautiously worded appeals, and a focus on the socioeconomic advancement of the Coloured people. This shift was noticeable within the *APO* newspaper as early as mid-1911, as it became progressively less outspoken and less aggressive in its demand for civil equality. Indeed, in 1919, the APO altered its name to the African People's Organization to reflect the change in emphasis.

This pragmatic incrementalism on the part of the APO was largely a product of the marginality and the intermediate status of Coloured people in South African society, which resulted in ambiguities and unresolved contradictions within Coloured identity, especially in the elite strata.[26] One of the most striking of these ambiguities, the tension between the ideal of nonracism and the practice of Coloured separatism, was clearly manifest within the organizational life of the APO and therefore also in its newspaper. In the early part of twentieth century, the Coloured petite bourgeoisie was under stress from contradictory social pressures. Although more and more Coloured families were growing wealthier and acquiring the means to sustain standards of middle-class respectability, their civil rights were being eroded. Their assimilationist overtures were rejected by whites, and they were subject to increasingly stringent segregation. Their marginality, moreover, prevented Coloured people from asserting themselves politically or penetrating the institutions, associations, and more prestigious professions of the dominant society to any meaningful extent. Thus, no matter what degree of "respectability" or personal accomplishment Coloureds achieved, they were nevertheless automatically branded as social inferiors by whites and were forced to accept second-class citizenship.

The Coloured elite was thus faced with a moral and political dilemma. As victims of racism whose ultimate objective was to assimilate into the dominant society, they embraced nonracial values as a matter of principle. But being marginal and having a subordinate status thrust on them, Coloureds had little option but to mobilize politically on the basis of this racial identity. Furthermore, the advantages of holding a status of relative privilege vis-à-vis Africans within the racial hierarchy provided the Coloured elite with added incentive for cultivating Coloured separatism. White privilege thus served to encourage racial exclusivity among members of the Coloured community by heightening their group consciousness and prompting them to rally together in defense of their rights.[27]

These ambiguities were clearly evident in the APO, which espoused nonracial and assimilationist ideals but in practice promoted Coloured separatism. Though its constitution did not contain explicit racial bars and though a few whites and Africans became members,[28] the APO saw itself as an organization expressly for Coloured people. Notwithstanding its name,[29] the organization did not seek to recruit Africans or to make common cause with African political organizations. In his presidential address to the 1910 APO Conference, Abdurahman confirmed that the APO was "an organization of the Coloured people only. . . . We have a deep interest in the native races of South Africa, and the Union Act of South Africa puts us all into one fold but it is my duty as President of the APO . . . to deal with the rights and duties of the Coloured people of South Africa as distinguished from the native races."[30] The APO was thus, in effect, a racially exclusive organization, its stated aim being the advancement of the Coloured people.

Although the *APO* displayed much sympathy for Africans as fellow sufferers under an unjust racial order, it was careful to demarcate them as a separate group that needed to minister to their own needs. The *APO* was highly sensitive to this racial distinction because it recognized that for Coloured people to be too closely associated with Africans would jeopardize their chances of acceptance into the dominant society. It was clear to the Coloured political leadership that the numerical superiority of Africans posed a threat to white supremacy in the long run and that their greater cultural distance from Western bourgeois norms evoked more virulent prejudice from whites. Consequently, they sought to stress the affinity of Coloured people to whites and to set themselves apart from Africans. This much was apparent from a description of the Coloured people that appeared in the first issue of the newspaper: "Everyone is well aware that in South Africa there is a large population of Coloured people as opposed to natives. . . . They are the product of civilization—in its most repellent manifestation according to some. They are of varying degrees of admixture. Their complexions vary from the black skin of the Kafir to a light tint that hardly discloses any trace of the Negro. The features of a large proportion of them are wholly Caucasian and their mode of life conforms with the best European model."[31]

The APO's assimilationism and Coloured exclusivism, however, did not preclude it from supporting the political initiatives of other black groups or decrying instances of racial discrimination against them. The organization, on occasion, even sought limited cooperation with other black political organizations in matters of common concern. The *APO* thus showed some interest in Gandhi's ideas of passive resistance and supported protests organized by the Indian community.[32] Similarly, the *APO* also supported African political initiatives. For example, it welcomed the founding of the South African Native National Congress (SANNC, ANC after 1923) in 1912 "as one of the most important events that has ever happened in South Africa" because it "has transformed them [Africans] from a congeries of warring atoms into a united nation."[33] Executive members of the two organizations met for discussion soon after the SANNC's inauguration, when it sent a delegation to Cape Town to protest against the Native Squatting Bill. Despite agreeing to cooperate on matters of mutual concern and to meet annually for discussion of such issues,[34] there was no collaboration between the two organizations until the late 1920s, when Abdurahman convened the first of a series of Non-European Conferences in response to the Hertzog Bills.[35]

The APO reconciled the contradiction between its rejection of racism and its acceptance of an inferior status for Coloureds relative to whites by adopting a political philosophy influenced by the ideas of Booker T. Washington.[36] The *APO* regularly quoted Washington and held him up as a role model for all black people to emulate.[37] Like Washington, the *APO* believed that a pragmatic strategy of incrementally improving the socioeconomic condition of the Coloured people would break down white prejudice and eventually win them civil equality within the dominant society. At the time, this line of reasoning seemed eminently sensible to the Coloured elite because the second decade of the twentieth century was one of relative optimism among the Coloured petite bourgeoisie in spite of the political setbacks they had experienced since the end of the Anglo-Boer War. Although they were apprehensive about the immediate future,[38] their progressionism persuaded the Coloured elite that these reverses were temporary and that it was only a matter of time before liberal values would be reasserted and Coloureds would resume their social and political advancement as South Africa evolved into a meritocratic society. The APO leadership was confident that by demonstrating their "rise in the scale of civilization," Coloured people would eventually overcome white racial prejudice and win acceptance into the dominant society.[39] After all, the most advanced members of their "race" already had a just claim to full equality with whites.

The APO's post-Union political strategy rested on these hopes of assimilation and were aimed at expediting the process through active promotion of Coloured self-improvement. Contemplating the most effective way for the Coloured people to gain "full political freedom and privileges," the *APO* paper asserted that "we have to better ourselves, improve our education, mode of living and environment, seek to become proficient in our callings and trades."[40] A later article explained that "we shall be required to prove that we are worthy of these and other rights which we claim as loyal British subjects."[41] The fallacy in this reasoning was that it was precisely when black people demonstrated competence that white prejudice tended to harden because of the fear of black economic competition and claims to social equality.

During the earlier years of Union, a new slant to the racial exclusiveness of the Coloured elite reinforced the APO's separatist tendencies. Although the pragmatism exemplified by Booker T. Washington remained dominant within the APO, the younger generation of educated and politicized Coloureds found the more assertive and self-confident stance of W. E. B. Du Bois more attractive.[42] The dominant theme of Du Bois's philosophy was the need for black people to take pride in their racial and cultural distinctiveness and not to adopt the negative image that whites held of blacks. Those influenced by Du Bois felt that Coloured people were too diffident and dependent on whites. They needed to build self-confidence and take the initiative in uplifting their own people.[43] Accordingly, exhortations for Coloured people to develop an affirmative group identity, or "race pride," became more frequent in the *APO*. Colouredness was increasingly rejected as a badge of derogation and was instead promoted as a positive and desirable quality. In a lecture to the Cape Town branch of the APO, Harold Cressy indicated a predilection for this more affirmative strain of thought when he complained of South African blacks lacking self-esteem and being too passive in promoting their communal interests.[44] He lamented: "In America, no people make a greater study of the Negro than the Negro himself. The same cannot be said of the Coloured and Native races of South Africa. . . . They have so little race pride and lack national feeling. Consequently they have taken little or no interest in questions that affect their welfare as a race."[45]

As attested by the influence of both Washington and Du Bois, politicized Coloureds were remarkably receptive to the political ideas of African American intellectuals in the earlier decades of the twentieth century. This was partly because black Americans appeared to be making real strides in their struggle for civil equality. Also, the African Methodist Episcopal (AME) Church, which had operated in South Africa since 1896, served as a conduit for these ideas. The AME Church had considerable influence within the Coloured elite, and several AME churchmen were intimately involved in Coloured politics. For example, William Collins, the first president of the APO, was a lay preacher for the AME Church, and Francis Gow, one of the most prominent leaders of the church in South Africa, was elected APO president in 1942.

Besides the focus on African American politics, the *APO* displayed a growing interest in the fortunes of black peoples in other parts of the world, especially those subject to colonial rule. It thus drew attention to ways in which Africans and Asians were being exploited by whites and painted an exaggerated picture of the progress made by blacks internationally.[46] Ironically, although the *APO* identified strongly with black people throughout the world, it sought to distance itself from Africans in South Africa itself for pragmatic reasons. The newspaper often pointed to the achievements of black people as proof that they had the potential for matching whites. Although the *APO* was prepared to admit that Coloureds and most other black peoples were "backward" compared to whites, it did not regard this inferiority to be inherent or permanent, as most racists did. The superiority of whites was assumed to be due to historically and environmentally favorable conditions that allowed the European peoples to outpace the rest of humanity. The *APO* thus endorsed the opinion that "the Negro, given the environment, the education, and the opportunity of the white man, will behave, think, and live in much the same way as the average white man."[47] To the *APO*, it was just a matter of time before black people caught up with whites, as Western education and technology spread to the rest of the globe.

After the exceptionally promising first two years of its existence, the *APO* gradually lost its vitality. Especially from the latter half of 1913 onward, the enthusiasm that had sustained the newspaper in the previous years waned as its circulation shrank, its advertising revenues declined, and it sank more deeply into debt. The organization itself was slowly declining into a state of dormancy. As production of the

APO became increasingly arduous, the reporting lost its incisiveness and the content became prosaic and suffused with a lassitude that reflected the demoralization of the Coloured elite in the aftermath of Union. World War I, however, provided the newspaper with a temporary reprieve. The war gave the Coloured elite hope of a new dawn after the conflict and provided the *APO* with sensational news that could be garnered with relatively little effort.

From August 1914, the content and editorial policy of the *APO* was completely dominated by the war. The paper's attitude toward the conflict was largely determined by the assumption that the war would mark a watershed in the progress of subject peoples the world over. The editors had little doubt that the Allied forces would triumph and hoped that much of the racial injustice suffered by black people would be eliminated by the need for governments worldwide to reconstitute social and international relations on a footing that would ensure peace and stability for the future. The *APO* trusted that the patriotism and the contribution of Coloured people to the war effort would be recognized and rewarded with an amelioration in racial discrimination and even its eventual elimination. It expected the Coloured people to be commended for remaining loyal to the empire whereas many whites had opposed South African involvement in the war and some had even revolted against British authority.

The newspaper thus supported the Allied cause with enthusiasm and ostentatiously displayed its loyalty to the empire and its patriotism for South Africa.[48] Indeed, the APO eagerly helped to recruit volunteers for the Cape Corps, an infantry regiment instituted to allow Coloured soldiers to serve in an auxilliary capacity during the war. The Coloured petite bourgeoisie took great pride in the Cape Corps, and several APO leaders either served on the Cape Corps Comforts Committee or helped with its fund-raising efforts.[49] Abe Desmore, a prominent APO member and a leading intellectual within the Coloured elite during the first half of the twentieth century, volunteered for service and wrote a book about his experiences. Echoing the feeling of his community, he described the Cape Corps as the answer to the "prayer of the Coloured community to be allowed to do their share in the toils of the Great War."[50]

War-induced inflation, however, undermined the commercial viability of the *APO* by increasing production costs and reducing circulation. The newspaper struggled along until November 1915, when, beset by financial difficulties, it ceased publication for nearly four years.

By the time the *APO* resumed publication in August 1919, it was clear that Coloured people could not expect to be rewarded for their patriotism and their contribution to the war effort. If anything, Coloured disappointment in this regard played an important role in making 1919 a year of revival for the APO. Not only did the organization resurrect its newspaper, it also organized a national conference for the first time since 1913. The period immediately after the war, in addition, witnessed a brief flurry of the activism that had marked the organization in the years prior to Union. Among other things, the APO tried, albeit unsuccessfully, to organize Coloured workers into labor unions under its aegis, and it petitioned the British government not to place South West Africa under South African control until Coloured political rights had been secured in that territory. After this request was brushed aside by the colonial secretary, the APO sent a similar appeal to the Paris Peace Conference in March 1919.[51] When its petition was ignored and the discriminatory franchise of South Africa was extended to South West Africa, it was apparent that the Coloured community would not reap any reward from its support of the allied cause.

Despite these disappointments and the intensifying segregationism, the period between the end of the war and the demise of the *APO* newspaper in 1923 nevertheless remained one of relative optimism within the Coloured petite bourgeoisie that they would ultimately achieve their quest for civil equality. The false expectations of the Coloured elite were nourished by their progressionist assumptions and continued faith that liberal values would somehow prevail in the end.[52] The setback of Union was rationalized as an aberration, and the worst of the onslaught on black civil rights still lay in the future. The Coloured petite bourgeoisie, moreover, was growing in size and gaining confidence in its ability to sustain the standards of white middle-class respectability. In addition, the Coloured vote was a growing force in the politics of the western Cape as Coloureds increasingly became politicized and able to meet the franchise qualifications.[53] Until the mid-1920s, the APO leaders also drew encouragement from opposition among Afrikaners to the South African government, especially when given violent expression as in the 1914 Afrikaner Rebellion[54] and the 1922 Rand Revolt.[55] They hoped that Afrikaner rebelliousness would serve as a foil for their patriotism and that, by comparison, Coloureds would be shown to be responsible, law-abiding citizens worthy of full acceptance into the dominant society. By ridiculing the extremism and lack of refinement of some white workers, the *APO* invited direct comparison between "respectable" Coloureds and the factious white working class.[56]

The *APO* was by far the most important newspaper specifically aimed at a Coloured readership prior to the emergence of a commercial Coloured press in the 1930s. The paper was important both in terms of the degree to which it represented Coloured opinion and in terms of the bulk and range of evidence it contained about the weltanschauung and social experience of the Coloured petite bourgeoisie. Facing the predicament of Coloured marginality and trying to capitalize on the intermediate status of Coloured people in the South African racial hierarchy, the leaders of the APO had to negotiate a tricky path between protest and accommodation, on the one hand, and between assimilationism and Coloured separatism, on the other. Continually adjusting their responses to white supremacism to gain the best compromise between these competing interests, the APO and its newspaper inevitably displayed ideological inconsistencies and were ambivalent in their political outlook. The next case study will confirm that these conclusions held true for the period following the demise of the *APO* and will also broaden the analysis to take into account class perceptions in the expression of Coloured identity.

Ambivalences of Race and Class
in the *Educational Journal*, 1915–40

The *Educational Journal*, published from May 1915 onward, was the official organ of the Teachers' League of South Africa, which had been founded in Cape Town in 1913 as a professional association expressly for Coloured teachers.[57] Representing what was by far the largest professional group within the Coloured community,[58] the league reflected the social experience and the worldview of the Coloured petite bourgeoisie. Although it started off as a relatively small organization, it had grown to the extent that it was able to draw the majority of Coloured teachers under its wing by the early 1940s. As the mouthpiece of one of the most influential Coloured communal organizations of the time, the *Journal* mirrored the values, aspirations, and frustrations of the Coloured elite.[59] With several of this social group's most eminent individuals and leading intellectuals within its ranks, the league and its periodical played an instrumental role in the ongoing process of Coloured self-definition and the construction of Coloured identity.

Although conditions of economic exploitation and class domination principally determined the sociopolitical status of the Coloured community, the racial dimensions of their situation were uppermost in the minds of the Coloured petite bourgeoisie and therefore of league members. They experienced their society primarily as members of a racial category, the Coloured people, and their consciousness was filtered through the prism of their identity as Coloureds. It was therefore racial oppression rather than class exploitation that informed their social perceptions and political outlook. As a result, class consciousness within the Coloured elite was attenuated and largely articulated in terms of their identity as Coloured people. This much is evident from the fact that the league was a racially exclusive body with the explicit aim of fostering the educational interests of the Coloured people.[60]

As explained earlier, their marginality and intermediate position within the society resulted in ambiguities and unresolved contradictions within Coloured identity and presented Coloured people with a series of dilemmas and paradoxes in their day-to-day living. This, in turn, led to inconsistent and equivocal behavior, which was particularly conspicuous within the Coloured elite and hence also in the *Educational Journal*. These inconsistencies reflected ambivalences inherent in the way in which Coloured people perceived themselves as a group and the manner in which they related to other social groups. Coloured identity was therefore highly sensitive to the immediate context in which it operated and had a degree of fluidity in any given situation. Because of their ambivalent position within the society and the insecurity that this engendered, Coloureds were continually modulating their reactions to their situation in order to strike a balance between their assimilationist aspirations, the realities of their exclusion from the dominant society, and their fears at being cast down to the status of Africans.[61]

The resultant ambiguities within Coloured identity were manifested in a range of inconsistent behaviors within the Teachers' League and in a disjuncture between the ideals and actions of its leaders. For example, within the Coloured community, the league demanded deference commensurate with its elite social standing, yet it often willingly accepted an inferior status relative to whites and meekly acquiesced in the humiliating treatment meted out to it by a bullying white officialdom.[62] More conspicuously, the *Educational Journal*, like the *APO*, opposed racial discrimination in principle yet endorsed the precepts of the South African racial hierarchy by zealously promoting Coloured privilege relative to Africans. The TLSA claimed to stand for a broad South Africanism and strove for the full integration of Coloured people into national life. Yet it failed to extend this cherished ideal of assimilation to Africans by doing all it could to distance itself from them. Another glaring inconsistency in the makeup of the league was that its leaders had a strong sense of social responsibility toward the Coloured laboring poor and were concerned about their welfare but often openly displayed disdain for the Coloured working classes. Class prejudice toward this sector consequently manifested itself in myriad ways within the *Educational Journal*.[63]

For the quintessential expression of such prejudice within the league, one need go no further than Dan Sampson's presidential address to the 1916 annual conference, in which he attempted a "class analysis" of the Coloured community.[64] Sampson's speech represents a comprehensive and vivid statement of the assumptions and prejudices that informed league attitudes toward the Coloured working classes. His speech is important for the coherence and frankness with which it delineated the Coloured elite's perception of the social hierarchy within the Coloured community. Furthermore, in his address, Sampson articulated the attitudes and assumptions that underpinned the league's civilizing mission toward working-class Coloured people and informed its struggle for educational reform throughout that period.

Sampson divided the Coloured people into three categories: the sunken, the sinking, and the uprising classes. Of the sunken class, he commented, "What an accumulation of filth, vice, dissipation and crime! Such a combination seems to defy all the influences of human healing. 'Past social redemption' we exclaim."[65] Though the sinking class was characterized as containing neither the "openly vicious nor the hardened criminal," its members were said to be indifferent to their own advancement and susceptible to corruption. Their "indispensable needs are not prison accommodation, reformatories or police officers, but schools and teachers, or in other words, education."[66] The uprising class, predictably, encompassed "those who, being concerned about their advancement in life, zealously watch over the moral and intellectual training of their offspring."[67] That the *Coloured Commission Report* more than two decades later made a similar tripartite class distinction within the Coloured population indicates that this was a common perception of social stratification within the Coloured community.[68]

A critically important assumption underlying Sampson's reasoning and one that was generally shared by the league was that hooliganism, crime, immorality, and social degradation were largely the result of "ignorance" or "a lack of knowledge." This ignorance was tied not only to such tangible concerns as illiteracy, the lack of economically useful skills, or mothers not knowing the basics of good nutrition but also to such elusive qualities as people's insensibility to "virtue" and their indifference to the "noble things in life."[69] In this respect, the religious and professional values of league members converged, so that there was an automatic association between ignorance and evil, on the one hand, and knowledge and virtue, on the other. "Ignorance" was seen to breed social degeneracy, whereas "knowledge" was the basis of progress, civilization, and all that was noble in humankind. The *APO* similarly contrasted ignorance as "the most soul-withering blight that can afflict mankind" with knowledge as "the wing that flieth to heaven."[70]

Consequently, it is not surprising that the *Journal* considered educational improvement to be the most powerful means for eliminating ignorance and remolding the Coloured working classes to fit its image of bourgeois respectability. Besides exposing them to the superior ways of the dominant culture, education would be the most effective vehicle for instilling the skills necessary for economic success and inculcating the values required to turn the mass of Coloured people into exemplary citizens. These attitudes were evident in the commonly expressed belief within the league that the school was the "bulwark of civilization."

This effort, however, required the cooperation of the state and the dominant society as a whole, for it was only through massive government intervention that sufficient educational facilities and other social services could be provided for the Coloured proletariat to be coaxed into the habits of "civilization." But this expression of goodwill was clearly not forthcoming. Having drawn attention to the "deplorable condition" of the Coloured masses, the natural question that arose for Sampson and the *Educational Journal* was, "Whence are the hooligans who throng our streets and fill our gaols; by whom were they created?" The answer he provided was typical of league reasoning on the matter: "The benevolence of a Creator intended them to be human, but the passivity of the State, with its mistaken economy is largely responsible for their degradation which brings them almost to the level of the brute."[71]

Sampson's reference to the "mistaken economy" of the state echoed a favorite refrain in the *Journal*'s periodic call for the reform of Coloured education. The league held that it was false economy and socially ruinous for the state to squander society's resources on law enforcement, the administration of justice, and other costs of endemic criminality. It instead advocated the preventative policy of providing all sectors of the population with adequate educational facilities. The league argued that this approach would, in the long run, benefit the whole of society by reducing expenditure on the police force, courts, jails, reformatories, hospitals, and the like.[72] Deploring the shortsightedness of the government for refusing to reform Coloured education, the *Journal* rhetorically asked of its policies, "What is the result but hospitals and prisons filled with human beings, who had but a little care and money been expended upon them when children, might have been a credit to the state and a source of happiness to their fellow men?"[73]

Besides altruistic motives, there was also an important element of self-interest in the league's incentive to raise the social condition of the working classes. Although league officials regarded the "advanced" sectors of the Coloured community to have attained the requisite level of "civilization" to merit acceptance into the dominant society, it was clear to them that the majority of Coloured people had not. The *Journal* recognized that, in the minds of whites, Colouredness was intimately associated with a range of negative, racially attributed characteristics. It was extremely conscious of white racist judgments of the sort that Coloureds were "a backward, lazy, debased people for whom it was better to build strong jails" and that they "lack sincerity of purpose, are too easy-going, poor in determination and possessing no stamina."[74] In addition, rowdiness, drunkenness, criminality, and the whole gamut of "immoral" and delinquent behaviors were sufficiently common among the Coloured working classes to embarrass so-called respectable Coloureds acutely. The *Journal*, for instance, was ashamed of the "Coloured hooligans and loud vulgar Coloured girls who perturb our streets, parks, public gardens, foreshore, trains etc."[75] League leaders realized that such behavior provided bigoted whites with ample ammunition to justify racial discrimination. They feared that individual Coloureds would not be able to take their rightful place in the society as long as they were being discredited by an unruly Coloured working class. The Coloured elite argued in vain that individuals should be judged on merit, that any community should be evaluated by its upper rather than its lower classes, and that the poor could not be held responsible for their predicament.[76]

Denied the option of quietly assimilating into the dominant society on the basis of individual merit, the Coloured elite adopted a longer-term strategy of implementing a civilizing mission toward the Coloured masses. Realizing that they would not be able to dissociate themselves from the Coloured laboring classes in the minds of whites, league leaders resigned themselves to the protracted task of raising the entire Coloured community to a "level of civilization" where there would be no justification for discrimination against them. The league therefore applied itself to the pragmatic and incrementalist strategy of doing what it could to raise the socioeconomic condition of the Coloured laboring poor and patiently demonstrating that there were Coloured people worthy of acceptance into the dominant society. Gradually eroding white prejudice in this manner appeared to be the only viable option.

For the *Journal*, an essential part of the civilizing process involved inculcating the Coloured masses with habits such as thrift, punctuality, honesty, cleanliness, temperance, moderation, dignity, and respect for authority.[77] These values were central to Western bourgeois perceptions of "civilized behavior" and the converse of traits attributed to the Coloured stereotype; mores that were taken to separate the "civilized" from the "savage" and the "progressive" from the "backward." The subjective connotations with which the league invested the quality of thrift provide a good illustration of the way in which such traits were imbued with racial significance. Discussing the need to instill the habit of providence into the Coloured people, "Advance," a regular contributor to the *Educational Journal*, asserted that "the savage races of man such as the Bushmen and the Australian Aborigines have no idea of providing for a future supply when food is plentiful" and concluded that "for a race to make progress, it is necessary that thrift habits be inculcated in the young."[78] Because they accepted this sort of reasoning, none of his colleagues contradicted E. C. Roberts when, in his 1937 presidential address, he attributed the "backwardness" of the Coloured people to "a lack of thrift."[79]

Ernest Moses, a prominent TLSA member and chairman of the Coloured Welfare Association, neatly summarized the rationale behind the league's civilizing mission:

> The progressive development of any nation or people is retarded and its vitality sapped by dire attacks of immorality, drunkenness, hooliganism, gambling and extravagance. . . . While the Coloured people of

South Africa have an aristocracy of their own they also have a large mass of uneducated, undeveloped individuals without ambition, who far outnumber the handful who have been blessed and privileged to develop a taste for the better and higher things of this life. . . . For many more years to come the Coloured people are to be judged according to the number of its weaker members, and that salvation lies only in the general uplift of the masses. . . . The weaker brothers and sisters should be schooled into virtue, and this can be done by no other method than by educational development.[80]

Thwarted in their attempts to shake off the automatic racial stereotyping of Coloured people and to be judged as individuals, league leaders, on occasion, expressed exasperation at both whites and the Coloured working classes for their predicament. Thus, Roberts complained that "it is astonishing to find men, good and sensible, . . . who consider hybrid people as possessed of vices only, with no virtues [and] relegate the hybrid people to the lowly position of hewers of wood and drawers of water."[81] In his presidential address of 1934, Ned Doman vented his frustration at the tendency of bigoted whites to "point with scorn and contempt at the lowest type of Coloured person he can find . . . as an example of the Coloured man" when those whites were, in fact, responsible for Coloured working-class degradation.[82] Similarly, an impatient John Abrahamse, despairing of the moral redemption of the Coloured people in his presidential address of 1938, proclaimed that "we are knee-haltered because a large portion of our people drag us down into a mire of filth."[83]

As the foregoing discussion demonstrates, class attitudes were inextricably bound up with racial perceptions within the league. Like white supremacists, the *Journal*'s editors tended to conflate class distinctions with racial differences, but unlike racists, they did not regard these differences to be inherent or permanent. Despite its contradictions and vacillations with regard to issues of race, the league ultimately believed that all human beings were potentially equal and that this fundamental truth would become increasingly evident as human society advanced to higher stages of civilization. It was on this premise that the *Journal* held out hope that Coloureds would, in time, be fully integrated into a society in which race would be irrelevant to social status. This partly explains why, despite intensifying segregationism throughout this period,[84] the Coloured political leadership and the league persisted with their pragmatic incrementalism and retained hope of their eventual acceptance into the dominant society.

Notwithstanding these aspirations, the league, in its daily affairs, still had to come to terms with the realities of the racially stratified society and the marginality of the Coloured people. In this regard, league leaders were faced with a dilemma common to the Coloured petite bourgeoisie as a whole. Because their primary objective was assimilation into the dominant society and because they were the victims of white racism, politicized Coloureds embraced the ideal of nonracism as a matter of principle. Their marginality, however, meant that they had little option but to mobilize politically by appealing to Coloured identity. Not only did the Coloured political leadership accept Colouredness and the inferior status that went with it as a social reality, they were also very aware that there were potential rewards consequent on their cultivation of Coloured separatism. Thus, in contradiction to their ideal of nonracism, virtually all Coloured political leaders chose to work within the racial system for the betterment of their community, thereby accepting the position of Coloureds within that hierarchy.[85]

As with the APO, this ambiguity manifested itself clearly in the organizational life of the league, which espoused nonracial and assimilationist ideals but for all practical purposes was racially exclusive. It is therefore not surprising that the league did not behave consistently in matters of race and that it vacillated, throughout the period under review, between accepting and rejecting the inferior status imposed on Coloured people. As a result, the organization developed an opportunistic attitude toward the racial system and Coloured identity. Given the inability of Coloureds to influence government policy in any meaningful way, the league realized that it needed to operate in a pragmatic manner and be flexible with regard to its organizational objectives. Perceiving no other option but to bow to white power, it deliberately set out to play the racial system to the minimum disadvantage of Coloureds, and it conceded that the pursuit of full equality with whites would be unrealistic for the foreseeable future. The *Educational Journal* thus tended to object to segregation when it was considered detrimental to Coloured interests but accept and even applaud racial discrimination when it was perceived to be to Coloureds' advantage. Its pragmatism therefore led the *Journal* to a qualified acceptance of segregationism and induced it to try and trade its acceptance of white privilege for concessions from the state.

The *Journal*'s readiness to accept an inferior status for Coloureds was, however, predicated on the condition that the Coloured people were not to be denied the opportunity of progressing at an acceptable pace. For example, Israel Oppelt, after pointing to the huge discrepancy between state expenditure on white and Coloured education in his 1927 presidential address, made it clear that he had "no quarrel with the state at differentiating. But that a difference out of all proportion be made . . . is unfair." His elaboration on this point typified the league's cautious incrementalism: "Though we may not succeed in shaking the conscience of the lawmakers so effectively as to obtain half the European child's grant, yet by consistently agitating we shall succeed in getting more than in the past."[86]

With the tightening of segregation against Coloured people throughout the 1920s and 1930s, the *Educational Journal* increasingly resigned itself to accepting racially discriminatory measures. It preferred to salvage whatever it could from a deteriorating situation and to maneuver within new constraints that were being placed on it rather than assert its rights or fight the system. This kind of meek capitulation and acquiescence in the people's denigration was demonstrated by the league's reaction to the exclusion of Coloured students from the Cape Town Technical College in 1925. Quite predictably, initial league objections at this racial bar were ignored by the authorities.[87] When it became clear that it could not reverse the decision, the league's executive tried to negotiate the best deal for Coloureds that it could manage. The *Journal* subsequently reported that "interviews with the College Council have been held and the matter discussed calmly and reasonably. . . . The League has recognized the spirit of the times as manifested in present-day ideals and prejudices and has made no pretentious attempt at trying to force the Council to open the doors to Coloured students."[88] The editor nevertheless felt that the league could "modestly congratulate itself" for having persuaded the college to allow Coloureds to register for segregated classes in a few subjects for which, it boasted, "the League had been the first to clamour."[89]

The *Journal* was even prepared to accept an inferior professional status for Coloured teachers. This was illustrated by the fact that the league did not seem to mind too much that white teachers in mission schools received a higher war bonus than Coloured teachers.[90] It did, however, object when Coloured teachers who had managed to pass for white qualified for the higher bonus. Apparently, it was especially female teachers who, "with the adventitious aids of rouge and powder—lots of it," were able to claim the higher bonus paid to whites.

This was an emotive issue within the profession, for, as a correspondent to the *APO* explained, it was unfair that distinctions be made between "European-Coloured" and "Coloured-Coloured" teachers.[91] The league's readiness to accept an inferior professional status was, however, nowhere more apparent than when it endorsed the Watermeyer Commission's finding that Coloured teachers had no claim to remuneration equal to that of white teachers.[92] The *Journal* conceded that "the European teacher will have the best pay. . . . No one will cavil at this." But the corollary to this acquiescence was that the league expected the Education Department to implement the commission's recommendation that Coloured teachers be paid between 60 percent and 72 percent of the equivalent white teachers' salaries.[93] The league was prepared to accept Watermeyer's proposals because they would have led to a substantial improvement in existing salaries.[94] To the league leadership, any improvement in prevailing conditions was welcome, no matter how small or how distasteful its implications. Their progressionism led league representatives to believe that such incremental improvements would eventually result in the attainment of their longer-term ideal of acceptance into the dominant society.

League leaders were prepared to compromise their nonracial ideals in these ways not only because it appeared futile to make demands for full equality but also because they considered it counterproductive to anger the authorities, to alienate possible allies, or to forgo opportunities for advancement, however small. They feared the damage that a white backlash or retribution from the state could do to their cause and their private interests.[95] Another reason the *Journal* editors did not want to complain too loudly about discrimination was that they did not want Coloured people to stand out too conspicuously as a group. Wishing nothing more than for Coloureds who had acquired the necessary social skills to filter quietly into the dominant society, they believed that to make too great a fuss about discrimination or to assert Coloured group rights too vigorously would have compromised their assimilationist aspirations.

However, the strains of adopting nonracism in principle but accepting the racial system in practice emerged from time to time. They surfaced most forcefully in the organization's ambivalent response to the government's 1938 announcement of its intention of implementing residential segregation for Coloured people.[96] G. J. Beukes, in his presidential message to the league, proffered the well-worn response of the *Journal* to the inexorable advance of segregation. He urged

Coloured teachers to strive for the social advancement of their community and tried to communicate a message of racial tolerance to the wider society. In a demonstration of the continued influence of the ideas of Booker T. Washington within the Coloured petite bourgeoisie, he pointed to the interdependence between the various racial groups in South Africa: "Let us remember that we who educate are also 'race-builders.' Let us instill racial pride into our pupils, make them love the members of their group. There need be no clash with other groups— no antagonism, as all the different groups in South Africa must be taught to be tolerant towards each other, with mutual understanding for the common good of the whole nation. As the five fingers make the one hand, so the different groups must needs comprise a happy and prosperous South African nation."[97]

But the extreme urgency with which politicized Coloureds viewed the issue of residential segregation was sufficient for the editor of the *Educational Journal*, Fred Hendricks, to depart from league custom and hit out at segregationists. In the process, he also administered an indirect censure to the president of the league for airing views that he himself had expressed as editor of the *Journal* on numerous occasions. He rejected the argument that the cultivation of Coloured separatism was beneficial to the Coloured community in that it stimulated the supposedly "enviable quality of race pride." This he held to be an absurd argument for Coloureds to make: "For to be proud of one's race is to be proud of one's language, ancestors, customs and achievements. And the language of the Coloured man is the language of the European; his forebears are Europeans; his mode of living is that of the European and what he has achieved thus far has been in collaboration with the European. Only idle fancy of a warped imagination can visualize for the Coloured people of South Africa a set of qualities or ideals entirely distinct from those of the European."[98]

The *Journal*'s rejection of race as a valid measure of human worth, on the one hand, and its propagation of Coloured separatism, on the other, were contradictory but not necessarily mutually exclusive positions. These contradictory ideas could be held simultaneously because they reflected different levels of consciousness among members and because they applied to different spheres of the organization's existence. The nonracism belonged to the rarefied realm of the ideal and of abstract morality that formed part of the ultimate goal of their striving, whereas the accommodation with racism was necessary for them to come to terms with the realities of everyday living. Although the league had utterly compromised its ideal of nonracism, assumptions about the theoretical equality of humankind continued to permeate its thought and discourse. These contradictory values existed side by side within the organization and continued to inform the thought and actions of its members.

In keeping with their nonracial ideal, the *Journal* editors intermittently denied the inherent inferiority of black people and made clear their feeling that racial prejudice and discrimination were unfair and immoral. This, for instance, was the spirit in which the *Journal* commented on such issues as the segregation of public transport and the habitual discourtesy of white shop assistants toward Coloured customers.[99] A *Journal* correspondent echoed league sentiment in this respect when he appealed for "social and economic standards and not colour" to determine access to rights and privileges within the society.[100] The league nevertheless recognized that there were substantive disparities in the objective abilities of different "races"—that some were indeed superior to others. This apparent contradiction needs to be understood in terms of the worldview of the league—in the way it perceived human diversity and the place of the Coloured people within this schema.

The league regarded humanity as consisting of distinct population groups, or races, although its concept of race remained vague and fluid. The *Journal*, for example, described the British Empire as consisting of "many races from the bronzed races of the East to the fur-clad tribes of North-West Canada."[101] It was accepted that some races or peoples were "advanced" and others "backward," with the basic division between the two being that of color. The league interpreted the undisputed global domination of the Western powers and their overwhelming technological lead as proof of the "superiority of the white man." Their daily experience appeared at every turn to confirm that the Coloured people were among the so-called backward races of the world. Assumptions of Coloured inferiority were clear in oft-articulated fears and self-deprecating statements such as that the Coloured people were "rapidly sinking to a level far below that of a civilized race," that Coloureds were becoming a "drink-sodden race of bestial degenerates," or that Coloureds were "at last emerging from the Dark Ages."[102]

The acceptance of Coloured inferiority did not necessarily contradict the league's egalitarian principles because the superiority of whites was assumed to be due to historically and environmentally favorable conditions that allowed them to outpace the rest of humanity.

The implication was that any of the "backward" peoples would, under the same circumstances, have developed at a similar rate and to an equivalent level.[103] The *Journal* advanced this thesis on the one occasion it broached the question of why the "White race is so much more intelligent than the Black." It explained that "this greater or higher mentality is second nature, due to favourable circumstances" and rhetorically asked: "If the black Negro were to be placed in similar favourable circumstances and remain free from all mixture with lighter-skinned races would he steadily become more intelligent and ultimately reach the level of the white race in mentality, while remaining black-skinned?"[104]

The assumption that Coloured inferiority was temporary and not due to innate racial disabilities was critical to the worldview and self-perception of the Coloured elite because it allowed them to square their acceptance of subordination with their assimilationist aspirations and nonracial ideal. Thus, although the *Journal* conceded that "the problem of the Coloured population is a difficult one," it argued that "there are forces and potentialities in it that are perhaps undreamt of at present."[105] The league firmly believed that Coloured "backwardness" would, in time, be overcome through improved education and exposure to the right social and cultural environment. Eventual parity between white and black was seen to be the inevitable outcome as the level of education of disadvantaged communities improved; as Western culture and technology spread across the globe; and as humanity progressed to its ultimate destiny of peace, prosperity, and racial harmony. A *Journal* editorial therefore rejected the "pathetic belief in the utter immutability of primitive nature."[106] And John Abrahamse, in his 1938 presidential address, explained that "there is truth in the advantages of birth bringing with it inherited qualities, but the claims of a race being inherently superior denies the evidence of education and opportunity being able to transform a backward people into a society of the highest culture."[107]

The *Educational Journal* pointed to the rapid advances made by black peoples the world over as proof not only that Coloureds had the potential to match whites but also that its prediction of future racial equality was becoming a reality, for blacks were starting to catch up with whites. Like the *APO*, the *Journal* drew attention to the achievements of black people, painting an exaggerated and romanticized picture of the progress being made by African Americans, West Indians, Africans, and Asians.[108] In this respect, the Coloured elite held special admiration for the Japanese, who had transformed an insular, tradition-bound society into a world power within a few decades. Coloureds were particularly enamored of the Japanese because they perceived them to be a "brown race" like themselves. There is no more revealing expression of Coloured petite bourgeois attitudes toward the Japanese during this period than J. R. Strydom's observations when a Japanese warship visited Cape Town harbor in 1922. Strydom, a regular contributor to the *Journal*, drew hope for the future of the Coloured people from those "little yellow men." "Commend me to the silent Japanese," he enthused,

> the wonderful little Japs . . . those little, narrow-eyed, high-cheekboned and determined-looking sons of the Land of the Rising Sun [who have] rapidly risen to one of the most exalted and powerful positions in the civilized world. . . . We saw them associating with our most distinguished and autocratic citizens on a footing of exact equality, and I believe it did our hearts good to see it all. Hopes were refreshed and revived. . . . Some saw our future in a different light and new possibilities appeared on the horizon, for here we saw the members of a race not quite dissimilar from ours in variegation of origin and the circumstances that attended their progress . . . in the civilized world.[109]

That Strydom attributed the success of the Japanese to their "ever moving, ever Westernizing" tendencies is an indication of the belief among the Coloured elite that Western bourgeois culture represented the apogee of human achievement and that the degree of conformity with its norms and values provided an objective scale for the measure of human development. Because they assumed Western culture to be an absolute standard of civilization, conforming to its practices automatically meant "progress" for entire peoples and communities and personal accomplishment for the individual. The Coloured elite therefore aspired to the acquisition of the social attributes and practices of white middle-class society because they genuinely believed Western culture to be inherently superior to other forms of human culture. Anxious to underscore its view that "culture" and "civilization" depended on more than just skin color, the *Journal* endorsed Sir John Carruthers Beattie's opinion that "it was not merely by having a white skin that we should maintain a white aristocracy but by being white in mind and spirit and achievement."[110]

The league's association with whiteness and its opportunistic attitude toward race were apparent in the way it defended and sought to take advantage of Coloureds' status of relative privilege vis-à-vis Africans within the racial hierarchy. Given its simultaneous commitment to racially egalitarian principles, the *Journal* displayed mixed feelings toward Africans. On the one hand, there was a genuine empathy for Africans within the league and a recognition that they were fellow citizens who suffered even more severe racial oppression than Coloureds. On the other hand, there was also a strong feeling that Coloureds were superior to Africans and deserved better treatment and higher social status.[111] By assenting to work within the racial system, the league automatically laid claim to the middle position within South Africa's three-tiered racial order. One of the reasons the Coloured political leadership was prepared to accept an inferior status for its people in relation to whites was because that stance allowed them to bargain for a position of relative privilege for Coloureds with respect to Africans. The result, as a *Journal* editorial once put it, was that "the Coloured people have quietly and steadily segregated themselves either voluntarily or under pressure of circumstances."[112] Calling on the league to capitalize on the increasingly rigid distinctions being made between Coloureds and Africans in the implementation of segregation, David van der Ross, in his presidential address of 1922, urged his colleagues to use their Coloured identity in more creative and affirmative ways to benefit their "race." He argued that "the classification of the races of this country under three distinct heads has come to stay, and is being more rigidly observed each day. It is expected of us now, as a people, to assert our individuality and to take the initiative in devising means for our advance."[113]

The tripartite racial ordering of the society was reinforced by the state and built into government policy. It found expression in education policy through the ever more rigorous separation of schooling into the three racial categories of white, Coloured, and African throughout the first half of the twentieth century. After the 1905 School Board Act achieved the state's primary aim of segregating white students from black and providing whites with compulsory public schooling, the Education Department progressively separated Coloureds from Africans in the education system in the ensuing decades.[114] The league's Coloured exclusivism was legitimated and encouraged by both church and state in a push to implement segregation even more rigorously within the education system throughout the period under consideration. Consequently, early on in its life, the *Journal* claimed to find the segregative policies of the Education Department to be a "welcome sign" that it was making "a genuine attempt to place Coloured education on a definite basis, apart from that of the Native and the European."[115]

Because they recognized that the primary racial distinction for whites was that between white and black, the Coloured elite often felt vulnerable to the possibility that Coloureds might lose their status of privilege relative to Africans.[116] These insecurities put the moderate Coloured political leadership at pains to underscore the affinity between Coloureds and whites and to stress their differences with Africans. The league therefore often responded to segregative measures by arguing that Coloureds and whites shared a symbiotic relationship and that by discriminating against Coloureds, whites would inevitably harm themselves as well.[117] This sentiment was evident when the *Journal* highlighted a quotation from the local press that "the Coloured population was now interbred throughout our whole social life and the well-being of the white depended on the well-being of the Coloured."[118] This was also the premise that lay behind Abdurahman's warning to whites, as reported in the *Journal*, that "the Coloured man is going to drag you down if you don't educate him."[119] And it was with the aforementioned considerations of color and class in mind that the league executive passed a motion thanking Canon Lavis for giving evidence before the Provincial Finances Commission that "it is a mistake to judge of the educational ability of Coloured children as a whole by the lower class only and one which happens to approximate more nearly to the Aboriginal. Colour is not one thing, but many, and in dealing with children who are perhaps 70 per cent European in blood, it should not be surprising to find that they have intellectual ability equal to that of European children, and expressing itself on European lines."[120]

The league's stress on the affinities between the white and Coloured communities and its concern to distance the Coloured people from Africans was predicated on an awareness that for Coloureds to identify too closely with Africans would erode their hopes of assimilation and diminish their case for relative privilege. Politicized Coloureds recognized that Africans suffered much more virulent prejudice than their own people did because of their greater cultural distance from Western norms and because their numerical preponderance posed a real threat to white supremacy in the long term. Thus, both the social aspirations as well as the political pragmatism of the Coloured elite dictated that the league distance itself from Africans.

Although the league did not initially include explicit racial bars in its constitution, it restricted its membership to Coloured teachers in practice. Earlier versions of its *Rules and Bye-laws* did not place racial restrictions on membership to the league, but later regulations stipulated that "membership shall be open to all Coloured teachers"; there was also a vague provision that "others" who were "interested in the advancement of Coloured education, may join as associate members."[121] In practice, this meant that the league allowed those few white mission school teachers who showed an interest to join the association but that it excluded African teachers. The *Journal* responded icily to a suggestion in the *APO* that African teachers be allowed to join the league. It replied emphatically that "the view held by the League has always been that our body stand for the Coloured teacher as distinct from the European and Native." Soon after this, when a group of African teachers volunteered to affiliate with the league as a separate branch, their advance was spurned.[122] It was only in 1934 that the TLSA was prepared to accept African teachers as full members, and this privilege was extended only to the handful of Africans teaching in Coloured schools. The necessary amendments to the league's constitution were made against the sustained opposition of a vociferous minority.[123] The *Journal* justified its racial exclusiveness by arguing that Coloured separatism was necessary for the Coloured community to develop its full potential as a people and that this would, in itself, help to make for more harmonious intergroup relations. The *Journal* therefore tried to reassure others that "we are not of those that preach antipathy toward any race in this land. Our profession is one that makes for harmony amongst the various peoples and communities."[124]

The *Journal* rarely confronted the moral problem of the exclusion of Africans from the association. The league's attitude to the matter—that Africans were a group apart and needed to attend to their own interests—was settled at the founding conference. This much was clear from the absence of African teachers at the inaugural gathering and the unanimous acceptance of the motion requesting that the Education Department separate statistics on black education into Coloured and African categories.[125] However, in his 1923 presidential address, Philip Scholtz berated the Coloured teaching profession for being too conscious of class distinctions within its own community and of racial differences in general: "We blame the European for making distinctions; and we do the same, in some cases with more severity." He quoted a couplet from Rudyard Kipling to drive his point home: "On our own heads on our own hands / The sin, and the saving lie."[126]

The men and women who formulated league policy and produced the *Educational Journal* were sensitive, compassionate individuals motivated by humanitarian ideals. The moral dilemmas of exploiting the racial system to the advantage of Coloured people did not escape them. Neither were they oblivious to the implications that their acceptance of a second-class citizenship held for their dignity. But in their hearts and minds, they did not accept Coloured inferiority as permanent or inherent, as evidenced by their assertions of a theoretical equality between human beings and their ideal of assimilation. They were willing to work for Coloured advancement within the framework of the South African racial hierarchy because they percieved themselves as having no realistic alternative. The ideological inconsistencies and contradictions within the pages of the *Journal* should therefore not simply be seen as hypocrisy and glib casuistry or the result of self-serving justification and opportunism, as radical critics were later wont to interpret them.

Contrary to the impression created by the current literature on Coloured history, the response of the Coloured petite bourgeoisie to the exclusionary political dispensation of Union and the ensuing upsurge in segregationism was not simply to protest and resist. As this examination of the *APO* demonstrates, the response of politicized Coloureds was more complex. There was opposition, to be sure, but there was also a degree of acceptance of the racial order and an attempt to work within this system for the benefit of the Coloured people. Despite a commitment to nonracial values, there was a perception that Coloureds needed to come to an accommodation with the racial order. And in spite of their overriding desire for assimilation into the dominant society, the Coloured elite believed that the only practical political option open to them was to mobilize by appealing to Coloured identity. These ambivalences and contradictions were a direct consequence of the marginality of Coloureds and their intermediate status within the racial hierarchy. The position of the Coloured community—and much more so the petite bourgeoisie—within South African society was ambiguous, and this was reflected in their ideology and behavior, as the examples of both the *APO* and the *Educational Journal* demonstrate. In the words of Shula Marks, "Ambiguity has been the price of survival in a contradictory world."[127]

The case studies in this chapter provide examples of the way in which Coloured identity operated in concrete social contexts, as opposed to the more generalized explanation provided earlier. The chapter explored the worldview of the Coloured elite, revealing, among other things, how they justified their beliefs and actions, tried to reconcile contradictions and ambiguities in their behavior, and devised strategies for coping with their predicament of marginality. Viewed as illustrative examples of the conventional expression of Coloured identity, they confirm the analysis presented in the preceding thematic chapters.

The next chapter will examine the impact of the rise of the radical movement in Coloured politics on the identity during the middle decades of white supremacist South Africa. Given Marxist dogma about the primacy of class and its penchant for uncloaking racial, ethnic, national, and religious mythology, it is not unreasonable to expect Coloured radicals to have rejected race as an analytical concept and, with this, any personal identification as Coloured.

4

The Hegemony of Race

Coloured Identity within the Radical Movement during the Mid-twentieth Century

This chapter uses two case studies to explore the ways in which the rise of the radical movement in Coloured politics influenced the expression of Coloured identity up until the early 1960s, when it was crushed by state repression. The first case study examines the *Torch* newspaper that appeared between 1946 and 1963. As the mouthpiece of the Non-European Unity Movement the *Torch* fell squarely within the Trotskyist tradition of the South African Left.[1] The second case study, drawn from the rival Communist Party faction, focuses on Alex La Guma's novella *A Walk in the Night*, written in the early 1960s.[2] Both case studies will demonstrate that analysts have exaggerated the impact of left-wing ideology and politics in the promotion of nonracism before the 1960s. It will also be argued that they have underplayed the extent to which conventional perceptions and attitudes toward Coloured identity held sway among radicals.

Discourses of Race and Identity in the *Torch* Newspaper

The idea of uniting black people within a single organization, not merely seeking cooperation between racially distinct bodies, was introduced into Coloured protest politics by the National Liberation League, the first radical political organization to gain significant support within the Coloured community after its founding in 1935. This development represented a significant advance in nonracial thinking, even if it was mainly confined to radical activists and intellectuals.

After its incubation in the NLL, which was defunct by 1940, the idea of black political unity as a precondition for the overthrow of white rule became the cornerstone of the Non-European Unity Movement, a number of whose leaders had cut their political teeth in the NLL.[3] The NEUM was set up as a federal body at its founding conference in Bloemfontein in December 1943 as part of a deliberate strategy to accommodate organizations and individuals from all sectors of society and to allow coordination of their activities without requiring that they surrender their separate identities. Besides building a united black political front, a core objective of the NEUM was to implement a policy of noncollaboration with white authorities, using the tactic of boycotting all racist institutions. The leadership positioned the NEUM as an organization for national liberation, with a set of minimum demands for full democratic rights outlined in the Ten Point Programme adopted at its inaugural conference. These transitional demands, it was theorized, would win the NEUM mass support within the black peasantry, urban proletariat, and petite bourgeoisie. Members of the white working class were not expected to play a progressive role in the early stages of the struggle, but it was believed they would, in time, realize that their fundamental interests lay with the rest of the working class as the movement grew in power and crises in the capitalist economy eroded their privileged status. When the struggle for national liberation had progressed to an appropriate stage, the radical demands of the working class would be asserted and provide the impetus for social revolution in South Africa.[4]

The NEUM's main affiliates, in turn, consisted of two federal bodies. The Anti-CAD was almost entirely Coloured and based in the western Cape, whereas the All African Convention (AAC) was almost wholly African and drew support mainly from the eastern Cape. These two wings had an overlapping leadership, most notably in the persons of Goolam Gool, his sister, Jane, and her husband, Isaac Tabata. Despite concerted effort, the NEUM failed to draw in either the African National Congress or the South African Indian Congress (SAIC). In 1948, however, it managed to attract a breakaway faction from the Natal Indian Congress, the Anti-segregation Council, into the federation.[5] These factions coexisted with varying degrees of unease within the federal structure of the Non-European Unity Movement for fifteen years until simmering tensions over differences in doctrine and strategy led to a split, largely along racial and regional lines, in 1958, each faction subsequently claiming to represent the NEUM. The AAC faction went on in 1961 to form a revolutionary wing, the African

People's Democratic Union of Southern Africa, which organized in South Africa's main urban centres as well as in some African reserves, most notably eastern Pondoland, before being suppressed by bannings and arrests in the latter half of the 1960s. The Anti-CAD wing, already largely inactive and isolated from the liberatory mainstream in the latter half of the 1950s because of an unwillingness to engage in mass campaigns, declined into dormancy in the face of state repression, particularly after the Sharpeville massacre. It has, however, managed to maintain a strident anti-imperialist and antiapartheid polemic in the *Education Journal*, which was kept alive by a handful of activists and still exists today.

The Non-European Unity Movement has built up a formidable reputation for its uncompromising stand on nonracism, and for decades, NEUM ideologues have been delivering incisive and scathing criticism of the racism evident in the assumptions, actions, and utterings of a wide range of individuals and organizations. Indeed, a puritanical insistence on the principle of nonracism has become one of the hallmarks of the NEUM's discourse and political philosophy. Bill Nasson, for example, wrote that the NEUM had "an abiding commitment to non-racialism. This was not only a tactical imperative to overcome 'enslaving' ethnic divisions . . . but also a fierce and uncompromising rejection of the very construct of 'race' or ethnicity itself. . . . The traditional position of Unity Movement thinkers has always been that race or racialism is a 'mere excrescence of capitalism,' its existence the bondage of forms of false consciousness."[6] Writing in 2000, Crain Soudien echoed these sentiments: "The movement was fiercely nonracial and challenged at every opportunity the racial labelling of South Africans."[7] Even more recently, Shaun Viljoen asserted that "a key progenitor and proponent of the concept of 'non-racialism' was the Non-European Unity Movement. . . . The ideology of the NEUM was marked by a strong internationalism and a non-racialism which challenged the notion of 'race.'"[8]

Scrutiny of the *Torch* and other NEUM documentation, however, indicates that nonracism had not always been a central tenet of the organization.[9] Generalized assertions that the NEUM was nonracist in the sense of rejecting the validity of race as an analytical concept or a social reality are exaggerated and do not reflect the intricacies of its ideology and political strategy or the complexities of its history. At the very least, such assessments need to be modified to take into account an acknowledgment by NEUM ideologues of the salience of racial distinctions within South African society, the very considerable concessions the organization made to various forms of racial thinking, and its own lapses into racial thinking in unguarded moments during the earlier period of its existence.[10] The NEUM's attitude to race and Coloured identity was more complex—and more pragmatic—than a blanket denial of the significance of race, as suggested by commentators. In fact, its uncompromising stance on nonracism was a feature of its *later* history, apparent only toward the end of the *Torch*'s existence. Viewed from the broader perspective of the development of Coloured identity and notions of political correctness through the twentieth century, to expect otherwise would be anachronistic.

At the time of its founding and through the years in which the *Torch* was published, it was clear that forging black unity and implementing a policy of noncollaboration with the white establishment were the primary objectives of the NEUM and that promoting nonracism was not central to its agenda. This much should be evident from the name of the organization, which spotlighted its stress on black unity. The very use of the term *Non-European* made an explicit racial distinction—between white and black. It also implied the existence of racial and ethnic differences within the black population because in response to the tacit question of who the Non-Europeans were, both the NEUM and white supremacist South Africa would have replied that they were the African, Coloured, and Indian people taken collectively.

Indeed, one of the most prominent leaders within the NEUM dismissed as unrealistic and politically premature the idea that racial differences within the black population could be ignored. In his highly influential address "The Background of Segregation," delivered to the first national Anti-CAD conference on 29 May 1943, Ben Kies, a founding member and key ideologue within the movement, called for the establishment of a united front of black political organizations and explained that

> when we speak of a united front of ALL non-Europeans we do not mean lumping all non-Europeans holus-bolus together and fusing them all together in the belief that, since ALL are non-European oppressed, the African is a Coloured man, the Indian is an African, and a Coloured man is either Indian or African, whichever you please. Only those who are ignorant of both politics and history can believe in this nonsensical type of unity. When we speak of the unity . . . of all

non-Europeans, we simply mean this: they are all ground down by the same oppression; they have all the same political aspirations, but yet they remain divided in their oppression. They should discard the divisions and prejudices and illusions which have been created and fostered by their rulers. . . . When they have thrown off the chains, then they can settle whatever national or racial differences they have, or think they have.[11]

Broadly, the NEUM worked from the premise that members of the white establishment of South Africa, the "Herrenvolk,"[12] were the "lackeys" of international capitalism, especially British imperialism. Whereas blacks had been subjugated and dispossessed to form a pool of cheap labor, the white working class had been co-opted as a labor aristocracy and bribed with part of the proceeds of black exploitation to act as "overseers" and "managers" for international capitalist, especially British imperial, interests. Segregationist policies were seen as a variant on the highly successful divide-and-rule tactic used by British imperialism throughout the world. Besides compartmentalizing the South African population into white and black, international capital further tried to split the black population into African, Coloured, and Indian sections. Interracial divisions were fostered by a policy of giving one group preference over another and by propagating "vicious racial myths" to set off one against the other. In addition, each of the racial groups was further segmented by fomenting tribal, religious, and ethnic divisions. According to the NEUM, this racist ideology had permeated the whole of society and had been internalized by black people themselves.[13] Kies graphically described the situation as one in which

the white minority looks upon the African as a "raw kaffir," and such he has been to the majority of Coloureds and Indians. The white minority looks upon the Coloured as a "bastard Hottentot" and such he has been to most of the Africans and Indians. The white minority looks upon the Indian as a "bloody coolie," and such he has been to most Africans and Coloureds. The African is told he is superior because he is "pure blooded"—and he has believed this. The Coloured man is told that he is superior because the "blood of the white man" flows in his veins—and he has believed this. The Indian has been told that he is superior because he belongs to a great nation with a mighty culture—and he has believed this . . . the slaves have taken over the segregationist ideology of their master.[14]

Hobbled by their racist outlook and the sectarian responses of a reformist leadership, the "oppressed" would thus never attain freedom
without uniting politically to fight white supremacism and capitalist
exploitation because their efforts were being "dissipated either in fruit-
less, isolated outbursts, or in meaningless argumentation over trifles,
or in the harmless channel of appeals, resolutions and petitions."[15]

This unequivocal acknowledgment of racial and ethnic differences
within South African society and the pragmatic disposition in dealing
with them by and large informed the NEUM's attitude toward race in
general and Coloured identity in particular until the early 1960s. That
Kies clearly regarded such distinctions as ultimately superficial did
not preclude him from recognizing their social reality and political
salience. What was needed for the overthrow of white supremacism
was not a sublimation of all racial distinctions but the political unity
of black South Africans, whatever their underlying racial or ethnic
identities. The point to note is that though the NEUM leadership was
nonracist in outlook and recognized that "the real cleavage is one of
class, not one of colour,"[16] it was prepared to make a tactical concession to the existence of racial identities within the ranks of its constituency for the sake of achieving the all-important preliminary goal
of national liberation. The key to understanding the movement's pragmatism with regard to race is to appreciate that the NEUM did not
see itself as a socialist party with a socialist program but as a movement for national liberation with a socialist leadership.

The NEUM operated in a world in which political correctness was
not yet a major consideration and a society in which virtually every
aspect of life had become racialized; as a result, there was inevitably
a fair degree of unconscious racial thinking and an automatic acceptance of racial categories in day-to-day life within its ranks. There
was also a general tolerance of inadvertent racial thought and expression within the organization, though any form of racist thinking
was clearly not acceptable. For example, when Tabata, the most
prominent leader and chief ideologue within the AAC, wrote that "a
single political party cannot represent a whole community or race
for the mere fact of belonging to the same race has nothing to do with
a man's political affiliations,"[17] the logic of his argument appears to
have been taken at face value; colleagues did not question his apparent acceptance of the construct of race. Similarly, when Wycliffe
Tsotsi, in his 1950 presidential address to the AAC, proclaimed that
"the African people look to the AAC for a lead," it did not result in

accusations that he was fostering racial division within the liberation movement.[18]

A purist nonracial stance was, however, already being taken during the early 1950s by a handful of ultra-Left Trotskyist intellectuals grouped within the Forum Club. Criticism that the NEUM's "Non-Europeanism" was a form of "voluntary segregation" that favored the interests of capital and the racist state came from these remnants of FIOSA, which advocated a strictly nonracial strategy.[19]

The *Torch*, named after the Bolsheviks' *Iskra*,[20] was a quarto-sized, weekly publication of eight pages and was more of a magazine in format and a political organ in content than a newspaper, as it has generally been described. Though by far the greater part of its readership was restricted to Cape Town and the western Cape, it did attract a significant readership in Johannesburg, and in its heyday, it was distributed as far afield as the eastern and northern Cape, Natal, South West Africa, and the protectorates.[21]

The *Torch*'s main fare consisted of local politics of interest to the NEUM. At various times, major areas of focus included protest against the Coloured Advisory Council (CAC), resistance to train apartheid, opposition to the city council's segregated housing schemes on the Cape Flats, the fight against the removal of Coloureds from the voters' roll, the boycott of the van Riebeeck festival, the implementation of the Group Areas Act, and state repression of left-wing political activity. The paper carried news from affiliates such as the Teachers' League, the Cape African Teachers' Association, the APO, and the Gleemoor Civic Association, as well as reports of protests, strikes, and social unrest. Because of the prominence of teachers in the NEUM, education and teacher politics were topics of particular interest in the paper's reporting. The *Torch* also maintained a vociferous antisegregationist polemic. The paper never tired of hurling invective at "quislings" and highlighting the absurdities of South Africa's racial system. It also pursued disputations with the ANC, the Communist Party, and the South African Indian Congress, among others, with a degree of gusto. There was some reportage of international developments in an anti-imperialist vein, particularly with regard to India, Indonesia, and China, but with surprisingly little comment on Africa. One feature of the newspaper was serialized articles on themes relevant to NEUM politics. A series could run for over two years—such as the 120 installments of "A History of Despotism," which examined aspects of South African history from an NEUM perspective—or relatively short—such as the more typical eight-part series "Problems within the Liberation Movement."[22]

The first issue of the *Torch*, which appeared on 25 February 1946, pledged "full and uncompromising support to the movement for full democratic rights for all, irrespective of race, colour or creed"; further, the paper would "be used to enlighten, to fight discrimination in every form and to unite the oppressed and exploited people." The editors rather disingenuously added that the *Torch* was "not tied directly or indirectly, to any political party" and that it was "neither the official or unofficial mouthpiece" for any political organization. In 1949, they repeated that the *Torch* "owes allegiance to no political sect or section of the oppressed," and for much of the paper's life, the staff tried to maintain the charade that it was independent of any political organization.[23] Careful not to create the impression that it supported any form of black chauvinism, the paper's first editorial also made it clear that the *Torch* would not allow its columns "to be used to foster racial ill-feeling either against the Europeans or any section of the Non-Europeans."[24] Besides wanting to keep the door open for the white working class to join the revolutionary movement, many believed that with racial tensions escalating in the society, there was a need to steer black people away from "race pogroms" and the possibility of a race war against whites.[25]

Given the Marxism of the NEUM leadership, there was surprisingly little radical rhetoric or class analysis in the *Torch*. The paper tended to approach the liberation struggle as one between white and black and thus to present social and political issues in racial terms. No doubt, this was in large part due to its conscious strategy of promoting black unity for the achievement of national liberation, but it can also be ascribed to the pervasiveness of racial thinking in South African society that resulted in an unconsciously racial approach to matters generally. The Marxist underpinnings of the newspaper's strategy did, however, surface from time to time and were usually presented in a simplified and racialized form intended to educate a readership unschooled in left-wing ideology. An excerpt from a *Torch* editorial explaining a basic Marxist insight furnishes a typical example: "What the Non-Europeans fail to understand is . . . that *all the wealth of the country is produced by them.* They are the workers on the mines, on the farms and in the factories. They create the wealth and the prosperity yet they do not enjoy the fruits of their labour. They create civilization for the whites yet they are not permitted to obtain the benefits of civilization."[26]

Like their moderate counterparts, the radicals responded to issues of race and Coloured identity in an ambiguous fashion, and the staff at the *Torch* was no exception. The columns reveal not one consistent outlook on matters of racial identity but a wide spectrum of perspectives and approaches. These responses ranged from an unconscious acceptance of race to a principled rejection of racial thinking, from confusion about notions of race and human difference to the tactical acknowledgment of racial identities to achieve broader political ends.

Viewed chronologically, the racial perceptions reflected in the newspaper passed through three recognizable phases. In the early years, until about the early 1950s, the discourse in the newpaper was decidedly racialized, with frequent lapses into inadvertent racial thinking. During that period, there was also a fair degree of inconsistency and confusion about the concept of race; one is left with the impression that the paper was grappling to find ways of dealing with a thorny issue in a rough-and-tumble milieu of political turmoil and rapid social change. In the second period, covering much of the 1950s, the paper was dominated by a more muted racial discourse that played down interblack racial distinctions with greater consistency and emphasized the cleavage between black and white as one of oppressed versus oppressor. The third period featured a politically correct approach to matters of race that was first evident in a tentative and inconsistent manner in the late 1950s but grew to a recognizable trend by the time the *Torch* ceased publication at the end of 1963.[27] Though these were identifiable phases in the development of a more self-conscious and consistent nonracism, the progression was by no means linear. They were distinct tendencies rather than categorical stages, for evidence of nonracial values can be found in the early years of the newspaper just as there were lapses into racial thinking in the later years.

Viewed thematically, at least four distinct discourses around issues of race can be discerned in the *Torch*. A pervasive approach to matters of race in the pages of the paper might be termed the tactical response, which coincided with the conscious political strategy of the NEUM in dealing with the problem of racial and ethnic divisions within the black population. This was the pragmatism advocated in Kies's *Background of Segregation*, which rejected the "nonsensical type of unity" of simply lumping all black people together and pretending that racial differences did not exist.[28] Within the tactical response, the acknowledgment of racial distinctions was accompanied by a calculated intention of undermining the racist edifice of South African society. The *Torch* editors made it clear that "we do not deny that the people are divided" but affirmed that "it is one of our most urgent tasks to destroy the barriers erected by the *Herrenvolk*."[29]

When in tactical mode, the *Torch* made a distinction between "Europeans" and "Non-Europeans," by which it meant the African, Coloured, and Indian people taken together. It self-consciously referred to each of the three racial groups as a "section" of the Non-European population.[30] Phrases such as "all sections of the Non-European oppressed—African, Coloured and Indian" and "European, Coloured, Indian, African—that is all South Africans" were common in the *Torch*.[31] Most of the time, the articles did not specify racial identities, but they frequently did identify people or organizations as either white, Coloured, Indian, or African when their racial identities were salient. In particular, racial categories were specified when reporting incidents of racial discrimination or racially motivated violence. Typical examples include the articles headlined "Coloured Youths and Constable Attacked by White Hooligans" and "Attack on Pretoria Coloureds," as well as reports of this sort: "Du Plessis, a European, was charged with assaulting a Coloured teacher, Eddie Baatjies."[32]

The *Torch*'s tactical discourse was racialized in other ways as well. At times, it might address the Coloured people directly on issues that affected them, such as when it asked "Will all Coloured people please note that . . . " or when it ran the headline "Boycott call to Coloured people" to draw attention to a TLSA resolution spurning all racially segregated institutions.[33] It also did not shy away from using racial terminology to attack racism or in polemical exchanges with opponents. On one occasion, sarcastically echoing cabinet minister Ben Schoeman's usage of the word *Hotnot* to refer to Coloured people, a *Torch* editorial dubbed the CAC the "Hotnot Advisory Council"; another editorial on disagreements between two "quisling factions" appeared under the heading "'Cape Boy' Politics."[34] Similarly, one of the articles denouncing the tercentenary celebrations was headlined "April Fool's Day for 'Hotnots' and 'Pankies.'"[35] And although the tone of the *Torch* was deadly serious, it occasionally allowed itself the luxury of using humor to attack racism, such as when it mocked prevailing attitudes toward interracial sex by quoting the following limerick:

> There was a young woman from Starkey
> Who had an affair with a darkey

The result of her sins
Was quadruplets not twins
One white, one black and two khaki.[36]

In its Afrikaans articles, the paper's use of the terms *Afrikaan* and its plural *Afrikane* to refer to Africans, in deliberate contrast to *Afrikaner* and *Afrikaners*, was one of the small but telling ways in which black claims to equality with whites was asserted. Besides, as the paper pointed out, the alternatives of *Bantu* and *Naturel* were derogatory.[37]

Within its tactical framework, the *Torch* not only depicted the Coloured people as a separate "section" of the Non-European oppressed but at times even encouraged their solidarity as a group. An example is provided by the *Torch* editorial that pondered the tragedy of sixteen-year-old pupil Billy Repnaar. Repnaar committed suicide after being forced to attend a Coloured school as the only darker-skinned child among five siblings in a family that was trying to pass for white. Criticizing those Coloured people who tried to dissociate themselves from their background, the editorial proclaimed, "We are proud to state that the majority of Coloured people . . . scorn subterfuges of this brand. They are for one not accepting the badge of inferiority . . . they take pride in their colour and greater pride in those who remain with them to lead them towards freedom from oppression."[38] In keeping with this sentiment, the *Torch* mockingly referred to those Coloured people who preferred to associate with whites as "Nearopeans" and as "European Non-Europeans."[39] The appeal for solidarity among Coloureds was also apparent in articles with large, front-page headlines proclaiming a "Rallying Call to the Coloured People"[40] or the "Biggest Anti-CAD Conference Ever: Authentic Voice of Coloured People."[41]

Moreover, the *Torch* sometimes treated the Coloured people as a group with a common history that had forged them into a distinct social entity. This attitude came through clearly in the TLSA's "Manifesto to the Coloured People," published in June 1953 as part of its rejection of the Commission of Enquiry into Coloured Education that had recently been appointed by the Cape Provincial Council. Described as "stirring" and quoted in full in the *Torch*, the manifesto started off by reviewing the history of the Coloured people: "The Cape Coloured People have always constituted a section of the oppressed majority of South Africa. Throughout the history of the country they have always been forced to hold an inferior and subservient position in the social system. For almost two hundred years many of their forebears were held in slavery and bondage and since then the laws and administration of the country have always been devised to maintain their subjection and oppression."[42] When in tactical mode, neither the NEUM nor the *Torch* could be described as nonracial because their discourse was overtly racial and marked by an acceptance of the reality of racial distinctions within South African society. And, as mentioned earlier, the aim of this particular tactic—building black political unity—was a manifestly racial agenda. Yet the ultimate goal of the *Torch* was to undermine the racist system. In terms of the NEUM's tactical approach, it was not so much the use of racial terminology or even racial thinking that mattered but rather its intent and effect. Thus, when the *Torch* accused others of being racist—it preferred the term *racialistic*—it was not because they acknowledged the idea of race or thought in racial terms but rather because they made negative judgments of people, discriminated on the basis of race, or in any way promoted racial sectarianism.[43] Thus, referring to people as African or Coloured was not in itself regarded as "racialistic," but asking that intermarriage between Coloureds and Africans be banned, as the Federal Council of Coloured Churches did in March 1956, certainly was; so, too, was demanding that those few African pupils attending Coloured schools be removed or claiming that Malay youths were more prone to becoming "*skollies*" (thugs) than their Christian Coloured counterparts.[44]

Intertwined with the tactical approach and shading into it was an unconsciously racial discourse with an a priori acceptance of the concept of race in which the conventional racial divisions of South African society were taken as given. For much of the time, the *Torch* blithely reported about Europeans, non-Europeans, whites, Coloureds, Africans, Indians, and Malays. It routinely used these terms and their Afrikaans equivalents and occasionally various racial epithets, such as "Bantu" for Africans, "*Ampies*" for poor or uncouth Afrikaners, "Negro" for African Americans, and "Yanks" for Americans (as in the headline "Yanks Arm Japs").[45] All of these racial terms were used without explanation or qualification, as if their meanings were self-evident. And often, they were employed when there was no real need to make racial distinctions or when the distinction between "European" and "non-European," for instance, would have sufficed. Although this racial terminology was accepted usage at the time (and to expect a more politically correct approach would be anachronistic), the very fact that it was used does indicate a considerable degree of unconscious racial thinking within the NEUM, contradicting unqualified assumptions that the organization was nonracial throughout its existence. Nevertheless, the *Torch* from time to time displayed an awarenes that the use of racial terms was problematic, such as when it criticized a new Afrikaans dictionary for using racist terminology, when it published an article by George Padmore on derogatory terms used for black people in Britain, and when it carried the caption "'Native' Education for Africans."[46]

In many instances, it was not clear whether particular examples of the use of racial terminology or concepts represented a tactical deployment of race or were lapses into racial forms of thinking.[47] Sometimes, however, the *Torch*'s slippage into inadvertent racial usage was clear-cut. Its story of "150 Coloured soldiers involved in a drunken brawl," its reference to "each of our four racial groups," and headlines such as "SA Coloured XV vs Bantu XV" or "African and Coloured Students Debate" are but a few of the myriad examples of lapses into unconscious racial reportage found in the pages of the *Torch*.[48] The paper's nonpolitical reporting—its sports news, the occasional human interest story, and the community news it carried—displayed a very clear racial orientation in that it was almost entirely focused on the Coloured community, which indicates that the paper was written largely with a Coloured readership in mind. This bias, though far less evident in its political reporting, is nevertheless noticeable there as well. For instance, a *Torch* editorial writer was justifiably indignant that the latest salary scales for teachers pegged the salaries of Coloured teachers at four-fifths of what their white counterparts were paid. However, no mention was made of the fact that the remuneration of African teachers was set at three-fifths that of whites.[49] The *Torch*, in addition, regularly ran racially exclusive employment advertisements inviting applications from "Coloured" nurses, teachers, clerks, and housekeepers.[50]

On more than one occasion, the nonracial discourse or the strategic use of race was compromised or contradicted by a lapse into unconsciously racial usage on the same page or even in the same article. One illustration is provided by the very first issue of the *Torch*. In the column right next to the editorial that pledged the newspaper to the promotion of the nonracial ideal, an article mentioned with great pride that in a local production of Shakespeare's *The Tempest*, "the carefully chosen cast is entirely Non-European." Echoing the assimilationist sentiment of despised moderate Coloureds, the article expressed confidence that the play would discredit white racist notions that "the artistic abilities of the non-European is limited to the Coons, Zonk and Kaatjie Kekkelbek."[51] Given the nonracial values it had espoused on the very same page, the *Torch* should have condemned this play produced by whites for an entirely "Non-European"—presumably Coloured—cast. Similarly, an article entitled "Race and Heredity," which reported on an eponymous lecture delivered to the New Era Fellowship by the prominent Coloured teacher and Unity Movement supporter Stella Jacobs, was confused and contradictory on the concept of race. Despite a strongly nonracial and egalitarian tone rejecting the drawing of any racial distinctions on the basis that "all human beings are descended from the same ancestor and belong to the same species," the piece nevertheless repeated Jacobs's claims that there "are three primary races namely, white, yellow-brown and black" and that the "Australian blacks are the purest race today."[52]

Part of the confusion over racial issues in the *Torch*'s reporting derived from its frequent efforts to combat racism using racial concepts and racial forms of thinking. For instance, one of the earlier *Torch* editorials in response to the xenophobic deliberations of parliamentarians over the "Anti-Indian Bill" laudably rejected the idea that there was such a thing as "white civilization" as well as the assumption that whites were the only creators of "civilization." The editorial, however, lapsed into a racialized mode of thinking when it tried to refute these racist assumptions by claiming that Simon van der Stel, governor of the Cape from 1679 to 1699, was "one of the most outstanding Coloured men in the history of South Africa."[53] Similarly, after making the commendable point that civilization "belongs neither to white or non-white people" and that it is "neither the product of any *race* or nation," the authors in the very next breath assert that civilization has "its roots embedded firmly and indisputably in cultures and *races* and nations in all corners of the globe."[54]

In addition to the tactical approach and the unconsciously racial discourse that together dominated the content of the paper, there were occasions when the *Torch* switched into a nonracial mode of discourse or analysis. These instances were relatively few and far between and were confined to specific articles in which the writers tried to debunk the myth of race and educate the readership in nonracial ways of thinking. This approach was apparent, for instance, in the article headlined "Professor Explodes Myth of 'European Race,'" which reported Meyer Fortes's evidence in a court case that the idea of a

"European race" had no scientific foundation at all.[55] A second example was provided by the article "Man and the Apes," which stressed the common ancestry and African origins of humanity.[56] The overall message of this discourse, which revealed the underlying nonracial outlook of the NEUM leaders, was that the concept of race had no scientific validity and that racial thinking was morally indefensible because of the essential unity of humankind. Their position was succinctly stated in an article entitled "Racialism—Weapon of Exploitation," which reported on Edgar Maurice's delivery of the A. J. Abrahamse Memorial Lecture: "Race and colour attitudes were not part of the nature of man; they did not develop of their own accord, but were a deliberate man-made product used to serve the interests of the dominant ruling classes in societies in which domination and exploitation of peoples of colour were part of the economic patterns of these societies."[57]

The preeminent example of this nonracial discourse in the *Torch* was, however, found in the series of twenty-five articles entitled "Science and Race," published weekly between May and October 1952.[58] This series was meant to educate readers in the basic tenets of nonracism and to debunk common racial myths. The opening article in this series stressed that all human beings "belong to one and the same species known as *Homo sapiens*" and that "the classification of people into 'races' is quite arbitrary"; it went on to make the important point that in any given "race," although "the group of people forming it have common characteristics, the differences among the individual people are just as great as the differences between the 'races' themselves."[59] Subsequent installments argued against various racial fallacies: that a superior race existed, that blacks were inferior to whites or all alike, that race determined character, that heredity occurred through blood mixing, that miscegenation led to degeneration, and so on.[60] The series examined issues of race with regard to Jews, Coloureds, Indians, culture, education, group areas, the child, and the individual, and in each case, it emphasized nonracial values and argued against popular myths, misconceptions, and abuses of racist ideas.[61]

The "Science and Race" series was significant not only because it confirmed the essentially nonracial outlook of the NEUM leadership but also because it provided a fairly systematic and detailed indication of the content of these ideas as well as of popular racist misconceptions it felt needed debunking. Inevitably, the series was also used to promote the NEUM's political agenda, which often detracted from its efficacy—as demonstrated by the article on "The Coloured People and Race." This article was disappointing in that it failed to address issues around race and Colouredness and instead did little more than denounce what it saw as a conspiracy by the Herrenvolk and the establishment press to sow division within the ranks of the Coloured people and to laud NEUM counter-strategies. The unintended subtext of this article—that the Coloured people formed an organic social entity—undermined the broader nonracial intentions of the series.[62]

A fourth approach to issues of race and Coloured identity was detectable in the columns of the *Torch* beginning in the late 1950s. Starting from about 1957, terms such as *Coloured, African, race, racial groups, Bantu, Kleurling,* and *Herrenvolk* were, with increasing frequency, placed in quotation marks, italicized, or prefaced with *so-called* to distance the paper from their racist implications. The growing incidence of phrases such as "'so-called' races," "persons described as Europeans," and, of course, "'so-called' Coloured" signaled this new sensibility,[63] as did the coining of terms such as *Bantuization* and *Colouredization.* Through the late 1950s and early 1960s, a self-consciously nonracial tone progressively pervaded the journalism of the *Torch*, so that by mid-1962, the practice of qualifying racial terms by using quotation marks or "so-called" became fairly consistent.

The development of this politically correct approach needs, in the first instance, to be viewed against the backdrop of growing international intolerance of racism after World War II, which had left a legacy of revulsion against racism. The U.S. civil rights movement, the shift toward African independence, the strengthening voice of the nonaligned movement that was founded in 1955, and an intensified global condemnation of apartheid fed nonracial sympathies worldwide. These developments impinged on the consciousness of the NEUM, which, because of the significance it attached to imperialism and global capitalism, had a more broadly international outlook than rival liberation organizations prior to the 1960s. On the domestic front, the implementation of apartheid social engineering, which kicked into high gear only in the late 1950s, also contributed to this growing antiracist sentiment. As segregation was more rigidly enforced and as petty apartheid measures intruded in people's daily lives, it became more and more probable that an antiracist counterthrust would assert itself among opposition groups. This was likely to occur as a gut reaction to apartheid, and it would also tend to raise the moral imperative and political salience of the principle of nonracism.

Although one would expect an antiracist position during this period of intensifying white chauvinism to have been a good strategy for gaining mass support among black people, a contrary dynamic was at play in the NEUM. As this political grouping became less active and politically more isolated through the latter half of the 1950s, pragmatic considerations that came with active political organization became less relevant, and the strategic approach to race was quietly abandoned. A more uncompromising and idealistic stance on most issues, including nonracism, became attractive, if for no other reason than for the NEUM to claim the moral high ground. Critics of the the organization have often accused it of using this principled stance as an excuse for remaining on the sidelines and thereby not exposing itself to either the hard work or the risks of mass mobilization.

It is clear that for the greater part of its existence, the *Torch* was not sufficiently self-conscious about its use of racial terminology and concepts for it to be described as nonracial. During the NEUM's politically active phase, political correctness had not yet become a major consideration internationally, and the nonracial ideal was not sufficiently important to its political agenda for it to be overly concerned with such niceties. Not until the early 1960s did the *Torch* scrutinize with any consistency its vocabulary and the concepts it used with a view to sanitizing them or distancing itself from their racist connotations. In this respect, NEUM ideologues, together with a handful of ultra-Left Trotskyist critics before them, were the first to develop a rigorously nonracial perspective and to start viewing Coloured identity in a different light.

That the *Torch* exhibited an ambiguous approach to race and Coloured identity prior to the early 1960s should not come as any great surprise. Without the etiquette of political correctness as a guide and with the prevalence of racial thinking at that time, there was bound to be varied usage of racial terminology and a degree of conceptual confusion. Moreover, in a newspaper turned out under the pressures of production deadlines, financial stringency, state harassment, polemical exchanges with opponents, political campaigning, and the vagaries of being dependent on part-time, amateur staff, one would expect close scrutiny to uncover inconsistencies. There was not necessarily a contradiction between the *Torch*'s nonracial discourse and the tactical concession to the social reality of race if one accepts that the goal of achieving black political unity took priority over the principle of nonracism. There are, however, clear contradictions between the nonracial and tactical approaches, on the one hand, and the unconsciously racial discourse, on the other. These contradictions were largely resolved in the early 1960s when the NEUM became much more self-conscious of its discourse around issues of race.

The *Torch* entered a long period of decline, a trend that was observable from as early as 1953 and that broadly reflected the fortunes of the Non-European Unity Movement. The NEUM had never attracted a mass following, and its organ had a small circulation that shrank as the movement became progressively less active from the late 1940s onward because of its refusal to mount or participate in mass campaigns or to confront the state directly. The organization was rent by ideological infighting through the 1950s and was especially vulnerable to state intimidation because a large proportion of its members were drawn from the teaching profession. Direct repression of the NEUM leadership started in the mid-1950s, with the dismissal of Kies and van Schoor from their teaching posts in February 1956 and a banning order being placed on Tabata the following month.[64] This deterioration was greatly exacerbated after the Sharpeville shootings, as the state cracked down hard on the extraparliamentary opposition.

As the paper went into decline through the 1950s, its tone became shriller and more denunciatory. Its content grew less diversified and more propagandistic, with less and less hard news and more and more condemnations of apartheid and Western imperialism. Its reporting also became repetitious, rhetorical, and jaded. The temporary closure of the paper when it was banned for five months during the state of emergency from the beginning of April to the end of August 1960 was disastrous, for it lost readers, revenue, and a significant part of its distribution network. Although publication of the *Torch* resumed in early September 1960, its parent company was under severe financial strain. By September 1962, the paper was in such dire straits that it published a front-page appeal for donations to avoid being scaled down to four pages. The climate of fear in left-wing circles in the early 1960s and the risks of bannings and detention made publication and distribution hazardous. It was the spate of banning orders served in the early 1960s on NEUM leaders—many of whom were involved in the running of the *Torch*, including its long-serving editor, Joyce Meissenheimer, and her replacement, Joan Kay—that finally crippled the newspaper.[65] The last issue appeared on 4 December 1963.

The *Torch* was the most important and representative of the serial publications produced within the Trotskyist tradition of left-wing politics in the Coloured community. Because there was no periodical within the rival Communist Party tradition that similarly shed light on Coloured identity, I have instead chosen to use Alex La Guma's *A Walk in the Night* as the second case study for this chapter. La Guma was a dedicated Community Party activist and had lived in the Coloured working-class area of District Six for nearly three decades. He wrote that novel with the intention of providing an authentic portrayal of life in "the District." That work is thus eminently suited to our present purposes.

Race, Identity, and Realism in Alex La Guma's *A Walk in the Night and Other Stories*

A Walk in the Night opens with the protagonist, a young Coloured man named Michael Adonis, alighting from a trackless tram on the bustling streets of District Six late one afternoon. Adonis is nursing a "pustule of rage and humiliation deep down within him" because earlier that day, he had been fired from his menial factory job for talking back to the white foreman. He goes to a local diner, where he meets his friend, Willieboy, a man who survives by hustling on the streets of District Six. He also meets up with Foxy and his gang, who are looking for an accomplice for a burglary they have planned for that night. After his meal, Michael makes his way to a nearby pub. En route, he is cornered by two white policemen, who search his pockets for *dagga* (marijuana) and accuse him of having stolen the money he has on him. Although outwardly compliant, Michael is furious at this racially motivated harassment. At the pub, he gets drunk on cheap wine before returning to his tenement. In the passageway, he meets fellow tenant Uncle Doughty, an elderly, alcoholic Irishman, who invites him to his room for a drink. With the liquor further fueling his rage, Michael takes out his frustration at being humiliated by whites on Uncle Doughty. He lashes out at the decrepit old man with a wine bottle, killing him. Michael escapes from the scene of the crime undetected, but Willieboy, who comes looking for Michael to borrow money, stumbles across the corpse of Doughty. Panic-stricken, he flees but is spotted by tenement dwellers and is blamed for Doughty's death. That night, Willieboy is hunted down by Constable Raalt, a sadistic white policeman, who shoots him in cold blood. Willieboy subsequently dies in the back of the police van. Later that night, Michael, after walking the streets of District Six, decides to join Foxy and his gang. His descent into crime has begun.

A Walk in the Night was first published in 1962 in Ibadan, Nigeria. La Guma started writing the novella during 1959 and had completed it by the time he was detained in April 1960 under the state of emergency declared following the Sharpeville shootings. He had little option but to publish overseas, for after being banned under the Suppression of Communism Act in July 1961, nothing he said or wrote could be published in South Africa. *A Walk in the Night* was La Guma's first substantive piece of fiction, and it won him immediate recognition as an exciting new author. In 1967, the novella, or "long story," as he preferred to call it,[66] was republished together with a selection of six short stories as *A Walk in the Night and Other Stories*. These works have a common theme in that they all deal with aspects of Coloured working-class life. Four of the short stories, as well as *A Walk in the Night*, are set in District Six during the late 1950s and early 1960s.[67]

Alex La Guma was born in District Six on 20 February 1925. He grew up in a highly politicized household because his father, James La Guma, was a lifelong political activist and a pioneering figure in the liberation movement. At the time of Alex's birth, Jimmy La Guma was general secretary of the Industrial and Commercial Workers' Union. A few months after his son was born, Jimmy joined the Communist Party of South Africa (CPSA) and was elected to the party's Central Committee the following year. During the latter half of the 1920s, he served as organizing secretary of the Western Cape Branch of the ANC and played a leading role in the creation of the fledgling black trade union movement of the 1920s and 1930s. Jimmy was, in addition, a founding member of the National Liberation League in the mid-1930s. He was serving on the Communist Party's Central Committee at the time of the party's banning in 1950 and was president of the South African Coloured People's Organization (SACPO) from 1957 to 1959. Jimmy died two years later.[68]

In 1928, he and his wife, Wilhelmina, whom he had married in 1923, set up home at 1 Roger Street, District Six, where Alex lived for the better part of three decades before moving to the middle-class Coloured suburb of Garlandale on the Cape Flats. Alex attended Trafalgar High School in District Six. He left school in 1942 to help support the family while his father was on wartime service with the Cape Corps in east and north Africa. He was nevertheless able to matriculate in 1945 by attending night classes at the Cape Town Technical College. La Guma found employment first as a factory worker and then as a clerk and bookkeeper. As early as 1946, he was initiated into active politics when he was fired for his part in organizing a strike among fellow workers at the Metal Box factory in Maitland. In 1947, he joined the Young Communist League, and the following year, he became a member of the CPSA. Alex La Guma rose to national prominence in the antiapartheid movement in the latter half of the 1950s after becoming a founding member of the South African Coloured People's Organization and serving on its executive committee. In 1956, he started working as a reporter for *New Age*, the unofficial mouthpiece of the banned Communist Party. In December of that year, La Guma was among the 156 members of the Congress Alliance who were charged with treason; in May 1958, he was the target of an assassination attempt. After his acquittal in the Treason Trial in 1960, Alex was banned under the Suppression of Communism Act in July 1961 and placed under twenty-four-hour house arrest in 1963. Subjected to continuous harassment by the security police, he left South Africa on an exit permit with his family in 1966. Both his political activism and his experience of growing up in District Six were essential ingredients in La Guma's writing of *A Walk in the Night*.[69]

The novella was written at a time when District Six had a reputation as a crime-ridden slum; life in the area had not yet gained the aura of romanticism that surrounds it today. It was only later, from the late 1960s onward with the mass removal of over thirty thousand inhabitants under the Group Areas Act and the demolition of the houses they had occupied, that District Six became an international symbol of the brutality of apartheid. Writing a decade before the Group Areas removals, there was no question that La Guma would romanticize life in District Six nor that he would succumb to the "we were poor but happy then" syndrome that afflicts so much of the more recent writing about the area.[70] Instead, he revealed District Six for what it was—a ripe slum. At one point in the novel, he characterized it as a "whirlpool world of poverty, petty crime and violence."[71] This, of course, is not to say that he did not write with sensitivity and compassion about its people or to suggest that District Six was not a vibrant community.

La Guma aimed to provide a faithful representation of working-class life in District Six as the setting for the novel. *A Walk in the Night* was inspired by a short paragraph that he had seen in a newspaper about a young "hooligan" who had been shot by police and later died in the back of their van. Wondering how and why this could have happened sparked his imagination and led La Guma to create his story based on "what I had thought life in District Six was really like." He confirmed that "most of the description of action or places in District Six is based upon actual characters and events."[72] His journalist's eye for detail and the insights gained from having grown up there gave La Guma's writing in *A Walk in the Night* a hard-edged realism and an incisiveness not attained in his subsequent work. And given the political messages he wanted to convey about the harshness of Coloured working-class existence and the inhumanity of apartheid, there was little place for sentimentality in his evocation of life in District Six. Contrary to latter-day romanticizers who idealize the spirit of District Six as a way of castigating the National Party government for having destroyed a vibrant community, La Guma wanted to show District Six in all its squalor as a means of condemning apartheid oppression.

Anyone familiar with "the District" of the 1960s will recognize the accuracy with which La Guma describes the crumbling tenements, the smell of decay that hung over the place, and the struggle of daily life for the majority of its inhabitants. Throughout the novel, he deftly details the wretched privation of the place. In a typical passage, he describes the landscape of District Six beyond the "artificial glare" of Hanover Street as consisting of

> stretches of damp, battered houses with their broken-ribs of front-railings; cracked walls and high tenements that rose like the left-overs of a bombed area in the twilight; vacant lots and weed-grown patches where houses had once stood; and deep doorways resembling the entrances to deserted castles. There were children playing in the street, darting among the overflowing dustbins and shooting at each other with wooden guns. In some of the doorways people sat or stood, murmuring idly in the fast-fading light like wasted ghosts in a plague-ridden city.[73]

His style of writing has, with some justification, been described as "revolutionary romanticism," but *A Walk in the Night* comes closest to La Guma's characterization of his own style as "socialist realism."[74]

Although Lewis Nkosi's judgment that "La Guma has written nothing since the appearance of *A Walk in the Night* which compels a fresh evaluation of his work" cannot be justified,[75] it is clear that the vividness and the gritty realism with which he portrayed Coloured working-class life in the novella was not matched in his subsequent novels. The literary merits of La Guma's various works are obviously open to debate, but there is little doubt that *A Walk in the Night* was his most convincing portrayal of social reality. The reasons for this are twofold.

First, having lived in District Six for much of his life, he was intimately familiar with life there and had a deep reservoir of personal experience on which he could draw in writing the novel. That he was writing about a community and a locality in which he had grown up accounts for the powerful sense of place in *A Walk in the Night*. The characters have an authenticity and the scenes a vividness not present in his later fictional writing. *And a Threefold Cord* and *The Stone Country*, both set in Cape Town and written while he was still living in the city, display La Guma's keen powers of observation but do not have the social perceptiveness and the depth of insight of *A Walk in the Night*, which draws on decades of lived experience. His later novels, *In the Fog of the Season's End* and *The Time of the Butcherbird*, written in exile and set in Cape Town and the Karoo, respectively, bear evidence of La Guma's separation from South Africa.[76] Whatever their literary merits, these works lack the intimacy and finely grained depictions of a particular social setting that mark *A Walk in the Night*.

Second, the progressive intrusion of a political agenda in La Guma's novels detracts from the realism of his writing. There is a fairly clear-cut progression in each succeeding novel: South Africa is increasingly depicted as a society polarized between black and white, with blacks becoming more and more militant and united in the struggle against apartheid. In the process, the complexities and the nuances of racial identity in South African society are blunted. Although the oppression of apartheid is ever present in *A Walk in the Night* and La Guma's political values pervade the novel, it is different from the works that follow in one important respect. In this novel, the depiction of the social reality of interblack racial prejudice takes precedence over the author's political conviction of the need to promote black unity and nonracism through his writing. In *A Walk in the Night and Other Stories*, racial exclusivity within the Coloured community is clearly evident, and although the author's private condemnation of such attitudes may be read as part of the subtext, the integrity of the characters is retained in this respect. Thus, for example, Michael Adonis, for whom La Guma clearly has much sympathy, is shown to harbor racial prejudice toward Africans, as was likely true of many residents in the District in real life.[77] By the time La Guma wrote his next novel, *And a Threefold Cord*, the political imperative of depicting racial harmony and solidarity between Coloured and African squatters took precedence over the likelihood of there being some degree of racial tension between them.

Scholarly appraisals of *A Walk in the Night* have tended to cast the work, especially the racial dynamic it depicts, in somewhat simplistic terms. On the whole, the novel has been interpreted as a parable about black and white in apartheid South Africa—hence, Abdul Jan-Mohamed's characterization of La Guma's fiction as depicting a Manichean world. As he asserts, "The life and fiction of Alex La Guma perfectly illustrate the predicament of non-whites in South Africa and the effects of apartheid on their lives. . . . Due to the *racial* basis of the South African social organization, his political and social experience can be considered generic to the extent that *all* non-whites are treated as interchangeable objects by the Afrikaner."[78] Kathleen Balutansky, in her exploration of multiple "dialectical oppositions" at play in the novel, endorses JanMohamed's view.[79] Cecil Abrahams also interprets the novel in terms of the unambiguous racial oppositions that apartheid is assumed to have spawned. Although Abrahams had himself grown up within the Coloured community and is presumably aware of the racial complexities underlying Coloured identity, he nevertheless chooses to construe the novel in racially dichotomous terms.[80] A more nuanced understanding of the social context informs the analyses of John Coetzee and Michael Wade, yet they do not explore issues of racial identity in the novel, for the theme is not directly relevant to their respective arguments.[81] Nahem Yousaf's sensitive analysis of the dialectic between writing and resistance in La Guma's novels similarly neglects the theme of Coloured identity in *A Walk in the Night*.[82] Balasubrian Chandramohan, by contrast, recognizes the "emphasis that La Guma placed on the ethnic specificity of the Coloureds" and notes the "neglect of ethnicity and community origins" in scholarly analyses of La Guma's work.[83] But having presented this significant insight, Chandramohan proceeds to dismiss the salience of racial and ethnic identity in La Guma's writing by emphasizing the extent to which it transcends ethnicity by "substituting racial divisions with class divisions" and portraying a situation in which "a community of poor people [is] oppressed by another community of privileged people."[84]

The Manichean oppositions of white and black, privilege and poverty, oppression and domination that critics have read into the social relations depicted in *A Walk in the Night* apply only in a limited sense. These stark contrasts are relevant only to specific situations in this volume, such as the encounters between white policemen and Coloured people and in "The Lemon Orchard," the short story about a Coloured teacher in a small town who is about to be flogged in a lemon orchard by a group of white vigilantes for having charged local white notables with assault.[85] Beyond these limited instances, in which La Guma tries to convey the racial arrogance of the white ruling class and Coloured resentment at this treatment, the writing in this volume is predicated on a much more sophisticated analysis of social relations and on a more complex perception of racial identity in South African society than critics have hitherto conceded.

Having grown up in District Six and espousing a Coloured identity himself, La Guma was very much aware of the nuances and ambiguities that permeated that identity. Although he does not explain these intricacies to the reader or explore them in any systematic way in the book, *A Walk in the Night* is nevertheless played out against this complex backdrop. To readers who have not had firsthand experience of the subtleties of race relations in South Africa, the work may well appear to be a story of stark contrasts about the racial dichotomies of apartheid South Africa. Presumably, this would account for the way in which JanMohamed, Balutansky and others have interpreted the novel in Manichean terms. The intricacies of the private politics of race and identity prevalent within the Coloured community are, however, clearly evident in this work. In the context of the novel, as in the reality of inner-city life in Cape Town, there can be no talk of "all non-whites" sharing an overarching, primary social identity, having a common social experience, or being treated as "interchangeable objects" under the apartheid system, as JanMohamed would have it. Nor can any credence be given to the idea that class solidarity superseded racial identity in the consciousness of most working-class Coloured people or the characters portrayed in *A Walk in the Night*, as Chandramohan asserts.[86]

The book was written at the time of La Guma's immersion in grassroots political activism, and he was deeply concerned with the problem of Coloured exclusivism and the implications this would have for the building of a multiracial resistance movement to oppose apartheid.[87] This is evident from the meanings vested in the title of the book. La Guma intended the name *A Walk in the Night* to resonate with readers on several levels. Most obviously, the novel derived its name from the main protagonists, Michael and Willieboy, embarking on several walks through the streets of District Six during that fateful evening, with each walk driving the plot forward and taking them to their respective destinies. At a more abstract level, La Guma depicts his characters as having little control over their lives. The story focuses on the underclass of District Six—the unemployed, petty thieves, gangsters, and outcasts, what La Guma at one point refers to as "the mould that accumulated on the fringes of the underworld beyond Castle Bridge."[88] Buffeted by a racially oppressive system, these people had few choices open to them and little prospect of improving their lives. Unable to shape their own destiny in any meaningful way, they react to events and try to roll with the punches that life throws at them. They might, in the words of Balutansky, be seen to be "walking the night of Apartheid."[89] La Guma also chose his title to symbolize the political conservatism and racial exclusivity of the Coloured community. In an interview with Cecil Abrahams in Havana in 1981, he explained: "One of the reasons I called the book *A Walk in the Night* was that in my mind the coloured community was still discovering themselves in relation to the general struggle against racism in South Africa. They were walking, enduring, and in this way they were experiencing this walking in the night until such time as they found themselves and were prepared to be citizens of a society to which they wanted to make a contribution."[90]

As explained earlier, Coloureds' marginality and intermediate position in the society resulted in ambiguities and unresolved contradictions within Coloured identity and presented these people with a series of dilemmas and paradoxes in their day-to-day living. The most conspicuous ambiguity at the political level was the contradiction between adopting nonracism in principle but accepting racial divisions in practice. La Guma was no exception. He clearly abhorred racism and devoted his life to the struggle for an egalitarian society. And as is well known, he suffered a considerable degree of persecution for the vigor with which he pursued this ideal.[91] Although this is never made explicit in *A Walk in the Night*, there can be little doubt that La Guma identified himself as Coloured and accepted Coloured identity as given. For example, he appealed to people's identity as Coloured to mobilize resistance to apartheid and had no qualms about being an officer of an organization, SACPO, that explicitly identified itself as Coloured. In his own life, La Guma manifested the contradiction of professing nonracial values in principle but having to come to grips with the reality of Coloured identity. This conundrum is also integral to *A Walk in the Night,* for in that work, the author who regards himself as Coloured ponders the very problem of overcoming Coloured exclusivism.

In his journalistic writing, La Guma's frequent use of words such as *we, our,* and *us* when writing about Coloured people indicated his personal identification as Coloured. At times, he even appeared to take pride in his Colouredness. Writing in 1955 about the upcoming Congress of the People, at which the Freedom Charter was to be adopted, he pronounced,"I look forward to attending it and hope that the example set by many other coloured people who are attending will be an inspiration to their people to come closer to the struggle for democracy in South Africa."[92] There were also occasions when he invoked the tripartite racial hierarchy of South African society while, ironically, espousing nonracial, egalitarian sentiments. For instance, reflecting on the political consequences of the declaration of a state of emergency in his *New Age* column,[93] Up My Alley, he declared, "We, who stand for a free, equal society of all South Africans, Black, White and Brown, have gained enormously in fellowship, in confidence and in allies."[94] Although he took Coloured identity for granted and accepted his membership of that social category as a matter of fact, he did not regard Colouredness as an inherent quality or in any way relevant to determining human worth: that much is evident from one of his very first Up My Alley columns: "The census declares that we [the Coloured people] are almost one and a quarter million. But if you identify people, not by names and the colour of their skin, but by hardship and joy, pleasure and suffering, cherished hopes and broken dreams, the grinding monotony of toil without gain . . . then you will have to give up counting. People are like identical books with only different dust jackets. The title and the text are the same."[95] Here, as elsewhere, there is the ambiguity of La Guma identifying himself as Coloured while at the same time dismissing Coloured identity as irrelevant.

However, he recognized that there was a high degree of race consciousness within the Coloured community at large and was particularly perturbed by Coloured antipathy toward Africans. This concern is present as an undercurrent in *A Walk in the Night,* but it comes to the fore strongly in the "The Gladiators," one of the short stories included in the volume. That piece tells the story of Kenny, a race-conscious Coloured boxer who was proud of his fair skin and Caucasian features. Epitomizing the intermediate status of Coloured people and their desire to assimilate into the dominant society, Kenny is, in the words of the narrator, "sorry he wasn't white and glad he wasn't black."[96] Kenny's racial arrogance leads him to underestimate his opponent because the man is African, and he is beaten to a pulp for this indiscretion.[97]

Politically, La Guma adhered to the multiracial strategy of the Congress Alliance, which replicated the racial and ethnic divisions of South African society in its political structures. On the surface, it might appear that he had embraced a pragmatic attitude toward race, but on closer scrutiny, it is clear that he did not consciously distance himself from Coloured identity, nor did he use it simply as an instrument for mobilizing people to further his political cause. In both his journalistic and fictional writing at that time, there was an ambivalence about racial identity and an uncomplicated acceptance of Coloured identity as given, indicating that La Guma had not yet fully come to terms with these contradictions for himself.

In one sense, it is not surprising that La Guma espoused a Coloured identity because he wrote before the rejection of that identity had become widespread. By the early 1960s, as demonstrated earlier, only a handful of intellectuals, among them those within the fold of the NEUM and FIOSA in particular, had questioned the validity of Coloured identity. The popular mind-set of the time, even within politically progressive circles, generally accepted the racial divisions of South African society as an immutable fact of life. La Guma, for instance, appears not to have questioned this racial segmentation of the Congress Movement in any way. He was a founding member of SACPO, served on its executive committee, and worked as a full-time organizer for the body between 1954 and 1956. He only gave up this position when he was forced to find employment because his wife, Blanche, a midwife, had to stop working while pregnant with their first child.[98]

Yet viewed in another light, it is quite extraordinary for La Guma to have accepted Coloured identity so uncritically. He was, after all, a committed socialist. For him, the primacy of the class struggle ought to have been gospel and the "false consciousness" of racial and ethnic identities obvious. Given that his life was dedicated to the eradication of a system of racial oppression and that he suffered severe persecution at the hands of the apartheid state, this particular blindness seems doubly surprising. What is more, by the early 1960s, the idea of rejecting Coloured identity was not an entirely novel one within the Coloured intelligentsia, of which La Guma was undeniably part. Nonracial thinking among Coloured radicals can be traced as far back as at least the mid-1940s, with the establishment of the Anti-CAD and the NEUM.[99] With Congress Alliance and Unity Movement ideologues in the western Cape engaged in a running polemic about the nature of black oppression in South Africa and the most appropriate strategy for overthrowing the state through much of the 1950s,[100] it is difficult to imagine La Guma was not exposed to the idea that Coloured identity was an artificial construction of the ruling classes, used to enslave black people and to divide and rule them. Though he was deeply troubled by Coloured racial exclusivity, the thought of rejecting Coloured identity appears not to have occurred to him at that stage.

Of all his novels, it is in *A Walk in the Night* that racial attitudes prevalent within the Coloured community are at their clearest. La Guma recognized that in the Coloured community, there was generally a high degree of sensitivity to racial features, especially skin color and hair texture. Even though racial traits were of little consequence to La Guma personally, he was nevertheless sensitive to them because he had been socialized into a community in which fine gradations of skin color and other racial characteristics were significant determinants of status.

Presumably because he recognized that these racial markers would have mattered to the characters he was writing about in *A Walk in the Night*, La Guma paid particular attention to shades of skin color and to hair texture in the book. One of the first things he notes in providing a physical description of Michael Adonis was that "he had dark, curly hair, slightly brittle but not quite kinky, and a complexion the colour of warm leather." Similarly, he introduces the other main character by noting that "Willieboy was young and dark and wore his kinky hair brushed into a point above his forehead." The skin colors of characters are variously described as "brown," "yellowish," "olive-skinned," "hammered-copper," "off-white or like coffee," "the colour of worn leather," "tan-coloured," "brown sandstone," "blue-black," and "like polish [*sic*] teak. Not exactly like teak because he's lighter." Hair is characterized as "coarse," "wiry," "stringy," or, most often, "kinky." He also notes that Kenny the boxer's nose is "a little flat from being hit on it a lot, almost like a black boy's nose." Moreover, disparaging racial epithets such as "Moor" for Indians; "hotnot" and "bushman" for Coloureds; "kaffir" and "tsotsi" for Africans; "boer" for Afrikaners; as well as "play-white," "pore-white [*sic*]," and "whitey" are scattered across the pages of the book, just as they would have peppered the conversations of the people he was writing about.[101]

La Guma goes beyond simply evoking the sensitivity of Coloured people and South Africans in general to racial traits. On several occasions, he invests his characters with racist sentiments and a sense of Coloured exclusivity that one might commonly have expected to encounter in the community he was writing about. For example, Adonis is greatly offended by his supervisor's referring to him as "black," thereby lumping him with Africans. "Called me a cheeky black bastard. Me, I'm not black. Anyway I said he was a no-good pore white." Similarly, Willieboy remonstrates with a brothel keeper that Americans and foreigners "have no right to mess with our girls." The internalization of the racist values of the dominant society by Coloured people is again depicted by Adonis's regarding himself as "brown," by his stating that "the negroes isn't like us," and by the way in which he attempts to justify his killing of Uncle Doughty to himself, "Well, he didn't have no right living here with us coloureds." Moreover, that Uncle Doughty, a white man, is made to utter the nonracial sentiments with which La Guma himself identified belies any idea that *A Walk in the Night* depicts a Manichean world. When Adonis challenges Doughty—"You old white bastard, you got nothing to worry about"—the elderly man replies, "What's my white got to do with it? Here I am, in shit street, and does my white help?"[102]

Although it takes fully eighty pages before La Guma identifies any of his main characters explicitly as Coloured, he signals their racial identity at the outset in a variety of ways. In case the location of the story and the physical description of Adonis and Willieboy leave any uncertainty about their being Coloured, he removes all doubt by giving his protagonist a surname almost exclusively found within the Coloured community. The name Adonis, like many others peculiar to the Coloured community, is a legacy of a servile past. Surnames corresponding with months of the year or with mythical Greek and Roman figures, such as Adonis, Appollis, and Cupido, are common within the Coloured community. Slaves were often given demeaning names as part of a process of dehumanization that helped to reinforce the master's control. Thus, a slave might be named after the month in which he or she was acquired or born or named after a Greek or Roman figure who exhibited a particular trait with which the slave was associated. The name Adonis—a youth of particular beauty and beloved of Aphrodite in Greek mythology—was usually bestowed in ironic fashion on a slave the master considered to be particularly

ugly.[103] Similarly, La Guma signifies the social status of other characters by using names such as Willieboy, Sockies, Foxy, Flippy, Banjo,
Gogs, Chips, Choker, and Chinaboy, which are typical of the nicknames assigned within the Coloured, urban working class.[104]

La Guma's use of colloquial language also signals that he is writing about the Coloured community. In this respect, he was faced with
a problem: the people he was writing about would normally speak
Cape Vernacular Afrikaans or *kombuis* Afrikaans, popularly stereo-
typed as a peculiarly Coloured manner of speaking the language. To
have rendered his characters' speech in colloquial Afrikaans would,
however, have made much of it incomprehensible to a large part of his
intended readership. La Guma instead paraphrased their speech in the
colloquial English that was distinctive to inner-city Cape Town, also
stigmatized as a Coloured, working-class variant of the language.
Thus, instead of speaking vernacular Afrikaans with a sprinkling of
English words as their real-life counterparts would have done, the
characters of *A Walk in the Night* are made to speak colloquial English
strewn with Afrikaans words and phrases.

Some examples of the Afrikaans colloquialisms La Guma uses are:
hoit/het pally (hello friend), *oubaas* (jail), *lighties* (youngsters), *stop*
(small parcel of dagga), *juba/burg/joker/rooker* (man, fellow), *laan* (big
shot), *squashie* (weakling), *goose* (young woman), *endjie* (cigarette butt),
metchie (match), *ching/chink/start* (money), and *beece* (bioscope). Where
he uses these colloquial Afrikaans words and phrases, La Guma either
translates them for the reader by having the characters repeat them in
English or expects their meanings to be deduced from the context. His
liberal use of discourse fillers such as *mos, ja, jong*, and *ou* does much
to make the conversation sound natural, as does the frequent occur-
rence of swear words such as *bogger* (bugger), "sonofobitch/sonso-
bitches," *blerry* (bloody), "bastard," and "eff/effing," a milder form of
"fuck."[105]

La Guma also puts a number of colloquial English words and phrases
generally associated with working-class, Coloured speakers of the
language in the mouths of his characters. Some examples are: "law"
(policeman), "make finish" (finish), "nervous like" (nervously), "braggy
like" (boastfully), "pull up" (beat up), "because why" (because), "don't
I say" (is that not so), "I'm just like this to him" (I said to him), "I
reckon to him" (I said to him), "how goes it with you?" (how are you?),
and "on the book" (on credit). In addition, he often imitates what is
typecast as the Coloured working-class pronunciation of English

words, as with: "gwan/garn" (go on, get lost), "fif" (fifth), "or'er" (order), "execkly" (exactly), "faktry" (factory), "reshun" (ration), "caffies" (cafés), "theff" (theft), and "awright" (all right). It is certainly no coincidence that in "A Matter of Taste," a short story about two Coloured workers who share their humble billy-can of coffee with a white drifter, La Guma has the white derelict saying "coffee" whereas the Coloured characters pronounce it "cawfee." Similarly, whereas John Abrahams, a Coloured character in *A Walk in the Night*, utters the words "law and or'er" and "execkly," Constable Raalt, who judging by his surname is Afrikaans-speaking, enunciates them as "law and order" and "exactly."[106]

It is clear that *A Walk in the Night* goes beyond the simple racial oppositions that a superficial understanding of racial identity in apartheid South Africa might suggest. Far from reflecting a Manichean world of white versus black in South African society, the novel operates in a more fluid milieu of complex social relations and multifaceted social identities in the specific urban setting of District Six. Because the author is intimately familiar with the private and public politics of Coloured identity, which he himself espouses, the novel reflects much of the complexity and irony of racial attitudes within the Coloured community as well as within the broader South African society. Adonis's denial that he is black and Doughty's dismissal of his own whiteness as inconsequential should be sufficient to dispel any thought that *A Walk in the Night* is played out in a Manichean world in which all black people are interchangeable entities under the apartheid system.

The case studies presented in this chapter contest existing scholarly understandings of the influence of Marxist ideology on Coloured identity. They belie any easy assumption that the radical movement in Coloured protest politics during the middle decades of white rule was nonracial in the sense that it rejected the salience of racial identity or of Colouredness in South African society and politics. The first case study demonstrates conclusively that neither the *Torch* nor the NEUM took an uncompromising stand on the principle of nonracism prior to the early 1960s. The study argues that though the NEUM's leadership had always had a nonracial outlook, the principle of nonracism was not always central to the group's political agenda. The NEUM's emphasis on nonracism evolved over a period of two decades, and it was only from the early 1960s onward that a nonracial discourse emerged as a consistent, self-conscious mode of expression within the

Unity Movement. The second case study attests to the hegemony of racial modes of thought by probing the ambiguities in the personal and social identities of Alex La Guma. Despite being a committed socialist and antiapartheid campaigner, he nevertheless operated within the conventional boundaries of the South African racial system in certain aspects of his thinking.

This chapter has shown that the influence of the radical movement on Coloured identity was relatively superficial. By the early 1960s, nonracial thinking in relation to Coloured identity was still confined to a tiny intelligentsia, an elite within the Coloured elite. It was only to start spreading, slowly at first, in the latter half of the 1970s, with the revival of the antiapartheid movement in which nonracial, democratic values were to become paramount. The next chapter assesses the impact of this trend on expressions of Coloured identity.

5

The Emperor's New Clothes

Coloured Rejectionism during the
Latter Phases of the Apartheid Era

This chapter will trace the trajectory of Coloured rejectionism, a development that started within a small section of the Coloured intelligentsia in the early 1960s and grew into a significant movement by the time it peaked at the end of the 1980s. It declined during the early 1990s, when the espousal of Coloured identity once again became acceptable in left-wing and "progressive" circles. Two in-depth case studies, supplemented by brief analyses of two complementary texts, will be used to document this tendency.

The Black Consciousness poetry of James Matthews, an internationally recognized Coloured writer from the Cape Flats, will form the basis of the first case study. Matthews's poetry of the first half of the 1970s is emblematic of a new consciousness of defiance and black solidarity within particular sectors of the Coloured population.[1] In the Coloured community, Black Consciousness ideology, with its stress on black unity and self-determination, appealed especially to the better-educated, urbanized groups outside of the NEUM's sphere of influence. It was particularly in the wake of the 1976 revolt that these ideas took root as a popular phenomenon within the Coloured community and were imbibed by an increasingly politicized student population. The second case study will focus on *South*, a newspaper published between 1987 and 1994. During the first half of its existence, *South* epitomized the populist nonracial approach to Coloured identity that characterized the extraparliamentary opposition of the

1980s. This movement, under the leadership of the United Democratic Front (UDF), initiated a substantial popularization of Coloured rejectionism and shifted the focus of the liberation movement away from the exclusivist and binary tendencies of Black Consciousness to a much more inclusive and strongly nonracial outlook. The history of the latter half of the newspaper's life will be used to illustrate the initial stages in the breakdown of this trend.[2]

In addition, a critical review of two supplementary texts will fill chronological and thematic gaps in the unfolding story of Coloured rejectionism. The first text, the *Educational Journal*, takes up where the last chapter left off in the story of the emergence of a politically correct approach to race and Coloured identity in the NEUM. From the early 1960s, the *Educational Journal* embodied a new antiracist discourse that became characteristic of the Unity Movement and that was highly influential among left-wing, Coloured intellectuals and political activists until well into the 1980s.[3] Early on, the *Journal* had been representative of moderate Coloured political opinion, but from 1944 onward, it became a mouthpiece of the Anti-CAD faction of the NEUM when the TLSA fell under the control of its minority radical wing.[4] The second supplementary text, the western Cape community newspaper *Grassroots*, will be used to complement the analysis of *South*, which appeared late in the 1980s. *Grassroots* was launched in early 1980 and published for almost exactly ten years; it was especially influential during the first half of the decade and was integral to the regeneration of the antiapartheid movement in the western Cape.[5]

Debunking *"Bruinmanskap"*: The *Educational Journal* during the 1960s

As noted in the preceding chapter, a growing political correctness relating to race and Coloured identity became evident in the *Torch* from the late 1950s onwards. A similar process was observable in its sister publication, the *Educational Journal*, at the same time. There, as with the *Torch*, words and phrases with racial connotations, especially the term *Coloured*, were increasingly qualified through the use of quotation marks, italics, and appended wording; certain sensitive terms were preceded by qualifying phrases such as *so-called, so classified, what is described as*, and *known as*.[6] Already in March 1958, there was an elaborate example in the *Journal*, in which the author wrote not of the "Coloured people," as had been the custom, but of "the section of the oppressed people who have come to be known and classified as the

Coloured people."[7] The *Educational Journal* clearly developed a more consistently nonracial approach somewhat earlier than the *Torch*, as a comparison of the 1958 issues of the two publications demonstrates. This was due partly to the *Journal*'s leisurely publishing schedule of just eight issues per annum. What is more, the *Journal* was under the editorial control of Ben Kies, whom many consider to have been the most accomplished intellectual in the Unity Movement.[8] Also, because the *Journal* focused on educational issues and was written by experienced educators who saw themselves as political activists from a distinct intellectual tradition, the content of this periodical was much more carefully considered.

Although elements of the nonracial rhetoric characteristic of later NEUM writing appeared in the *Torch* during the early 1960s, sustained examples were not yet to be found in the paper by the time it folded. The first mature examples of such rhetoric were, however, already appearing in the *Educational Journal*, which would become the main voice of the Anti-CAD faction of the NEUM in its dormancy. In this respect, its April 1962 article entitled *"Ons Bruinmense"* (Our Brown People), written under the pseudonym I. M. Human, is something of a landmark, as it represents the first full-blown example of the nonracial rhetoric that came to be the hallmark of the NEUM from the early 1960s. The biting sarcasm, the scorning of "quislings," and the implacable antiracist stance of this article is vintage NEUM— in its politically dormant phase, that is:

> An examination of the techniques employed to establish the sub-species "Bruin-man" reveals . . . Piet Botha, I. D. du Plessis and company were given the job of creating the political *Bruinman*. His identity was founded on the Separate Representation of Voters Act which gave him a temporary *bywoner* [sharecropper] status until such time as he could "come into his own." . . . To establish their "separateness" and *eiesoortigheid* [uniqueness], the "special" needs of the *Bruinmense* were "recognized," and a benevolent Government, ever anxious to reward those who were prepared to accept inferiority, set aside "their own" Department of State to cater for their social needs. . . . Outa Tom and his *handlangers* [lackeys], at every secret session with foreman Botha, ask for bigger and better doses of *apartheid* in housing schemes, on the trains, in post offices, in employment, in prisons.[9]

By that time, the TLSA and the NEUM had abandoned the strategic approach of recognizing the reality of racial divisions within the society. This much is clear from the *"Ons Bruinmense"* article, which ended with the warning that any acceptance of Colouredness marks those thus classified under apartheid with the "badge of inferiority, of being less than human." Coincidentally, in another article on the same page, the *Educational Journal* stated the opinion of the Teachers' League and the NEUM on the nature of Coloured identity in its simplest and starkest form when it characterized Colouredness as "a concept legislatively and socially created, with intent" (to divide, rule, and exploit).[10] The unequivocal rejection of Coloured identity by the Unity Movement in the early 1960s marked the start of Coloured rejectionism as a recognizable movement.

Through the early 1960s, the discourse of the *Educational Journal* became rapidly homogenized along the lines of that exhibited in the "*Ons Bruinmense*" article, as more and more of the content was written by a handful of like-minded TLSA stalwarts and less and less of it was drawn from the broader membership. That membership had already started dwindling in the late 1940s, and it contracted sharply during the late 1950s and early 1960s when its leadership started being banned. The more moderate members were alienated by the radical leadership that took control in the mid-1940s, and the less committed withdrew during the latter part of the 1950s for fear of retribution from the apartheid state; some younger members, dissatisfied with the inactivity of the leadership, also broke away in the early 1960s. By the end of 1963, the TLSA was effectively dormant, as its branch structure had atrophied and its last conference was held in June of that year. By that point, the uncompromising nonracism and ascerbic tone of the NEUM and TLSA were standard fare in the *Journal*.[11] For the rest of its existence, the *Educational Journal* held true to the principle it proclaimed in April 1965: "The TLSA has no colour bar in its constitution, practices no colour bar and does not classify people racially."[12] On one occasion, however, a *Journal* editorial grudgingly conceded the stubborn persistence of the "myth of Colouredism." Besides continuous reinforcement through apartheid propaganda and the expediencies of "collaborators," Colouredism, it explained, insinuated itself subtly into people's thinking because they had no option but "to live in a 'Coloured' location, to go to a 'Coloured' school, to obtain a teaching licence labelled 'Coloured'"; as a consequence, "a good many honest people carelessly or unthinkingly refer to 'our school' or 'our musical talent' or 'our doctors.'"[13]

Until the 1980s, this nonracial outlook and the Coloured rejectionism that went with it was highly influential within those sectors of the Coloured elite with left-wing sympathies, especially in the western

Cape. This rather restricted constituency had narrowed further through the 1960s and the first half of the 1970s, as the influence of the NEUM waned and the strictures of the apartheid state limited its ability to function. Its ideas were, however, kept alive within a small elite of radical intellectuals, in a handful of schools where the TLSA retained influence, and within the small NEUM discussion groups, or "fellowships," in which university students were prominent.[14] The NEUM's nonracial philosophy would nevertheless have a significant impact on the mass democratic movement that emerged in the western Cape in the early 1980s. First, many politicized Coloured people, including Black Consciousness supporters, were exposed to NEUM thinking and its critique of Black Consciousness in educational institutions and through its literature without necessarily becoming members of the organization or consciously supporting it. The *Educational Journal*, for example, scorned Black Consciousness as "nothing but racialism (with perhaps a dash of American dressing)—using the Panthers and Soledad Brothers to make the racialism more palatable."[15] For some, such as journalist and former Black Consciousness adherent Rashid Seria, this exposure prompted them to question both the morality and the political wisdom of countering white racism with black exclusivism.[16] Journalist and UDF political activist Zubeida Jaffer spoke for many when, in an open letter to Richard Dudley and the New Unity Movement in 1992, she stated: "I have never been a member of the Unity Movement but I will always appreciate the guidance and information provided by your organization in the seventies. . . . Those of us in Cape Town who were nurtured by your organization, although often unknown to ourselves, would distort history if we did not acknowledge the role played by so many of our brave teachers when the times were much darker."[17] Second, defectors from the Unity Movement—Dullah Omar and Trevor Manuel being the most prominent examples—helped infuse these ideas into the UDF-dominated mass democratic movement of the 1980s. The influence of the NEUM was, by and large, restricted to the educated middle classes. The self-consciously working-class James Matthews, for example, claims that the Unity Movement had no influence on his thinking.[18]

From Manenberg to Soweto: The Black Consciousness Poetry of James Matthews

James Matthews was born on 25 May 1929 in a run-down tenement in the predominantly Coloured working-class neighborhood of Bo-Kaap, along the lower slopes of Signal Hill bordering Cape Town's central business district. Matthews was forced to end his schooling at Trafalgar High School while in standard VIII [grade 10] to supplement the family income. He held a series of menial jobs, which included selling newspapers on street corners, running office errands, and working as a night telephone operator and clerk before pursuing a career as a reporter at the *Golden City Post* and the *Muslim News* during the 1960s and 1970s.[19]

Matthews felt an acute and personal sense of grievance at the injustices suffered by black South Africans, and in the latter half of the 1950s, his political awareness matured through incidental exposure to Communist Party teachings. He remembers that the impromptu "talks" that Wolfie Kodesh delivered to clusters of locals on street corners in his neighborhood while selling copies of *New Age*[20] were particularly influential in "crystallising . . . my political awareness." Matthews, however, resisted joining the Communist Party or any other political organization because he felt the need, both as a writer and an independent thinker, to maintain a personal autonomy, free from the constraints that came with allegiances of that sort.[21] He claims to have developed the ideas of black pride and solidarity expressed in his writing independently of the local Black Consciousness Movement and to have been influenced mainly by the philosophy of the Black Panthers in the United States and the ideas of negritude in the writings of Léopold Senghor, Cheikh Anta Diop, and Aimé Césaire.[22] The closest he came to a direct political affiliation with any particular organization was serving on the executive committee of the Black Consciousness–inspired Union of Black Journalists that was formed in January 1973.[23]

In the meanwhile, having published his first piece of fiction in the *Sun* newspaper at the age of seventeen, Matthews had made a name for himself as a short story writer, beginning in the mid-1950s. He confirms that he started writing less out of any ambition to become an author than as a form of catharsis, "just to get a lot of shit out of my head."[24] His stories were published in a range of newspapers and magazines, including the *Cape Times, Cape Argus, Drum, Hi-Note, Africa South, Transition,* and *New African,* as well as in several anthologies of South African prose.[25] Two stories in particular—"Azikwelwa," first published in 1958, and "The Park," in 1962, both of which had strong antiapartheid and black solidarity themes—gained international recognition. It was particularly in Sweden, West Germany, and Holland that he gained a following.[26] In 1973, Matthews started his own publishing house, BLAC—the acronym standing for Black Literature, Art and Culture—which he used to publish his own work and that of other township artists.[27] Matthews's writing career was stunted by the apartheid state's refusal to grant him a passport, which not only cut him off from international contacts and a large part of his readership but also prevented him from taking up numerous opportunities to present his work overseas and to broaden his artistic experience. It was only through the intervention of the West German government in 1980 that he obtained a passport to allow him to attend the Frankfurt Book Fair. The passport being valid for five years, he was able to travel abroad and returned to Germany in 1984 to receive the freedom of the towns of Nuremberg and Lehrte.[28]

All of Matthews's work, though not necessarily always overtly political, commented in one way or another on the experience of black people under apartheid. His stories described the squalor, degradation, and humiliation of the lives of those oppressed by apartheid but also testified to their anger, their defiance, and, above all, their humanity. Drawing on his own rich experience of Cape Town's working-class life, including the male street-corner culture of drinking, gambling, smoking marijuana, and petty gangsterism (he was a member of the Cluster Buster gang),[29] Matthews's writing mediated the harsh realities of life in the city's townships and inner-city localities. And despite indulging in the decidedly middle-class pursuits of journalism and literary production, he remained fiercely loyal to his working-class roots. Recalling their first meeting in the mid-1950s, longtime friend and fellow author Richard Rive testified that Matthews looked "ostentatiously working class" and stated, "I realized immediately he saw in me everything he despised. I not only looked Coloured middle class, but I spoke Coloured middle class and behaved Coloured middle class."[30] In 1988, Matthews, with characteristic self-effacement, dismissed himself as "just another ghetto writer."[31]

When Matthews switched to poetry as his main form of artistic expression in the early 1970s,[32] he found himself at the forefront of a new wave of black protest poetry that primarily addressed a black readership rather than a general audience or the white or Western conscience, as earlier protest poetry had tended to do.[33] Wally Serote acknowledged Matthews as its leading exponent—"At the head of this group was James Matthews, who set the standards of how we were going to deal with things around us"[34]—and Mbulelo Mzamane was of the opinion that "Matthews was an influence on, and not influenced by, Black Consciousness."[35] He is also generally recognized as the angriest of the Black Consciousness poets who wrote before the 1976 uprising, being described by Hein Willemse as a "despatcher of raging Black Consciousness poetry."[36]

The bulk of Matthews's poetry of this genre is to be found in the aptly titled *Cry Rage!* which appeared in 1972 and also contained a collection of poems by Gladys Thomas, a long-standing friend. Other poems of similar complexion appeared in the 1974 anthology *Black Voices Shout!* which was edited by Matthews,[37] and a few more were published individually in newspapers and magazines.[38] In his Black Consciousness poetry, Matthews gave voice not only to the anger that many Coloured people felt but also to the embryonic feeling of solidarity with Africans that was to grow significantly after the Soweto revolt and the death of Steve Biko. Matthews was ahead of his time in these respects in that very few people, particularly within the Coloured community, were as outspoken as he was in *Cry Rage!* which, he claims, had the distinction of being the first volume of poetry to be banned by the National Party government.[39] It was only after the Soweto revolt that Black Consciousness sentiment flourished in the Coloured community and that the public expression of outrage became more common.

In the opening poem of the *Cry Rage!* compilation, Matthews made it clear that

> I am no minstrel
> who sings of joy . . .
> but the words I write
> are of pain and of rage . . .
> my heart drowned in bitterness
> with the agony of what white man's law has done.

He did not believe that what he wrote should be labeled poetry. According to Gareth Cornwell, Matthews preferred to call his poems "protest songs" because of his intention that they serve a consciousness-raising function and because the urgency of his message did not allow for indulgence in the luxury of "literaryness."[40] Matthews himself has, on several occasions, referred to his poetry as "gatherings" or "expressions of feelings."[41]

In line with Black Consciousness thinking, Matthews sought to transcend his personal identity—and his classification by the apartheid state—as Coloured by taking pride in his blackness. In a memorable section of verse, he affirmed this broader identity:

> I am Black
> my Blackness fills me to the brim
> like a beaker of well-seasoned wine
> that sends my senses reeling with pride

Pride in his blackness kindled within Matthews a sense of fellowship with Africans in the rest of South Africa:

> Our pain has linked us
> from Manenberg to Soweto

as well as with black people globally:

> I share the pain of my black brother
> and a mother in a Harlem ghetto
> with that of a soul brother in Notting Hill

At times, Matthews pushed his identification with the suffering of Africans to the point of imagining that he personally experienced their oppression, as he did when writing about influx control measures that restricted their freedom of movement by confining them to poverty-stricken rural reserves and preventing them from seeking work outside of the strictly regulated and highly exploitative migrant labor system. Honing in on the system's destruction of African family life and the personal distress it caused, he rhetorically asked of "the white man":

> can he feel my pain when his laws
> tear my wife and child from my side
> and I am forced to work a thousand miles away? . . .

> is he with me in the loneliness
> of my bed in the bachelor barracks[42]

In Matthews's Black Consciousness poetry, there is a clear-cut opposition between black and white—pitting oppressors against the oppressed and persecutors against the dispossessed. He continually contrasted black poverty, suffering, and rightlessness with white opulence, hypocrisy, and lack of compassion, at one point describing South Africa as

> ... my fair land a'dying of the stench
> of valleys of plenty

Although he mainly focused on antiapartheid themes, such as the human toll of influx control, forced removals, immorality legislation, police brutality, deaths in detention, and the iniquitous effects of "sad, sick segregation," Matthews also wrote of colonial dispossession and economic exploitation:

> the fields that were ours
> our cattle can no longer graze
> and like the cattle we are herded
> to starve on barren soil
>
> we die in the earth's depth
> to fill his coffer with gold
> his lust for shiny pebbles
> outweighs his concern for our lives[43]

Matthews lashed out at whites in general, at one point crying out in anguish:

> White South Africa
> you are mutilating my soul

And he made no apology for his heavy-handed excoriation of white South Africa, stating in the introduction to *Cry Rage!* that it was his intention to "show contempt for white man's two-faced morality." He thus had little compunction in cursing them:

> Goddam them!
> They know what they've done

passing judgments of the sort that

> the word of the white man
> has the value of dirt

or dismissing whites with contempt:

> . . . and white man
> should you die
> i won't even
> laugh or cry . . .
> to waste on
> you as much
> as a sigh

He even threatened whites with violent revenge:

> rage as sharp as a blade
> to cut and slash
> and spill blood
> for only blood can appease
> the blood spilled
> over three hundred years[44]

Some of Matthews's strongest invective was reserved for liberal whites, whom he readily lumped together with the broader racist establishment. In one angry outburst, he wrote:

> . . . the hypocrisy of your pious double-talk
> of sharing my pain and plight sickens me
>   white man
> get lost and go screw yourself
> you have long-gone lost your soul[45]

It needs to be pointed out that in these instances, Matthews's anger, was directed at those liberal whites who wanted the best of both worlds—dissociating themselves from apartheid yet continuing to benefit from it—for he did salute that tiny minority of whites who were prepared to make personal sacrifices in their stand against apartheid. He thus paid homage to the Reverend Bernard Wrankmore:

> that priest upon the hill
> who fasted for freedom

and to the University of Cape Town students who were beaten by police when they protested against apartheid education on the steps of the St. Georges Cathedral in the center of Cape Town in 1972.[46]

In accordance with Black Consciousness principles, Matthews wrote scathingly not only of black opportunists and collaborators who sought to profit from apartheid but also of black people mimicking white behavior—and by implication, especially Coloured people's association with whiteness—which he saw as a betrayal of their black heritage:

> white syphilization
> taints blacks
> makes them
> carbon copies . . .
> the women
> faces smeared
> skin bleached
> hair straightened
>
> wake up
> black fools!

In the same vein, he decried what he regarded as subservient behavior on the part of black people. On the one occasion he used the term *Coloured* in a normative sense in his poetry, Matthews upbraided participants in the coon carnival:

> Coloured folks garish in coon garb
> Sing and dance in the hot sun
> Their faces smeared a fool's mask
> Happy New Year, my baas, a drunken shout
> To whites who applaud and approve
> Their annual act of debasement

This represents a significant about-face for Matthews, who had been a coorganizer of the prominent coon troupe, the Ragtime Millionaires, during the 1960s.[47]

Because of his stress on black unity, Matthews made explicit racial distinctions between black people in only three instances in this poetry.[48] However, he freely made such distinctions indirectly, through the use of place-names or by mentioning the different forms of oppression apartheid visited on different sectors of the black population. References to the people of Illinge, Dimbaza, Sada, and Limehill or to suffering inflicted by the pass laws signaled that he was writing about

Africans,[49] whereas mentions of Manenberg, Heideveld, Lavistown, and Group Areas removals were signifiers for the Coloured community. On the second of the two occasions in which he used the term *Coloured*, it was with reference to the race classification system, and he put the word in capitals to indicate that it was not his wording but official terminology.[50]

Although Black Consciousness strongly tended toward a Manichean view of South African society, it nevertheless recognized the existence of racial and ethnic differences within the black population, most notably through its definition of the black community as consisting of Africans, Coloureds, and Indians. A 1970 *SASO Newsletter* editorial explaining the movement's stance cautioned: "By all means be proud of your Indian heritage or your African culture but make sure that in looking around for somebody to kick at, you choose the fellow who is sitting on your neck. He may not be as easily accessible as your black brother but he *is* the source of your discomfort."[51]

Being a member of a minority group generally characterized as occupying an intermediate status in the South African racial hierarchy and in which racial characteristics were an important determinant of status, Matthews was sensitive to these differences. Although at no point in his poetry did he try to explain or deconstruct his own identity as Coloured or even make explicit reference to it, Matthews nevertheless regarded himself as Coloured throughout his life, and his adherence to Black Consciousness did not cause him to reject this identification.[52]

In his strongly autobiographical novel, *The Party Is Over*, described by Hein Willemse as "reality disguised as fiction," the central character, David Patterson, struggles with the frustrations of being a Coloured writer and the expectations placed on black artists.[53] At one point, Patterson declares, "I can't really be classified as a Black African writer." When asked, "Why not?" he replies, "'Let me put it this way: I don't come from a tribal background, neither do I speak an indigenous language. I'm not white, but I am not African either.' David fell silent. It would be a waste of time to explain to these misguided people that he sometimes felt that the Coloureds had become the new lost tribe of Israel."[54] An earlier draft of this section, published in the mid-1980s, has Patterson explaining in addition: "I can't truthfully say that my soul is one with that of Africa. There is a gulf between me and the [African] . . . Culturally my outlook is most certainly European. . . . Racially, it's the African who pushes me aside, labelling me as Ama-Bushman."[55] Interviewed in 1999, Matthews clearly stated, "I have no problem being Coloured, but it is not an issue, unless its taken in a bantustan approach. . . . We shouldn't be treated differently."[56] For Matthews, there was no real inconsistency in embracing Black Consciousness yet regarding himself as Coloured. In a 1998 newspaper article in which he reflected on the nature of Coloured identity as well as the history and aspirations of this community, he explained: "For those who have absorbed the policy of Black Consciousness, the acceptance of being coloured and black is not as contradictory as it might appear, because being black does not mean rejecting being coloured. Being black is part of their political stance—a stance they still feel necessary now—and does not exclude them from their place in coloured ranks."[57]

The significance of Matthews's Black Consciousness poetry is that it heralded a growing acceptance of ideas of black solidarity within the Coloured community during the latter part of the 1970s and helped coax this tendency on its way. It was also a harbinger of the popular fury of the post-Soweto era that periodically boiled over into mass protests and rioting. Though the number of committed Black Consciousness activists in the Coloured community remained small, the impact of the ideology, on the youth in particular, was considerable.[58] Much of the political turmoil in Coloured townships and educational institutions during the second half of the 1970s was informed by Black Consciousness thinking, albeit often in inchoate, rudimentary ways. For many Coloured people, especially among the younger, newly politicized cohorts that provided the main impetus to the protest movement, exposure to Black Consciousness philosophy—even at the simplest level of sloganeering that "Black is beautiful"—entailed raising questions about Coloured identity, about its significance and legitimacy, and about the implications of espousing it. Although Black Consciousness tended toward a binary view of South African society, it nevertheless encouraged the interrogation of received notions of Coloured identity.

For most people at that time, as the example of Matthews demonstrates, embracing Black Consciousness did not necessarily entail the rejection of Coloured identity. For the majority, Colouredness was still too solid a social reality to be dismissed as merely a white, ruling-class invention, though its use as a means of dividing the black population was clearly recognized. Accepting the tenets of Black Consciousness did, however, mean consciously displacing Colouredness from its pedestal as their sole or primary social identity and according it a secondary status, if only in the arena of politics or for symbolic reasons. For many politicized Coloured people, most notably those who were to become active in the mass democratic movement of the 1980s, this was a step toward the complete rejection of Coloured identity.

It is ironic that just when one would have expected Matthews's most wrathful and anguished outburst—during and immediately after the 1976 revolt, when the anger of black South Africans reached unprecedented heights—the poet's next offering consisted of a collection of pensive, introspective poems. The incongrously titled *Pass Me a Meatball, Jones* was written during his detention in solitary confinement in Victor Verster Prison in Paarl between September and December 1976.[59] In this somber collection, there is no explicit social commentary and no ranting against the system but rather an intensely personal evocation of the loneliness, fear, and despair that Matthews experienced during his imprisonment. His next volume of poetry, *No Time for Dreams*, marked a return to social and political commentary. His "raging" had, however, subsided considerably, and the emphasis on black solidarity was supplanted by a nonracial outlook more accommodating of progressive whites. This more mellow and considered stance shines through most clearly in the final poem of this collection, in which Matthews proclaims:

> Freedom is not the colour of my
> black skin . . .
> freedom coloured by blackness is
> a dream
> There is no time for dreams . . .
>
> the blood that will bring
> about freedom
> is an offering from the bodies
> of the many freedom fighters
> believers in the togetherness of people
> and not the colour of their skin[60]

By the early 1980s, Matthews had moved beyond Black Consciousness thinking and embraced a more inclusive approach that, among other things, recognized the valuable role that progressive whites could play in the struggle for freedom. This later writing reflected the liberation movement's swing away from the binarism of Black Consciousness after the movement had been crushed by a spate of bannings and arrests in the aftermath of the Soweto revolt, toward the nonracial democratic ethos of the 1980s. Matthews was influenced by this reorientation, and served on the first editorial board of *Grassroots*, which was emblematic of this new outlook.[61]

"We Don't Fit the Ethnic Stereotypes": Irony and Ambiguity in *Grassroots* and *South*

Although the Soweto revolt resulted in the crushing of the Black Consciousness movement by the apartheid state, it also marked the revival of ANC influence in the internal opposition to apartheid. The collapse of white supremacist regimes on South Africa's borders allowed the exiled wing of the ANC, reinvigorated by several thousand youthful exiles as a result of the Soweto uprising, to establish regular contact with supporters inside the country and to mount an armed resistance campaign from the latter half of the 1970s onward. The burgeoning black trade union movement as well as proliferating youth and community organizations of the post-Soweto era generally identified with the banned ANC. Many former Black Consciousness adherents turned their backs on black exclusivism and embraced the nonracial position of the ANC enshrined in the Freedom Charter it adopted in 1955. Escalating protests and growing grass-roots organization culminated in the August 1983 formation of the United Democratic Front, an umbrella body with which more than six hundred political and community organizations were affiliated, to coordinate this resistance. From its inception, the UDF associated itself with the inclusive, nonracial stance of the ANC.

The revival of the ANC-aligned resistance movement spawned a wide range of alternative newspapers, newsletters, and other media projects,[62] of which *Grassroots*, starting in 1980, and *South*, published from 1987 onward, were the most important examples in the western Cape. In Ineke van Kessel's judgment, *Grassroots* was "a pioneering effort to forge a new genre of local community newspapers,"[63] and as its name was meant to convey, it was very much part of the political strategy envisioned in the Freedom Charter of building community-based organizations to oppose apartheid. *Grassroots* was the product of a new generation of energetic, young, and generally well-educated political activists who regarded themselves as Marxist. And though they were predominantly Coloured and Indian, they eschewed any ethnic or racial affiliation in accordance with Marxist principles. *Grassroots* editors sought to go beyond simply raising political awareness or articulating the views and interests of the working classes; they also wanted to mobilize the working classes against apartheid and capitalist oppression. *Grassroots* staffers saw themselves not as journalists but as media activists, their credo summed up in the acronym POEM, which stood for Popularize, Organize, Educate, and Mobilize.[64]

In the first half of the 1980s, *Grassroots* was a dynamic project that made a significant contribution to the liberation struggle in the western Cape. In this earlier phase, the paper was integral in creating a community of activists and extending the network of youth, community, and social service organizations that underpinned the democratic movement. In addition to some political reporting, *Grassroots* focused mainly on community issues such as everyday struggles involving rent, housing, the cost of living, labor, and health. Its strategy was to mobilize people around workaday issues of immediate concern to them rather than to focus on "high politics." It strove to achieve attainable goals through community action and thereby to raise the consciousness of people politically and induct them into the broader struggle for democracy and a socialist future. *Grassroots* thus tirelessly promoted the message that it was only through collective action that the "racist capitalist system" that oppressed them could be combated and people's lives improved. *Grassroots* activists did indeed help to mobilize people around a number of local issues, and they could claim a few victories, albeit small ones.[65] Given these intentions, *Grassroots* from the outset adopted an unequivocally antiracist approach in its reporting, stressing the overriding importance of unity and "people power."

By the middle of the 1980s, however, the *Grassroots* project had become marginalized, and in the latter half of the decade, it was increasingly irrelevant to the liberation struggle. First, intensified state repression after the declaration of a state of emergency in July 1985 disrupted the production and distribution of the paper. Staff members were forced into hiding, several were detained, and the newspaper's offices were raided by security police and gutted by fire in October 1985. The following year, *Grassroots* organizer Veliswa Mhlawuli was seriously injured in a failed assassination attempt.[66] Second, the collapse of community organizations and the inability of *Grassroots* organizers to operate openly meant, in the words of Ineke van Kessel, that "*Grassroots* operated in a vacuum. Cut off from its community links, the newspaper became the tool of a limited and mainly introverted circle of militants."[67] This new reality was reflected in its content, which shifted focus from community organization to straightforward political reporting as a mouthpiece of the UDF.[68]

By the mid-1980s, the antiapartheid struggle in the western Cape had expanded to the point at which community newspapers such as *Grassroots* and its offshoot, *Saamstaan*,[69] were of limited value. Its slow publishing cycle of five weeks,[70] as well as the restricted volume of news it could carry, made *Grassroots* unsuitable for the populist political agenda that now dominated the liberation movement in the western Cape. The focus of community newspapers was too narrow and their penetration too limited to service these needs. Media and political activists increasingly believed it would take a mass-circulation political newspaper to provide the democratic movement with an effective channel of communication with its wide, informal following as well as one through which it could promote its vision of an alternative society. Such a paper could also be used to counter the biased and watered-down reporting of "struggle news" by the establishment press,[71] which either openly supported the National Party government or practiced a high degree of self-censorship by complying with state curbs on the media and reporting only antiapartheid news that was safe enough to avoid retribution from the state.[72] Media activists, moreover, hoped that a left-wing commercial newspaper, if run as a successful business, would free them from dependence on donor funding and generate capital to underwrite other antiapartheid projects.[73] These were some of the main considerations behind the establishment of *South*, an independent weekly newspaper launched in the western Cape in March 1987 by a group of media activists who had been instrumental in setting up and running the *Grassroots* project.

South was born of one of the most troubled times in South African history. The apartheid state had entered its most turbulent phase in the latter half of the 1980s. From late 1984, popular revolt and mass insurrection in black townships greeted the imposition of the tricameral parliamentary system on South Africa. As the crisis deepened and organized resistance escalated, the National Party government responded with brutal repression. From July 1985, successive states of emergency were proclaimed annually to clamp down on the extraparliamentary opposition. The emergency regulations armed the government with a number of authoritarian measures to block the free flow of information on politically sensitive issues and to muzzle dissenting voices, making the latter half of the 1980s the bleakest years in the annals of press freedom in South Africa.[74]

South was the first left-wing newspaper to be published in the western Cape in twenty-five years,[75] after papers such as the *Guardian* and *Torch* had been snuffed out in the repression of the early 1960s. After a decade and a half of calm, the revolt of 1976 and the widespread civil disturbances of the 1980s created what appeared to be a viable niche for a left-wing political newspaper in the media market of the western Cape. As the populist campaign of the United Democratic Front gathered momentum in the mid-1980s, media activists felt that the western Cape generated enough antiapartheid news to justify a regional newspaper. And as the number of community and youth organizations mushroomed in black residential areas in the region, so did the demand for news about unrest and for radical political commentary. A glaring absence of news from black townships and rural areas appeared to be another weakness of the mainstream media that could be exploited.[76]

Although the deteriorating political climate created the opportunity to publish an independent radical newspaper in the western Cape, it was the frustration of the handful of black journalists who worked for the white-owned, mass-circulation newspapers in the region who provided the impetus for the establishment of *South*. Black journalists in the western Cape had to contend with an alienating work environment, in that the newspapers for which they worked reflected the concerns of the ruling white minority and their media strategies were seen to be supportive of the status quo.[77] The initiative for establishing *South* came from two such media activists— Rashid Seria, who became the first editor of *South*, and Moegsien Williams, who succeeded him in November 1988.[78] Seria, who had been mulling over the idea of establishing a left-wing commercial newspaper since the late 1970s, conducted a feasibility study with the help of Williams toward the end of 1985, after his release from an eighty-day spell in detention.[79] They used the results of this study to consult with key political leaders and progressive journalists about the possibility of starting a mass-circulation weekly. Encouraged by positive responses to their proposal as well as the success of the recently launched *New Nation* and *Weekly Mail*, Seria enlisted the aid of Allan Boesak to secure funding to the value of R450,000 (US$150,000–225,000) for the project from the Interchurch Organization for Development

Co-operation (ICCO), a nongovernmental organization sponsored by Dutch Protestant churches.[80] The appearance of the first issue of *South* on 19 March 1987 is a milestone in the history of dissenting journalism in the western Cape.

The main objective of *South*, in the words of its founders, was "to articulate the needs and aspirations of the oppressed and exploited in the Cape and in so doing serve the interests of the working class people."[81] There was thus no question of *South* identifying itself as a Coloured newspaper or following a narrowly racial agenda. Its more immediate political aims were to provide the extraparliamentary protest movement, particularly the United Democratic Front, with a voice and to keep the public informed of news and information the apartheid government wanted to suppress. Furthermore, it sought to challenge the monopolistic control of the media by the government and a few large corporations.[82] The newspaper thus concentrated on news relating broadly to extraparliamentary politics and the injustices of apartheid in the western Cape. It seldom reported news from outside of the western Cape, and it carried virtually no international coverage. The paper did not attempt to provide conventional news coverage, except for some social, community, and sports news. Yet despite its noble intention of serving the working class, *South* was largely bought by the politicized sector of the Coloured middle class as well as by Left and liberal white sympathizers who wanted to keep abreast of struggle news in the western Cape.

South fiercely proclaimed itself to be "the independent voice of the people of the Cape" and asserted that it was "free from vested interests and financial manipulation from any quarter."[83] It also asserted a nonsectarian political stance, claiming that "we will not be dictated to by any political party or organization."[84] Despite these pronouncements, however, *South* was, in effect, the mouthpiece of the United Democratic Front in the western Cape and thus firmly within the camp of the ANC. This should come as no surprise, as the newspaper was founded by UDF activists and its political philosophy was informed by the values of the Freedom Charter. Williams made it clear that he was under no illusions that "the raison d'etre of *South* was to promote the ANC in the western Cape."[85] *South* was, however, less partisan than one might have expected, because the staff saw its role as fostering unity within the broader antiapartheid movement and avoided a formal relationship with the UDF. Editors also jealously guarded the paper's editorial autumy.[86]

From its fifth issue onward, *South* adopted the motto "You have the right to know" to signal its intention of challenging curbs on press freedom by reporting antiapartheid news that the mainstream newspapers did not dare publish.[87] Printing news that the National Party government was intent on suppressing called for courage and a caliber of brinkmanship that would continually test the limits of government tolerance for the propagation of dissident views. The editors at *South* walked a tightrope in deciding the limits to which they could push censorship laws without having the paper banned. Despite the paper's determination to break with the compliant reporting of institutionalized journalism, Seria readily admits that *South*, like other newspapers, exercised a degree of self-censorship.[88] The survival of the newspaper depended on a judicious evaluation of all political reporting, as the greatest threat it faced during the 1980s was proscription by the apartheid state.[89]

The government's main strategy in persecuting the alternative press was for Stoffel Botha,[90] the minister of home affairs and communication, to use his powers under the emergency regulations to attack these newspapers.[91] Several issues of *South* were banned in 1987, and in May 1988, the paper was served with an order banning its publication for three months. Williams estimates that as many as twenty-four court actions were brought against *South* by the state during the 1980s and that in early 1989, it simultaneously faced seven lawsuits under the emergency regulations. State harassment of this sort was extremely damaging to the newspaper, as it took up much of management's time, entailed costly litigation, and added greatly to the insecurity of the staff.[92] Ensnaring the paper in a web of legal regulations and wearing it down in a courtroom war of attrition seemed to be the conscious strategy of Stoffel Botha, a lawyer by training.[93] The paper was also under continuous surveillance from security police, and its journalists were regular targets for harassment and intimidation by shadowy operators within the state's security aparatus.[94]

Being severely undercapitalized, *South* operated on a shoestring budget, its resources stretched to the limit. Its premises were inadequate, its equipment was rudimentary, and the entire project was chronically short-staffed. High expectations among an intensely politicized staff regarding progressive employment practices and the quality of the newspaper they wanted to produce, on the one hand, and the pressures of getting the paper out on time every week as well as financial stringency, on the other, made for an extremely volatile working environment, especially during the first two years of its existence. There was often a great deal of tension between colleagues, and long, acrimonious meetings were regularly held to thrash out differences.[95] Despite these tensions and stresses, one of the paper's great strengths was its ability to draw on a team of people who were committed to the antiapartheid struggle and who were prepared to make sacrifices for the paper. Intent on implementing the egalitarian values that informed the antiapartheid struggle, management ran *South* along scrupulously nonracial and democratic lines, eliminating as far as possible the usual hierarchies of the workplace. There was a deliberate attempt on the part of all involved to banish any recognition of race. One concession to racial thinking, however, was the preference given to the training and employment of promising African journalists.[96]

With justification, *South* criticized the weak-kneed reporting of the mainstream press as tantamount to praising the emperor's new clothes.[97] Yet the paper was itself guilty of praising the naked emperor's garb in its treatment of Coloured identity. *South* adopted the left-wing orthodoxy of the 1980s of not only rejecting Coloured identity but also treating it as if it did not really exist except as a fiction created by white supremacists to divide and rule the black majority. In reaction to the overt racism of the apartheid order, the democratic movement in the western Cape embraced an ever more dogmatic nonracism and refused to recognize the reality of racial identities and ethnic exclusivisms in South African society. In terms of these values, any recognition of Coloured identity was condemned as reactionary and racist. Investing the concept of Colouredness with the conspiratorial intent of the divide-and-rule tactics of white supremacism and refusing to acknowledge its existence became a common political and polemical counter to apartheid ideology in left-wing circles in the 1980s. From its inception, this had been the stance of *Grassroots*, one of the pioneers of Coloured rejectionism as a popular movement.

Given *Grassroots*'s meticulously nonracial line, only a handful of references to race appeared in the entire run of the paper. It instead simply made reference to people, residents, communities, workers, trade unionists, students, and so forth. The paper's staffers shut their eyes to the racial divisions in South African society, even refusing to use terms such as *white* or *black* and glossing over distinctions between Coloured and African people.[98] Rather, they focused on the opposition between "bosses" and "workers" or wrote of "oppressors" and "oppressed," both sets of terms in effect functioning as substitutes for black and white. As was fashionable among left-wing activists at the time, *Grassroots* often referred to "the People" or "the Community" as if they represented a readily identifiable and homogeneous group. Where greater specificity was needed, individuals were usually identified in terms of their place of residence and communities in terms of geographic location. Because of the highly segregated nature of South African society, this served as a proxy for racial identification, allowing readers to work out from these and other clues the racial identities of particular people. Thus, reports about the "community of Schotsche Kloof" or "Lotus River" were obviously about Coloured people; similarly, references to the "residents of Mbekweni" or the squatter camps of "KTC, Nyanga Bush, Modderdam and Crossroads" pertained to African people. In the few instances in which *Grassroots* resorted to racial terminology, it was necessitated by the need to make sense of one or another apartheid-induced situation.[99] Thus, there was little option but to use racial terms in an article condemning the government for raising the salaries of Coloured but not African nurses and another providing advice on how to negotiate the apartheid bureaucracy to obtain state pensions. In both instances, the paper resorted to the use of quotation marks to indicate its aversion to racial terminology.[100]

At no point did *Grassroots* confront issues of race or Coloured identity, even at the level of explaining how race was used to divide and rule black people or the workers of South Africa. Its viewpoint, summed up in a letter to the editor stating that "the people only know about the Human race, not about 'Coloureds, Indians, Whites and Blacks,'"[101] was taken for granted, and there appears to have been an assumption that by cultivating a working-class consciousness, racial identities would melt away. The closest the paper came to tackling these issues was in a cartoon strip published in the latter part of 1984 and early 1985 that depicted the ideal the paper wanted to help bring to fruition. In the opening sequence, Mrs. Williams, a factory worker from Manenberg, welcomes the Tricameral Parliament on the grounds that "we coloureds are getting the vote at last."[102] It is not long, however, before a UDF activist canvassing the neighborhood convinces her that to vote for tricameralism would be to vote for "more suffering, more hardships, more oppression for our people."[103] Later, she buys a copy of *Grassroots* and learns about the Freedom Charter and how the capitalist system exploits workers. Interaction with her fellow workers, including an African man who holds a menial job but is highly knowledgeable about the freedom struggle, as well as a series of unpleasant encounters with her rude and exploitative employer reinforce her awareness of her status as a worker. Her nascent working-class consciousness causes Mrs. Williams to respond to a scolding from her boss with the thought, "One day, Mr. Measly, we'll make the laws. One day, we'll control the factories and your days of rudeness and bossing will be over."[104]

This fantasy was, of course, nowhere close to the social reality of a South Africa rent by racial tension and ethnic exclusivism, of which the antipathy between Coloureds and Africans was not the least significant. *Grassroots* itself was, with some justification, viewed as a Coloured paper in the African townships. Not only did Coloured activists continue to predominate in the running of the publication but there was a clear Coloured bias in its reporting. Despite initiatives to make the paper more representative, such as printing more news from African townships, hiring African organizers, and publishing a few articles in Xhosa, *Grassroots* was never able to shake off its image as a Coloured paper. Van Kessel points to the irony that in the late 1980s, when the paper was run by an introverted group of militants and had lost touch with its constituency, it came to be seen as an African paper by many Coloured people who were unable to identify with its radicalism.[105] An even more delicious irony that testifies to the pervasiveness of racial identities and the hegemony of racist values was that *Grassroots* occasionally carried advertisements for hair straightener and skin-lightening treatments.[106]

Like *Grassroots*, *South* adopted a nonracial stance and avoided references to racial and ethnic identities whenever feasible. Having to meet a much more demanding production schedule and having to report hard news, *South* was significantly more flexible in its attitude to race, making many more direct and indirect references to it. The paper nevertheless remained true to a core objective of promoting the establishment of "a non-racial democracy in a unitary South Africa."[107] *South* thus studiously avoided using the word *Coloured* throughout the 1980s. References to Coloured people were usually either subsumed under the generic term *black* or included in some wider categorization such as "the people," "the community," or "the oppressed." Racial identities were, however, usually obvious from the context of the discussion. When the word *Coloured* was used, it was typically employed to highlight the unjust and arbitrary racial distinctions imposed by apartheid laws or to expose the racist thinking of the dominant white minority. The word was usually placed in quotation marks or prefaced with *so-called* to signify its superficiality and to distance the paper from the values implicit in its use. Sensitivity to the label "Coloured" within the democratic movement in the western Cape was further demonstrated by *South*'s practice of *not* placing other racial labels, such as "white," "Indian," and "African," in quotation marks.[108]

The only time *South* addressed the issue of Coloured identity in the 1980s—and then only obliquely—was in an article entitled "Quisling or Realist?" based on an interview with Richard van der Ross when the freedom of Cape Town was about to be conferred on him. Van der Ross, who represented moderate, middle-class political opinion within the Coloured community, made it clear that he embraced Coloured identity fully but did not support any form of segregation or differential treatment, such as wanting "a university of coloured people for coloured people." In a barb directed at the politically correct Left, he asserted: "I have no hangups about being called coloured. Don't put the word coloured in inverted commas. As for those who speak of so-called coloured people, I've never understood what that means."[109]

Despite its avowed objective of promoting nonracism, *South* nevertheless consciously targeted the Coloured working class. This contradiction did not escape those associated with the paper. The matter was thoroughly debated, and despite some misgivings, the paper retained an underlying racial focus. The targeting of a Coloured readership was justified on several counts. First, it made business sense because this was a market segment in which the founders of *South* had extensive experience and one that did not have a dedicated newspaper after the demise of the *Cape Herald* in 1986.[110] Indeed, Derek Carelse, art director at *South* between 1987 and 1988, claimed that the paper deliberately copied the look of the *Cape Herald*.[111] Second, writing for a working-class African readership posed insurmountable problems of language, skills, and resources. Also, *South* did not wish to go into competition with *New Nation* and *City Press*, which were being distributed in Cape Town. Importantly, there was a recognition that the Coloured working classes tended to be racially exclusive and politically reactionary. The editors of *South* thus adopted the spreading of the message of nonracism to the Coloured working classes as part of their mission. With this went the hope that *South* would help to secure political support for the UDF and later the ANC within this constituency.[112]

Seria and Williams were greatly encouraged in this regard by the perception that deep-rooted exclusivist tendencies within the Coloured community were at long last breaking down in the 1980s. Widespread social unrest in both urban and rural areas of the western Cape from the mid-1980s onward convinced them that the Coloured community was shedding its insularity and was prepared to make common cause with Africans against apartheid. Williams saw "the community pushing out people" such as Ashley Kriel, Ashley Forbes, and other youths from Coloured townships, who joined Umkhonto we Sizwe as conclusive evidence of a sea change within the Coloured community.[113] Thus, although some saw the antiracist position of denying the existence of Coloured identity as little more than a knee-jerk reaction to apartheid, to *South* editors, promoting this fiction was a pragmatic strategy necessary to the building of a nonracial society.[114] The contradiction between maintaining a nonracial facade and targeting a Coloured readership was reflected in ambiguities over Coloured identity in the content of the paper. Most notably, although its political reporting was nonracial, *South*'s reporting on sports, social, religious, and human interest stories focused almost exclusively on the Coloured community.[115] This was emphasized by the disproportionate attention paid to Mitchell's Plain, a sprawling, almost exclusively working-class set of Coloured housing estates of over 400,000 people.

There was much optimism at the time that *South* was indeed helping to foster a nonracial ethos in the western Cape. Williams's favorite metaphor then was to liken *South* to the footbridge spanning the railway line separating the Coloured housing estate of Manenberg from the African township of Nyanga. In the light of the subsequent resurgence of Coloured exclusivity and growing tensions between Coloureds and Africans, Williams admits to having been naive in thinking that ingrained racial antipathies could so easily be overcome. He feels that it would have been much more productive to have faced up to the ugly reality of racism within the Coloured community than to have swept it under the carpet as *South*—and the democratic movement as a whole—had done in the 1980s.[116]

On 2 February 1990, F. W. de Klerk's epochal opening address to parliament launched South Africa on a four-year transition to democratic rule. The state of emergency was lifted, outlawed political organizations were unbanned, political prisoners were freed, and a wide range of political parties and organizations entered into negotiations to chart the transition to representative government. Despite continuing social unrest and political turmoil, it was clear that circumstances had changed fundamentally. The management of *South* realized that if the newspaper was to survive, it would have to change with the times and reposition itself in the media market. *South* needed to change from being an organ of struggle, dependent on donor money and justifying its existence on moral and political grounds, to a commercially viable concern. As the prospects for democracy improved, it became obvious that *South* could no longer be driven mainly by an antiapartheid agenda, nor could it for long escape the realities of the marketplace. It was also evident that political change would make donor money increasingly difficult to procure, as funding shifted from financing political activism to redressing the legacy of apartheid.[117]

From its inception, *South* had been unable to sustain a circulation that would make it commercially viable. Its management finally conceded that there was no real market for a left-wing political newspaper in the western Cape and decided to transform it into a publication with popular appeal. *South* thus embarked on a series of changes designed to make it commercially viable, culminating in the launching of a revamped newspaper on 27 February 1992 under the slogan "News for New Times" to signal its fresh outlook.[118] *South* now tried to marry serious political reporting with racier sex and crime stories in an attempt both to satisfy its traditional readership and to appeal to Coloured working-class readers. Stories on drug abuse in schools, gang warfare, the lifestyles of gang leaders, family murders, child rape, sexual harassment in the workplace, and breast implants now jostled for space with the usual fare about worker militancy, apartheid exploitation, and popular protest. The relaunch, however, was not a great success. These changes did little to improve the commercial viability of the newspaper, and the financial position of *South* became ever more precarious.[119] The new format lost *South* many of its traditional readers but failed to attract significant working-class customers. Ongoing problems of inferior-quality production, poor marketing and distribution, and potential advertisers' perceptions that *South* was "too radical" continued to plague the paper.[120]

Political changes of the early 1990s also affected *South* adversely. As the incidence of local unrest died down and public attention shifted to the drama of negotiation for a national political settlement, the newspaper started losing much of its relevance to its traditional readership. Interest shifted from the western Cape to the violence on the Witwatersrand and in Natal. *South*'s regional focus was a liability at a time when the key questions of the day related to national issues such as whether a third force was operating to destabilize the society and whether the political center would be able to hold against extremists of both the Right and the Left in the quest for a political compromise. Newspapers such as the *Weekly Mail* and the *Sunday Times* became more attractive weekend reading for *South*'s primary constituency. Also, as the emergency regulations were lifted and the more tolerant atmosphere of de Klerk's presidency took hold, the establishment press started encroaching on the terrain of the alternative newspapers, rendering the political reporting of papers such as *South* less distinctive.[121] As early as July 1991, Gabu Tugwana, the editor of *New Nation*, complained that "the mainstream newspapers have moved more like opportunists . . . our market has been sort of eaten."[122]

Very importantly, with the lifting of media curbs and with liberation organizations able to operate freely, *South*'s role as the voice of the democratic movement was greatly diminished. Its intimate relationship with the western Cape UDF was broken when the unbanning of the ANC changed the nature of extraparliamentary opposition politics virtually overnight. Hopes in early 1990 that *South* would somehow "ride the wave of the ANC" did not materialize.[123] On the contrary, the relationship between *South* and the democratic movement, according to Rehana Rossouw, a media activist and *South* reporter, soured rapidly once free political activity was allowed, and *South* started asking awkward questions about inefficiencies and possible corruption within its ranks. The rapidity with which *South* became sidelined is demonstrated by the ANC "forgetting" to invite representatives from the paper to its press conference the day before the Groote Schuur talks of 1 May 1990. The reality was that *South*, with its limited reach, had become expendable to the democratic movement that now pursued national and even international agendas.

As the political climate changed in the early 1990s and it became more acceptable to use racial terms and ethnic labels in public discourse, there was a noticeable shift in *South*'s reporting. From mid-1991, it started shedding the politically correct pretense that racial identity did not exist and began confronting issues of Coloured exclusivism, particularly racism toward Africans. The practice of putting the word *Coloured* in quotation marks was dropped, and racial identities and labels were much more commonly used in its reporting. The initial hesitancy in resorting to the use of racial terminology within the mass democratic movement as a whole during the early 1990s was reflected in the opening lines of a letter to the editor analyzing the poor reception of the ANC within the Coloured community, even among those who had been enthusiastic supporters of the UDF: "I apologize for the frequent use of certain terminology in this letter. However, to clear certain matters, this is unavoidable."[124] By September of that year, *South* had become sufficiently adventurous to refer to the earliest Coloured recruits to the National Party as "Hotnats"—a play on the racial slur *Hotnot*.[125] The paper avoided gratuitous use of racial and ethnic labels, though, and remained true to its objective of fostering a nonracial democratic ethos in the society.

Already in June 1991, *South* noted the unseemly haste with which "so many coloured people are prepared to forgive the Nats their trespasses."[126] Issues of Coloureds' racial exclusivity, their antipathy toward Africans and the ANC, and their preference for associating with whites, including those parties and leaders who had been directly responsible for their oppression, were particularly topical in the run-up to the 1994 elections and the postmortem on the failure of the ANC to win the Western Cape provincial election.[127] The reality of racial tensions in the region was brought home forcefully to the paper when *South* staffers themselves fell victim to African hostility toward Coloured people. In August 1993, angry protesters from the Pan Africanist Student Organization turned on *South* journalists covering a march to demand the release of suspects arrested for the St. James Church massacre. When photographer Yunus Mohamed was felled by a brick that hit him in the groin, a protester was heard to shout, "One settler down!" and reporter Ayesha Ismael was sworn at and taunted with being a "coloured settler."[128]

Although *South* steadfastly maintained a nonracist stance throughout its existence, it could not avoid being seen by many as a Coloured newspaper. A double irony is that even though it claimed to be nonracial and to address the working class as a whole, *South* not only was perceived to be a Coloured newspaper by this same working class but also actively targeted the Coloured component of the working class. *South* made no real attempt to reach the African working class and was virtually unknown to African readers, except for a circumscribed circle of activists and intellectuals. The assertion by a *South* editorial that "we don't fit the ethnic stereotypes. We're not a coloured newspaper—nor white nor black nor anything else"[129] confirmed the editors' sensitivity in this regard. It is no coincidence that this denial came precisely at a time when *South* was focusing even more narrowly on the Coloured community as a result of a restructuring to make the paper commercially viable.

Because of continuing losses, financial mismanagement, and the failure of a number of urgent measures to stave off closure, *South* went into liquidation at the end of 1994.[130] Its demise was essentially due to a combination of being in no position to compete directly with the establishment press and being unable to find a niche large enough to sustain the paper. However, although it was a commercial failure, *South* could lay claim to considerable journalistic and political successes.[131] Both *South* and *Grassroots* were very much products of the antiapartheid struggle, and it is not entirely surprising that they did not survive the apartheid era.

Moegsien Williams refers to *South* as having been "schizophrenic."[132] Indeed, the paper was engaged in a continuous juggling act to balance the demands of the marketplace with those of the political arena, of trying to square the reality of its middle-class readership with the unrequited desire to attract working-class patronage, and of attempting to reconcile a studied nonracism with its targeting of a Coloured readership. *South* management greatly underestimated the degree to which working-class Coloured people actively disagreed with the radical politics of the UDF and of *South* itself. As one of its columnists, Sylvia Vollenhoven, put it, "The politics of a relatively calm Mitchell's Plain is not the politics of a burning Spine Road."[133] Although the Coloured working classes were aggrieved at being victims of apartheid, they did not necessarily subscribe to the radical politics of the UDF, nor did they embrace the democratic movement's nonracial egalitarianism. This much is evident from the majority of working-class Coloured voters heeding the National Party's racist appeal and flocking to its banner in the April 1994 elections.

This chapter has demonstrated that although Coloured rejectionism had grown into a significant movement by the time it climaxed at the end of the 1980s, it was never a broadly based, popular current taken up by the mass of the Coloured people. Rather, it was generally confined to a highly vocal and politicized minority active within the antiapartheid movement. Furthermore, although Coloured rejectionism sprang from such worthy motives as wanting to banish racist thinking, expose racial myths, and foster unity in the face of the divisions imposed by apartheid, it was generally not a credo held with deep conviction, in the sense that most of its proponents actually believed that Coloured identity did not exist or have any social relevance, even though this may have been proclaimed with gusto from political platforms or forcibly asserted in countless heated arguments over race, identity, and strategies for ending apartheid.[134] To most of those who renounced their identity as Coloured, this renunciation was, in the first place, a refusal to countenance apartheid thinking, and to many others, it was also a recognition that such a renunciation was a necessary step in the creation of a truly nonracial society. Contemplating the charade of nonracism and Coloured rejectionism in the democratic movement during the 1980s, Vollenhoven commented, "I heard so much talk of nonracialism and saw so little evidence. . . . Through it all there has always been a part of me that felt like the child in the crowd who saw no new clothes, only a fat, foolish, naked emperor."[135]

6

New Responses to Old Dilemmas

Coloured Identity in a Transforming South Africa

The overarching argument of the book has been that Coloured identity remained remarkably stable and experienced relatively little fundamental change in the way it operated throughout the era of white domination. The postapartheid period has, however, witnessed significant and swift changes in the ways Coloured identity manifests itself. The first part of this chapter analyzes a relatively short-lived perspective on Coloured identity and the community's history that gained currency among "progressive," especially ANC-supporting, elements within the Coloured community during the dying days of the apartheid order. The second part seeks to explain why Coloured identity is experiencing rapid change and an unusual degree of creativity in the ways it is finding expression in the postapartheid environment.

Resistance, Protest, and Accommodation: A Progressive Perspective at Apartheid's End

This section will use Hein Willemse's 1993 article on Straatpraatjes,[1] a newspaper column that appeared in the *APO* from its inception in 1909, as a case study. This scholarly article, written toward the end of white rule, analyzed a text that was not only produced during the formation of the South African state but also commented extensively on the process. The broader outlook represented by Willemse in this piece, usually characterized by an underlying tone of triumphalism in anticipation of a decisive victory over white supremacism, exaggerated Coloured people's resistance to white supremacy as well as their association with the African majority by stressing their identity as black. Though rejectionist in spirit, this view grudgingly acknowledged the salience of Coloured identity, since outright denial was no longer tenable by the early 1990s.[2] In this case study, I will contest Willemse's interpretation of Straatpraatjes as one of the earliest examples of a tradition of resistance to white domination and self-assertion among black Afrikaans-speakers.[3] I will argue that it is misleading to characterize Straatpraatjes as the product of black Afrikaans-speakers or to suggest that it was aimed at a black readership. On the contrary, the column confirmed the existence of profound ambiguities in Coloured identity and cannot simply be construed as an expression of black or even Coloured resistance to white domination.[4]

Straatpraatjes was a satirical column that appeared in the Dutch-Afrikaans section of the *APO* newspaper between May 1909 and February 1922. It was written in a variety of Cape Vernacular Afrikaans that was spoken in particular by the Coloured working classes residing in the inner-city areas of Cape Town.[5] It was narrated by Piet Uithalder, a fictitious character, and told of the social experiences and the political encounters of Piet and his friend, Stoffel Francis. Piet and Stoffel were former shepherds from the Kat River Settlement who had managed to acquire some education and had become politicized as a result. They had migrated to Cape Town, where they joined the APO and Uithalder attached himself to the organization's head office staff as a voluntary worker. Piet, who was portrayed as socially unsophisticated and somewhat naive, could speak only Afrikaans. He relied on Stoffel, who had a rudimentary grasp of the English language and some knowledge of middle-class social etiquette, to act as his guide and interpreter.[6] Using this vernacular with wit and ingenuity, Uithalder brought some humor to a newspaper otherwise given to high seriousness.

Among other things, Piet related his experiences at dinner parties, picnics along Cape Town's Atlantic seaboard, and a wide variety of APO functions. He also gave his impression of public events, such as the celebration of the king's birthday, election meetings, and the Stellenbosch Agricultural Show. Uithalder often inveighed against white racism and took particular delight in ridiculing uncouth whites, especially *boere* (Afrikaners) from the backveld. In addition, he chided Coloured people for being too color-conscious and poked fun at the social pretensions of the Coloured petite bourgeoisie. Straatpraatjes, at one time or another, also delivered commentary on all of the key political issues confronting the Coloured community during that period. Lampooning rival Coloured political organizations was one of Uithalder's main preoccupations. He was relentless in his ridicule of their leaders and his parodying of their meetings. Piet and Stoffel, moreover, regularly visited parliament and satirized the racist attitudes of parliamentarians and the passage of segregationist legislation.[7]

Straatpraatjes was one of the most effective weapons in the APO's journalistic arsenal. The combination of Uithalder's razor-sharp wit and the novelty of writing in colloquial language gave the column a popularity and political punch not matched by the rest of the paper. From the time it appeared in the *APO*'s first issue, Straatpraatjes was an integral part of the newspaper's agenda of furthering the aims of the APO and articulating the interests of the Coloured community. Piet clearly saw himself as a spokesman for the Coloured community as a whole and did not shy away from sensitive or controversial issues. If anything, Straatpraatjes had the virtue of allowing Uithalder to say in jest what the *APO* did not feel comfortable articulating in its normal reporting.[8] Although the newspaper never revealed the identities of the authors of Straatpraatjes, the evidence suggests Abdullah Abdurahman wrote nearly all of the columns.[9]

The name Uithalder had meanings that resonated with the readership of the column at several levels. Most simply, *uithalder* meant "clever" or "smart," and Piet Uithalder, being the equivalent of Smart Alec, was an eminently suitable pseudonym for the author of a column of this nature. But as Hein Willemse points out, the term can also mean "excellent" or "the best" and could thus be construed as a conscious challenge to the stereotyping of Coloured people as intellectually limited and socially inferior.[10] Most significantly, however, the name held strong connotations of black resistance to white domination for politicized Coloured people during the early twentieth century. Willem Uithalder was a prominent leader of the Kat River Rebellion of 1851, and Piet was presumably a descendant of the rebel leader.[11]

The Kat River Settlement had a special place in the hearts and minds of the Coloured petite bourgeoisie of the early twentieth century because they saw the land grant of 1828 on which the settlement was founded as emblematic of Britain's recognition of their loyalty to the empire and their claim to full citizenship rights. Its symbolic importance was evident from the way Uithalder equated Kat River with equal rights when describing his first encounter with W. P. Schreiner, the former prime minister of the Cape Colony and the most noted liberal politician of his day: "After Stoffel introduced me the discussion really got going. Mr. Schreiner told me about the Kat River equal rights. Slavery, excise, rebellion, Botha and so forth." The loss of this land, however, was attributed to settler greed and racism of the sort with which they still had to contend. The Kat River Rebellion has faded from present-day popular memory, but at that time, it was recalled with pride within the Coloured elite. At one point, Piet thus warned racists that "Kat River Hottentots . . . know how to remove a boer from behind a rock."[12]

Although it is not clear how the idea of writing Straatpraatjes originated, it appears to have been partly prompted by the Parlementse Praatjes (Parliamentary Talk) column in *De Zuid Afrikaan*, the leading Dutch daily newspaper in Cape Town at the time.[13] Written in an urbane, lightly humorous vein, Parlementse Praatjes reported on the doings of parliament in language that is best described as an educated, white, middle-class version of Afrikaans, in contrast to the formal Dutch used in the rest of the newspaper. Thus, the *APO* established Straatpraatjes to voice Coloured interests in the language of the Coloured community in the same way that Parlementse Praatjes represented the white supremacist interests of the Afrikaner in the language of the Afrikaner. As the title of the column indicated, it was the intention of Uithalder to contrast his Afrikaans of the street and kitchen with that of white speakers of the language, which he associated with parliament and parlor. By writing in the language of the Coloured working classes, Piet consciously identified with the Coloured people and used the vernacular to appeal to their identity as Coloured. Resorting to this highly expressive vernacular heightened the comic effect of Uithalder's satire, and hitting out at their opponents in a code recognizably their own clearly added to readers' pleasure. Despite their Anglophilia, the APO leaders nevertheless recognized that this stigmatized vernacular had deep emotional appeal to their constituency.

Straatpraatjes, unlike other examples of this patois in early Afrikaans literature, was as authentic a replication of the Afrikaans vernacular spoken within the urban Coloured community of the western Cape as one could hope to find in print. The authors of the column were clearly native-speakers of the dialect, and because there were no formal spelling and grammatical rules to follow, they wrote the language as they themselves spoke it. In addition, the monologic format of the column meant that Piet Uithalder addressed the readers directly, as if he were speaking to them. In nearly all instances where this patois occurred in early Afrikaans literature, it was used by white authors to caricature blacks, their language being distorted for comic effect and reinforcing negative racial stereotypes.[14] In Straatpraatjes, however, Piet addressed his readers in the distinctive code of his community in order to demonstrate that he was one of them. He wanted to create an emotional bond and gain their confidence. It was therefore important that Uithalder's language come across as genuine. The popularity of Straatpraatjes and the enthusiastic response from readers clearly testified to its success in this regard. Thus, in Straatpraatjes, Coloured people were invested with a dignity and the language they spoke was accorded a propriety not found elsewhere in early Afrikaans writing.

Although both the authors and the majority of the column's readers were members of the Coloured elite, it is clear that they were intimately familiar with the social practices and the language of the Coloured laboring poor, for, as indicated earlier, there was no great social distance between the Coloured petite bourgeoisie and the Coloured working classes. People such as Uithalder, who aspired to middle-class status, and other Straatpraatjes characters, including Mrs. Janewari and Mrs. Shepherd, who were described as being *pertikelaar* (particular),[15] continued to socialize with working-class friends and relatives and were fluent in Cape Vernacular Afrikaans. Nonetheless, this elite's preference for English and the connotations of social inferiority they attached to Afrikaans were clearly evident in Straatpraatjes. Uithalder's humble origins were, for example, signaled by the variant of Afrikaans he spoke, whereas Stoffel's social aspirations were evident from his determination to speak English even though he was hardly proficient in the language. Similarly, on numerous occasions, Uithalder caused *rouwe boere* (raw boers) to betray their lack of refinement through their broken English or by conversing in *kombuis Hollans* (kitchen Dutch).[16] The identification with English culture was also reflected in the anglicized personal names adopted by characters in Straatpraatjes. Thus, the Gedults preferred the surname Patience, Miss November tried to disguise her Afrikaans background by calling herself Miss Wember, and Mrs. Margaret Shepherd would have been mortified to be called *"ta Grietjie Skawagter,"* as she was

known back in Kat River. Uithalder himself preferred the name Out-
holder when in refined company.[17]

Straatpraatjes was a very successful column and remained one of
the *APO*'s most popular features. Piet Uithalder's perceptive observations and his penchant for broaching sensitive issues in a forthright
manner provided unique insights into the social identity and political
attitudes within the Coloured community during the early years of
Union. Published at a time when the direct testimony of Coloured
people was relatively sparse, Straatpraatjes added nuance and texture
not found elsewhere in the historical record. What is more, Uithalder
was a pioneer of satirical writing in Afrikaans, employing satirical
techniques thought to have been introduced into the language in the
mid-1920s by C. J. Langenhoven, a leading Afrikaner literary figure.[18]
Indeed, Straatpraatjes was so successful that it spawned an English
equivalent, The Office Boy's Reflections, authored by Johnny, the
APO's "office boy." The *S.A. Clarion*, the mouthpiece of the rival United
Afrikaner League and its National Party sponsors and so often at the
receiving end of Piet Uithalder's invective, paid Straatpraatjes the ultimate compliment by copying the idea and publishing its own Straatpraatjes column.[19]

In a September 1993 article published in *Stilet*, the journal of the
Afrikaans Literature Association, Hein Willemse, who would be regarded as Coloured in the context of the South African racial system,
explored the weltanschauung of Piet Uithalder's Straatpraatjes column, focusing in particular on the implications his discourse held for
the racial stereotyping of black Afrikaans-speakers.[20] In this article,
Willemse, at the time a lecturer in the Afrikaans Department of the
University of the Western Cape, presented Uithalder's writings as an
unequivocal challenge to white cultural hegemony and the perception
of black people as inferior, especially within the Afrikaans-speaking
sector of the ruling minority. He also argued that Uithalder's discourse represented a form of intellectual resistance to colonial domination that laid the basis for later, more effective means of resisting
white supremacism.

Willemse prefaced his analysis of the column by explaining that
Afrikaans language and literature are, on the whole, elite, white-
centered cultural constructions produced by generations of Afrikaner
culture brokers. Voices raised in opposition to these ruling perceptions, he argued, were either absent as a result of illiteracy and social
domination or, when they arose, were effectively silenced by being

marginalized or ignored. To restore Afrikaans to its rightful status as a multivocal medium, it was necessary to resurrect these silenced voices. Piet Uithalder, Willemse asserted, represented one such voice, with his choice of a Coloured working-class variant of Afrikaans being a conscious act of resistance to white domination. Straatpraatjes therefore provided a rare opportunity to explore an early counter-hegemonic voice from within the community of black Afrikaans-speakers. Willemse contended that Uithalder's column challenged fundamental assumptions underpinning the colonial order and white supremacist ideology in South Africa. He focused on four aspects of Uithalder's discourse, namely, the significance he attached to education, his deprecation of the consumption of alcohol among Coloured people, the status he assumed as traveler and independent observer, and his attitude toward whites. All four, Willemse maintained, defined the relationship between oppressed and oppressor in significant ways and were effectively used by Uithalder to undermine colonial categorizations.[21]

First, Willemse pointed out that Uithalder often railed against discrimination in the education system because it impeded Coloured people's access to skilled employment and social advancement. Besides educational attainment in itself being a status symbol, Uithalder recognized that education was a fundamental source of power because literacy and the access it provided to advanced technologies underpinned colonial domination. Second, Willemse held that Uithalder's antiliquor campaign was largely motivated by his perception that alcoholic abuse among Coloured people was symbolic of their subjection. Not only did whites induce alcoholic addiction through the tot system of paying labourers part of their wages in daily rations of cheap wine to ensure a docile labor force, they also used liquor to manipulate Coloured voters. Third, Willemse claimed that through his incisive observations and independent reportage during his travels in South Africa and England, Uithalder broke the stereotype of blacks as intellectually inferior to whites, fit only for subservient roles. By presenting Uithalder as an autonomous, reflective individual, Straatpraatjes challenged the deeply entrenched assumption of Afrikaner paternalist ideology that it was the destiny of Coloured people to be subservient to the Afrikaner. Most significant of all, in Willemse's view, was Uithalder's attitude to whites in general. In addition to being highly critical of racially prejudiced whites, he demanded "equal rights" and portrayed *boere* and poor whites as socially inferior to middle-class blacks, which further subverted the stereotyping of black people as inferior, degenerate beings incapable of civilization. Willemse concluded by arguing that notwithstanding his identification with English culture, Uithalder's writings represented the beginnings of the intellectual liberation of black Afrikaans-speakers, his assimilationism being part of the creation of a worthy self-image.[22]

Willemse's interpretation of Straatpraatjes is open to challenge on a wide front. Given the racial exclusivity of the APO, there can be no doubt that Uithalder did not see himself as black but self-consciously identified himself as a Coloured person and wrote specifically for a Coloured readership. After all, the first thing Uithalder did was to introduce himself as *een van de ras* (a member of the race) to stress that he was Coloured.[23] He characterized himself as a *bruine mens* (brown person) and often voiced opinions about and on behalf of *onse bruin mense* (our brown people) and *onse ras* (our race).[24] Indeed, not only was he comfortable with his racially exclusive identity as Coloured, he also appeared to accept prevailing racial categories as natural. He thus, for example, freely used racial terms such as *boer, hotnot* (Hottentot), *half-naatje* (half-breed), and *slams* (Muslim) to describe people.[25] And although he clearly had sympathy for Africans as fellow sufferers under an unjust racial system, Uithalder had no compunction about using the pejorative *kaffer*[26]—or even *rouwe kaffer* (raw kaffir)[27]—when referring to Africans. Uithalder also, as a matter of course, drew distinctions between *kleurling* (Coloured) and *swartling* (African); *bruine en kaffer; bruine en swart* (black); and *kaffers* and *hotnots*.[28]

Willemse's description of Uithalder as a *swart rubriekskrywer* (black columnist) and as representative of black Afrikaans-speakers is thus misleading.[29] Uithalder certainly did not have a racially dichotomous view of South African society, and the distinctions he drew between white English-speakers, Afrikaners, Coloured people, and Africans were central to his political outlook and his understanding of South African society. What is more, at no point did Uithalder evince allegiance to a wider black identity, nor did he ever describe himself as black in this sense. It also needs to be noted that his assimilationism, though it may have aided in the making of a positive self-image, also functioned to associate Uihalder with the dominant society and thereby distance himself from Africans.

Thus, although Piet abhorred racial discrimination and castigated white supremacists, he was not able to rise fully above the racist ideology that so powerfully shaped the worldview of his society. The resultant ambiguities were abundantly evident in Straatpraatjes. Despite his frequent challenges to the ruling order with assertions of the sort that "we are all South Africans" and "colour does not give one a good character,"[30] Uithalder just as often displayed acceptance of the racial categorizations imposed by the dominant society. Given the dilemmas that came with Coloured marginality and trying to capitalize on their status of privilege relative to Africans, as argued earlier, the APO continually vacillated between protest and accommodation, on the one hand, and between assimilationism and Coloured separatism, on the other. Continually modulating its responses to white supremacism to strike a balance between these competing interests, the APO was inevitably inconsistent and ambivalent in its political outlook, and this was clearly reflected in Straatpraatjes.

Uithalder's choice of language also did not represent an uncomplicated act of defiance by a black Afrikaans-speaker intent on asserting the worth of his particular code of Afrikaans, as Willemse seemed to think. The use of colloquial Afrikaans in Straatpraatjes was fraught with tensions and ambiguities, not least because it was written by authors—and for a readership—that preferred English even though Afrikaans may have been their mother tongue. As demonstrated earlier, Afrikaans was associated with social inferiority, cultural backwardness, and Afrikaner racism in the minds of the Coloured elite, whereas English was revered as the language of culture, civilization, and progress. Rather than simply being an act of resistance, the decision to write in colloquial Afrikaans was, in part, also a grudging concession to the prevalence and deep emotional appeal of the language among its constituency by a modernizing elite that wanted to distance itself from "barbarous Cape Dutch." Thus, despite its appropriation of the Coloured working-class patois and despite providing true-to-life descriptions of their popular culture, Straatpraatjes largely embodied the values and aspirations of the Coloured elite.[31]

Published over a period of thirteen years—albeit with a break of six years between 1913 and 1919—the 102 surviving Straatpraatjes columns inevitably reflected the changing social and political context in which it operated. It also mirrored the changing fortunes of the APO, from the optimism and vigor that marked its protest campaign of 1909 and 1910 through the steady decline after Union and the revival of the organization in 1919, as outlined earlier. Willemse failed to recognize the critical changes in Uithalder's social and political outlook over that period. Instead, he presented a static and oversimplified picture of uncompromising resistance on the part of Uithalder.

Straatpraatjes came into being at a time of heightened concern among Coloured people about the erosion of their civil rights and the implementation of segregationist measures. The assimilationist overtures of the Coloured petite bourgeoisie had been firmly rejected by the dominant society, and the elite experienced a hardening of racial barriers in the years following the Anglo-Boer War. Avenues for social advancement, particularly in education and employment, were being closed, and their civil rights were under serious threat. Frustrated by the deterioration in their social status, the Coloured elite rallied behind the APO, which grew rapidly under the dynamic leadership of Abdurahman.[32] Riding the wave of Coloured anger and apprehension at the imposition of a racially exclusive political settlement on South Africa with the making of Union, the APO was at its most vigorous and Straatpraatjes at its most spirited during that period. The pressures of intensifying segregationism thus pervaded the Straatpraatjes column, and each new discriminatory measure drew ascerbic commentary from Uithalder, who displayed a remarkably creative impulse both in his use of the vernacular as well as in conjuring up images and scenes of great hilarity. This was also the time when Piet was at his most defiant and his satire at its most trenchant.

Not long after Union, though, a subtle change was observable, as Uithalder's satire started losing some of its bite. This was largely the result of a demoralized APO having changed its strategy and its political outlook in the aftermath of Union. Enervated by its inability to stem the tide of segregation, the APO slowly declined, falling into a state of dormancy by the beginning of 1914. This decline was reflected in Straatpraatjes, for although Uithalder managed to retain a tone of strident protest throughout, after 1912 he seldom wrote with the flair and humor that marked the earlier episodes. Also, the column appeared less regularly, and a hint of despondency crept into the writing. At one point, Uithalder lamented that "the good days are gone. All that one can do now is to sit and wait to hear what Hertzog or one of the greybelly farmers have to say. Sometimes I get so depressed I feel like taking a drink just to keep up my spirits."[33] In October 1913, the "Straapraatjes" column was discontinued for six years without any reason being offered to the readers.

The stresses and strains on the APO and its leadership in the post–World War I period, as detailed earlier, were clearly manifest in the revived Straatpraatjes column. By the time he took up the pen again in August 1919, Piet Uithalder had lost his sense of humor and assumed a hectoring tone. His creative impulse and resourcefulness with the vernacular had deserted him. The column became repetitious and perfunctory, and it appeared less regularly. During that period, Piet Uithalder was almost exclusively concerned with discrediting its main rival, the United Afrikaner League, which was allied to the Cape National Party.

A measure of the change in the APO's political outlook that had occurred in the meantime was demonstrated by Uithalder's retreat from the defiant challenge he issued to the white supremacist establishment in 1912: "We have for long enough crawled like animals to the white man. It is now time that we stood up straight . . . and no longer with hat in hand and on bended knee saying 'please master' and 'yes master.'" By 1922, this defiance had changed to frustrated resignation: "We are always tardy when we have to do something for ourselves. . . . When are we going to take an example out of the white man's book?"[34] Even more striking was the about-face in Uithalder's attitude toward the South African Party, which governed until its defeat in the 1924 elections. Whereas the likes of Jan Smuts and Louis Botha were given short shrift in earlier columns and were characterized as "greybellies" and "the enemy," Uithalder praised Smuts as "a smart man" and "a brave leader" in the revived column.[35] On Smuts's return to South Africa after the signing of the Treaty of Versailles, Uithalder even went so far as to welcome him home with a fawning "Yes Smuts . . . we missed you a lot."[36]

This volte-face on the part of Uithalder was very much a consequence of the dilemma faced by Coloured people in the party political arena due to their marginality. The APO had little option but to back the political party best served Coloured interests, especially at election time. In effect, this meant that the APO was forced to choose the lesser evil among various racist parties. The APO's predicament in this regard was abundantly clear in the very first episode of Straatpraatjes, when Uithalder gave vent to his disappointment at the Unionist Party's support of the draft South Africa Act. As the political home of Cape liberalism, the APO had depended on Unionists to defend Coloured civil rights. After 1920, when the Unionist Party disbanded and most of its members joined the South African Party, the APO found itself with little choice but to switch its allegiance to the party of Botha and Smuts, which it had formerly castigated as racist and unprogressive. The only alternatives were to support the even more racist National Party or Labour Party or to pursue a policy of boycott, which it regarded as utterly futile.

The oppositional element of Uithalder's writing cannot, therefore, be characterized as resistance—*verset*, in Willemse's parlance.[37] In this regard, a distinction needs to be drawn between the concepts of protest and resistance. At the very least, the concept of resistance, whether violent or passive, implies rejection of the ruling order and the desire to embrace a social and political system informed by alternative norms and values. Given their assimilationism and the degree to which they were prepared to come to an accommodation with the South African racial system, the APO's political strategy and, by extension, that of Straatpraatjes can hardly be described as resistance. The political strategy of the APO, of which the column was an integral part, conformed much more closely to the concept of protest, the essential features of which were outlined by Donald Crummey: "Protest assumes some common social and political order linking protesters and those to whom the protesters appeal. Protesters tend to direct their energy to the redressing of grievances arising from that order."[38] It is abundantly clear that Uithalder did not want to overthrow the system he was satirizing; he merely wanted to change it sufficiently for Coloured people to share fully in its benefits.

Although there was a dimension of defiance in the Straatpraatjes column, it is clear that Piet Uithalder's response to white domination was something more complex than resistance per se. As this examination of Straatpraatjes and of the *APO* newspaper earlier on has demonstrated, the response of Uithalder—as, indeed, of most politicized Coloured people of the time—was characterized by a profound ambiguity in its racial perceptions, in its attitude toward the white ruling establishment, and in the political strategy it deployed. Though he opposed white supremacism and helped to undermine it in many ways, Uithalder had come to an accommodation with the South African racial order in other ways, and he attempted both to work within the system and to work the system for the benefit of Coloured people. Uithalder's growing conservatism and his chastisement of Coloured people for not taking "an example out of the white man's book" in the last column he wrote demonstrated that the impetus for assimilation and accommodation in his discourse came to overshadow his impulse to resist.

The argument presented by Willemse and the sentiment underpinning it typified opinion within the "progressive," largely ANC-supporting minority faction of the Coloured community that, at the close of the apartheid period, entertained exaggerated notions of Coloured resistance to white rule and their identification with Africans as comrades in oppression. The subtext of Willemse's argument was that this tradition of resistance—of which Straatpraatjes was held to be one of the earliest examples, if not the first, to be expressed in Afrikaans—was to grow from strength to strength through the twentieth century, culminating in an important contribution by Coloured people to the impending victory of the nonracial democratic movement over apartheid in the mid-1990s. Not only is it ahistoric to read such assumptions back into Coloured responses to white supremacism during the early decades of the twentieth century, but there is very little evidence to support such an interpretation. There is no identifiable tradition of resistance, intellectual or political, of this sort dating back to the early twentieth century. Such an outlook can first be observed in very tenuous form from the mid-1930s onwards with the emergence of the radical movement in Coloured politics and then more substantively from the late 1970s onward within the nonracial democratic movement. On the contrary, as the present analysis has shown, Straatpraatjes provides evidence of a tradition of ambiguity between the egalitarian values of nonracism and assimilationism, on the one hand, and racial exclusivity driven by a desire to protect a position of relative privilege, on the other.

The romanticized and transient perspective that informed Willemse's analysis was rudely shattered when the majority of Coloured people gave expression to their alienation from the new order by voting for the National Party in the April 1994 elections. Many Coloured people on the progressive Left whose wishful thinking had blinded them to the extent of Coloured racial chauvinism were shocked and shamed into more realistic appraisals of sentiment within the Coloured community generally. Despite preelection surveys indicating heavy defeat for the ANC in the Western Cape, the prominent activist who became premier of the Western Cape in 2004, Ebrahim Rasool, confirms that the response of left-wing activists was nevertheless one of disbelief: "We were shell-shocked . . . we somehow didn't believe that the [Coloured] community of the Western Cape would in the worst days be able to vote for the National Party."[39] Emille Jansen (aka Emille YX), cultural activist and leader of the Cape Town hip-hop group Black Noise, which actively supported the ANC, most notably by performing at preelection rallies, expressed his disappointment with the 1994 election results more candidly: "I couldn't fucken believe it, *my bra* [my brother], like yoh! . . . I was *kak* [shit] upset!"[40] Rasool correctly diagnosed the activists' misreading of the situation as largely stemming from their conflation of the defeat of apartheid with a change in mind-set within the Coloured community as well as from an assumption that popular support for the UDF was evidence of growing nonracism among Coloureds and would automatically translate into approval of the ANC.[41]

"Not Black Enough": Coloured Identity in Postapartheid South Africa

In contrast to its stability under white supremacy, expressions of Coloured identity have undergone rapid transformation in the post-apartheid environment. The period since 1994 has been a time of flux and of unprecedented change in the way Colouredness has operated and, indeed, has needed to operate as a social identity. The new democratic dispensation has brought with it a degree of freedom of association and possibilites for ethnic mobilization that were inconceivable under white domination. It has also undermined, even invalidated, some of the most basic assumptions and practices that were at the foundation of Coloured identity from the time it crystallized in the late nineteenth century. And with the racial hierarchy that had regulated social relations in white-ruled South Africa having broken down in important respects, intergroup relations have become more complex and expressions of social identity more fluid. This has, on the one hand, compounded the confusion and controversy that have dogged the identity in recent decades, but on the other hand, it has opened up opportunities for new ways of conceptualizing Colouredness and brought forth more varied and creative responses to questions about the nature of Coloured identity and its role in South African society. It is thus not surprising that the new political paradigm and ongoing, swift social transformation have stimulated innovative attempts at marshaling Coloured ethnic resources. This section seeks to explain why Coloured identity, given its prior history of relative stability, has experienced fast-paced and, in some respects, thoroughgoing change from the early 1990s. The new social and political dynamics informing these shifts will also be explored.

Despite the emergence of a vocal, Coloured rejectionist voice within the nonracial democratic movement of the 1980s, the subsequent period has witnessed a resurgence of Colouredism, with many people

who had rejected the identity reembracing it. Fear of African majority rule, perceptions that Coloureds were being marginalized, a desire
to counter pervasive negative stereotyping of Coloured people, and
attempts at capitalizing on the newly democratic environment in
pursuit of political agendas have all played a role in fueling Coloured
assertiveness in the new South Africa.[42] It has become commonplace
for Coloured people disaffected with the new South Africa to express
their disgruntlement by lamenting that "first we were not white
enough and now we are not black enough." This claim has very rapidly become clichéd because it reflects popular sentiment within the
greater part of the Coloured community and highlights key dilemmas
Coloured people face in coming to grips with the postapartheid environment. Besides accentuating their interstitial position within a
transforming South African racial hierarchy, the phrase very neatly captures Coloured people's perennial predicament of marginality. Though
the adage "the more things change, the more they stay the same"
rings true for many Coloured people regarding their position in the
new South Africa, few will deny that their lives have been profoundly
affected by changes since the transition to democracy. Though the responses of the majority are still informed by apartheid-style thinking,
elements within the Coloured community have nevertheless been
creative about the manner in which they express their social identity.

The most obvious reason why expressions of Coloured identity
have shifted rapidly in postapartheid South Africa is because change
was forced on the Coloured community with the sudden and drastic
alteration of the political environment after de Klerk's landmark
speech of 2 February 1990. A radical reordering of the political landscape during the transition to democracy compelled a reassessment of
allegiances and a realignment of priorities throughout South African
society. The swift pace of social and economic transformation has ensured a fluid milieu, conducive to the remolding of all social identities,
not least of all Coloured identity.

Importantly in the case of Coloured identity, political reform
brought with it a significant increase in the political clout of the Coloured people, which heightened the salience of the identity. For the
first time, democratic government gave the Coloured community voting power commensurate with its demographic profile. This influence
came into play well before 1994, in that soon after the unbanning of
the ANC, leaders and organizations across the political spectrum
started lobbying with increasing urgency for support within the Col-

oured community, in anticipation of the need to strengthen their hands in negotiations and in expectation of having to mobilize for forthcoming elections. Because Coloureds were concentrated in the western third of the country, where they formed a majority of the population, it was clear to all from the start of negotiations for a new dispensation that Coloured support was essential to political success in those areas that were later to become the provinces of the Western and Northern Cape.[43] Nelson Mandela's 1992 urging of the ANC to recognize "Coloured ethnicity" as a political reality was an important step in the public acknowledgment of the existence of Coloured identity by the radical Left.[44] These appeals to Coloured group consciousness had the effect of reinforcing Coloured exclusivity because they contributed to the reification of Coloured identity, undermined the nonracial stance of the rejectionist movement that had developed during the 1970s and 1980s, and promoted the expression of political interests along racial lines. Strenuous attempts to win the Coloured vote and hand-wringing responses to Coloured voting patterns have subsequently served only to accentuate Coloured exceptionalism and reify the identity further.

The use of overtly racialized political tactics has declined since the mid-1990s. Most political parties in the new South Africa claim to be nonracial, but they are more accurately described as multiracial in that they work with essentialist concepts of race and often openly try to exploit racial identifications. The black peril tactics of the National Party during the 1990s, particularly in the run-up to the 1994 elections, were undoubtedly instrumental in heightening race consciousness within the Coloured community. More recently, Democratic Alliance strategies for winning Coloured support have openly played on fears of African domination. The ANC clearly also contributed to this process both by sidelining the UDF-affiliated antiracist lobby of the western Cape soon after its unbanning and by directly soliciting Coloured support. Given the continued prevalence of racial thinking in postapartheid South Africa, no political party aspiring to mass support could afford to ignore the popular mind-set in this regard.

A concomitant influence promoting innovation in the expression of Coloured identity stems from the abolition of apartheid and the advent of the democratic order having provided Coloured people with a degree of personal liberty and freedom of association never before enjoyed. One aspect of this newfound freedom is that people now have the option of expressing their social identities and ethnic preferences in any way they please. A few organic intellectuals within the community have, for example, sought to mobilize Coloured opinion primarily through an identification with a slave past, others are trying to reinvent a Khoisan ethnic identity, and yet others retreat into a laager of Coloured exclusivism. Some Coloured people have sought to promote an identification with Africa, others identify with various forms of rainbow nationalism, and a few adhere to an antiracist universalism. Since 1994, a motley marketplace with distinctly idiosyncratic elements has developed for ideas and movements related to Coloured identity. It includes the eccentric claims of "Chief" Joseph Little to the chieftainship of the Hamcumqua Khoi tribe; the suggestion that a "ganster party" be formed;[45] the emergence of the provocatively named Kleurling Weerstandbeweging (Coloured Resistance Movement),[46] which drew most of its support in the Coloured townships of Gauteng; and the solitary effort of maverick Peter Abrahams, who styles himself as "Instigator" of the Movement for the Expulsion of Non-Blacks. However, the majority of Coloured people, particularly within the working classes, have continued to adhere to a racialized conception of Colouredness, with strong affinities to whiteness and a defensive racism toward Africans that draws heavily on apartheid-style values. This new creativity in manifestations of Coloured identity is part of a wider flowering of cultural expression encouraged by the tolerant atmosphere of postapartheid South Africa that self-consciously celebrates racial and cultural diversity.

It is ironic that with the abolition of legally binding race classification, as enshrined in the Population Registration Act and other apartheid legislation,[47] Coloured identity has gained even greater salience in South African public life than it had in the latter phases of the apartheid era. Now that those who had forcibly been classified as Coloured are at liberty to identify socially and politically in whichever way they desire, the majority have chosen to emphasize their Colouredness, and many have done so in ways that are hostile to Africans and even, at times, flagrantly racist. Such anti-African sentiment has surfaced most strongly at election time, fanned by opposition party rhetoric and a voyeuristic press. The oft-heard dismissal of Nelson Mandela as "just another kaffir" during the first years of democratic rule captures the racially motivated contempt and alienation felt within large swaths of the Coloured working classes toward the new order. The subsequent emergence of the colloquial acronym JACK, an abbreviation for "just another confused Kaffir"—usually reserved for the scornful dismissal of prominent Africans, particularly politicians or government spokespeople—is an indication that these sentiments are still common.

A principal cause for Coloured dissatisfaction with the new order and thus an important determinant of the way the identity has found expression is that members of the Coloured community, especially the working classes, see themselves as having gained little, if any, tangible benefit from the new dispensation. Although the skilled and well-educated Coloured middle classes have profited from the extension of civil liberties and many have been able to take advantage of opportunities that have become available to formerly disadvantaged people through affirmative action and black economic empowerment initiatives, the Coloured working classes have been victims of jobless economic growth and an increasing desire among employers in the formal sector to hire Africans in order to have a more racially representative workforce. In the Western Cape, the unwinding of distortions caused by the Coloured Labour Preference Policy is not only affecting the Coloured community adversely but is also perceived to be the result of government policy unfairly advantaging Africans. Civil rights such as the franchise and freedoms of expression and association, which have clearly enhanced the lives of the Coloured middle classes, have meant little to their working-class counterparts, who remain mired in poverty and feel marginalized. Having the right to live where you want, marry whom you want, and send your children to the school of your choice is of little consequence to the laboring poor of the Coloured townships.

Furthermore, although large sections of the African poor have benefited from the provision of basic services such as electricity, sanitation, and running water since the mid-1990s, only a relatively small section of the Coloured proletariat has experienced any improvement in living standards that can be attributed to the coming of the new order. Because of Coloured people's status of relative privilege under white domination, the apartheid regime had, by and large, provided these services to Coloured communities and in the sub-economic housing estates erected to accommodate the hundreds of thousands of people relocated under the Group Areas Act. Very importantly, because social services and welfare payments have now been extended to the African masses that were neglected under apartheid, the benefits received by Coloureds have, in most cases, been diluted, dropping below the relatively privileged levels of the past. This has caused real hardship within the Coloured proletariat and is generally seen to be the result of inequitable government policies favoring Africans. Some have even chosen to interpret government policy in this regard as a way of punishing Coloured people for not supporting the ANC. Though such claims are clearly unfounded, they nevertheless feed Coloured suspicion of the ANC government, as well as resentment toward Africans in general.

Indeed, a very common perception within the Coloured working classes, as well as among elements within the lower-middle-income group, is that they are worse off under the new dispensation than they were under apartheid. They cite shrinking employment opportunities especially as a result of affirmative action, escalating crime, deteriorating social services, and the rapaciousness of corrupt government officials, among other reasons, to support the view that they were "better off under the white man." There is a strong feeling that the Coloured people have traded one set of oppressors under apartheid for a larger, even more unscrupulous set of oppressors since 1994. Relying on apartheid-style reasoning, disaffected Coloured people often present themselves as victims of inherent racial traits of Africans, be it their propensity for violence, their innate corruptness, or their inborn tendency to favor their own kind. Award-winning Coloured actor Anthony Wilson recently captured popular sentiment within the Coloured community when he claimed that "the Boers stole, but at least they budgeted and did not steal everything. They stole the cream, but the darkies are stealing the cream, the milk and the bucket. . . . We [Coloureds] are being victimized. We are being turned into the new slaves of our country. . . . We swapped five million farmers for 34 million blacks [as our oppressors]."[48]

Although it is all too easy to dismiss such negativity toward the new South Africa as a product of irrational racism, there is a growing body of evidence that the living standards of the Coloured proletariat have suffered significantly since the early 1990s. A study by Stellenbosch University economists Servaas van der Berg and Megan Louw found that even though the poverty headcount ratios of all other race groups declined between 1990 and 2000, only among Coloureds did it increase during that period.[49] Their growing impoverishment has manifested itself in various ways within the Coloured working class. Not surprisingly, more and more people in this social category have found it increasingly difficult to keep up with escalations in the cost of municipal services since apartheid-era subsidies were phased out and the ANC government implemented a policy of full cost recovery for such services. On the basis of a national survey conducted in collaboration with the Human Sciences Research Council, David McDonald, director of the Development Studies Programme at Queens University, Canada, found that 20 percent of Coloured respondents were regularly unable to pay for basic services such as water and electricity and that many had suffered service cutoffs or even evictions as a result. Even people in lower-middle-income groups were not immune to service delivery cutoffs. Having committed a large slice of their income to mortagage or rent payments, they were unable to afford all the services they needed.[50] Another important indicator of social stress is that crime statistics show a hugely disproportionate rise in the homicide rate among Coloured people from the early 1990s onward. Recent studies claim that Coloured people are more than twice as likely to be murdered than people from other race groups. Although this is partly a legacy of the breakdown of communal and family bonds as a result of forced removals, the violence has been exacerbated in recent years by rising unemployment, increasing drug and alcohol abuse, and a growing prevalence of gangsterism and criminal activity in working-class Coloured areas.[51] Whatever else one may read into these studies and statistics, it is clear that there is some material basis to Coloured people's disenchantment with the new order and thus to their racial antagonisms toward Africans.

In the wake of the 1994 elections, a stereotype of Coloured people as being particularly prone to racist behavior has emerged. Given the continued prevalence of racial thinking and stereotyping and of interracial hostility between various groups in South African society, there is no justification for singling out Coloured people in this regard, and any suggestion that their attitude is somehow inherent is indefensible. What can be said, however, is that members of the Coloured community are highly sensitive to issues of race. This sensitivity emanates, first of all, from their marginality, which has made them vulnerable in a society in which race remains the primary form of social identification and therefore of social and political solidarity. Second, their intermediate position in the racial hierarchy has helped sharpen Coloured people's awareness of racial issues that affect them both personally and as a group. It needs to be stressed, though, that Coloured racial hostility toward Africans is essentially defensive in nature and arises from their position of weakness and feelings of vulnerability. This is a key reason why these antagonisms have not yet erupted in a single instance of serious interracial violence perpetrated by Coloureds against Africans. This racial animosity has hitherto been restricted to the trading of verbal insults and at worst has resulted in tense standoffs over African squatter invasions of land that a particular Coloured community regarded as its own or over government allocation of housing to Africans to which Coloured people felt they had a prior claim.[52]

Coloured feelings of marginality—and of betrayal among some disillusioned former supporters of the antiapartheid movement—have been deepened by a perceived loss of status in the new South Africa. Coloured people had enjoyed a position of relative privilege in the past, but many now regard Coloureds as the lowest in the pecking order of the new South Africa because the African-dominated government advantages its own racial constituency; meanwhile, whites, who continue to dominate the economy, increasingly favor Africans in order to ingratiate themselves with the political elite. Of course, this highly selective view ignores the impoverished mass of Africans and instead finds justification by focusing on high-profile African individuals and a rapidly growing and conspicuous African middle class. There can be little doubt that Coloured anxieties have been exacerbated by ongoing African racial chauvism toward Coloured people and an African triumphalism that, on occasion, emanates from within the ranks of the ANC itself. Coloured unease has also not been calmed by the shift in emphasis from reconciliation under the Mandela presidency to the more Africanist tone of Thabo Mbeki's administration.[53]

Perhaps the most fundamental reason why Coloured identity needs to be expressed in new forms is that the discrediting of racist ideologies and the abolition of apartheid have undermined the racial basis on which the identity has operated from the time of its late-nineteenth-century genesis. Colouredness has always been constructed as a racial identity in the popular mind—and in much of academic writing, one might add—and was sustained by racist ideology. There can be little doubt that the driving force behind Coloured exclusivism under white rule was the promotion and protection of the relative privilege enjoyed by Coloured people in the South African racial hierarchy. Coloureds' assertion of a separate identity was originally founded on their claim to higher social status and better treatment relative to Africans, since they were assimilated to Western culture and were partly descended from European colonists. Unable to win first prize of assimilating into the dominant society because of white racism, they laid claim to an intermediate status in the racial system, which in turn underpinned their espousal of a separate Coloured identity. By and large, the white supremacist state and the ruling establishment sanctioned this claim to relative privilege because it resonated strongly with the dominant society's perception of what the social order should be, whether viewed as God-given or natural. Privileging Coloureds above Africans was also useful as part of a broader divide-and-rule strategy.

The precipitate change in the political and moral climate in which Colouredness has to operate in the new South Africa has been deeply disconcerting to many of the political, communal, and intellectual leaders of the Coloured community. These individuals have been wrestling with the unenviable problem of reorienting and rearticulating a profoundly racialized identity, a task complicated by a widely-held perception of Coloured complicity in maintaining white supremacy in the past. The new order, with its emphasis on multiculturalism, nation building, and the egalitarian values enshrined in its proudly progressive constitution, has invalidated what had all along been the principal strategy behind the espousal of a separate Coloured identity in white supremacist South Africa. With the Coloured community's racially based claim to relative privilege no longer acceptable, there has been an urgent need for politicians, community leaders, and organic intellectuals to find a new basis for the espousal of the identity and new strategies for fostering Coloured group interests.

One possible response to the postapartheid situation has been the assertion of nonracism. The popularity of this option in its purist, antiracist form has declined markedly from its apogee in the heady days of the late 1980s, when the antiapartheid movement, most notably the UDF, had considerable success in promoting it to counter apartheid ideology. In the polarized world of apartheid South Africa, it was relatively easy to promote nonracism as an ideal. Fostering nonracism has become much more difficult in the postapartheid environment, where racial and ethnic identities have greater legitimacy and are a potent means for marshalling support. Despite the political correctness and rainbow rhetoric that veneers much of South African public life, the reality of racial politics in day-to-day living and the pervasiveness of racial forms of thinking have made nonracism an impractical option for those seeking to mobilize a popular following. In the new South Africa, the terrain of antiracism appears largely to have been abandoned to intellectuals and to some former antiapartheid activists who continue to reject Colouredness as a form of false consciousness or white-imposed identification.[54]

Since the reality of Coloured identity cannot be wished away or ignored in the political arena or other areas of public life, a more practical alternative to the strictly nonracial position has become necessary for those hoping to steer expressions of Coloured identity in a more progressive direction. The most common response in this regard has been for organic intellectuals, community leaders, and activists within the Coloured community to espouse a rainbowist position that accepts the reality of racial and ethnic distinctions and their identity as Coloured but embraces the multiculturalist precepts that all communities be accorded respect and receive equal treatment. Support of the ANC, generally viewed as the most representative and progressive party, appears to be the most popular political option among those who have adopted this stance.

An early example of an attempt to affirm Coloured identity and realign it within a progressive, multiculturalist framework is provided by the December 1st Movement that came into being in Cape Town in the latter months of 1996. The movement, which drew its name from the freeing of slaves on 1 December 1834, sought to invigorate a despondent and disunited Coloured community by kindling within it an identification with a common slave past. Finding little resonance among the mass of Coloured people and widely criticized for fostering Coloured separatism, the movement was allowed to lapse after its first commemorative gathering on 1 December 1996. This initiative foundered on the contradiction of its desire to maintain a politically progressive approach while mobilizing under the aegis of a discredited racial identity.[55] A personal and more subtle attempt to come to terms with the racial baggage of Coloured identity is furnished by Zimitri Erasmus's introduction to the edited collection of essays *Coloured by History, Shaped by Place*, published in 2001. Erasmus argues that the only way to rupture the racialized modes of thought in which the identity is mired is to confront the reality of Coloured racism and its complicity with white supremacism head on. Any form of denial or resort to essentialist notions of identity, as has been the case since the advent of democracy, will only perpetuate Coloured marginality and discomfort with the new dispensation. Most important, not only the Coloured community but also the whole of South African society will need to develop a new mind-set and a new kind of "reflexive political practice" to relieve itself of the burden of the apartheid past. Accord-

ing to Erasmus all South Africans need to recognize "racist sentiments and practices as part of our everyday reality and the shaping of
all our selves" and Coloured identity as part of a "shifting texture of
broader black experience."[56]

For the greater majority of Coloured people, however, there are serious drawbacks to broadly South Africanist approaches of the sort
proposed by Erasmus or the December 1st Movement. For many, racial
thinking is so deeply entrenched that racially unifying approaches to
politics or intergroup relations are automatically discounted as unrealistic or even delusional. Because of continued and deep-seated
antipathy toward Africans within the Coloured community and perceptions of being victimized by an African-dominated government,
South African political and economic life is seen as necessarily adver-
sarial, with cleavages drawn along racial lines. Even among those who
profess to subscribe to multicultural values, there is a fear that Coloured interests and needs will be overlooked within any broadly South
Africanist or nonracial approach. Indeed, for many, the marginalization of Coloured people in the new South Africa is already a reality.
Rainbow nationalism has proven to be an arid ideology that is long on
rhetoric but short on practical solutions to racially defined problems
of South African political life. It has already become something of a
cliché among Coloured people to dismiss rainbowism with the protes-
tation that "there is no brown in the rainbow."

Under these circumstances, one might have expected Coloured
separatism to have had strong appeal and for some organization or
movement professing Coloured exclusivist ideals to have gained widespread popularity. The reality is that initiatives such as the Kleurling
Weerstandbeweging, the Brown Nationalist Front, the Brown Democratic Party, and the Coloured Forum have remained completely
marginal or have existed in name only. The only separatist movement
to have struck a chord within the Coloured community—and a relatively feeble one at that—is Khoisan revivalism, the first prominent example being the 1994 decision of the Pan Africanist Congress' former
secretary-general, Benny Alexander, to renounce his conventional name
in favor of Khoisan X. The revivalist movement reached its apogee
when over 440 delegates representing 36 Khoisan communities and
organizations came together at the National Khoisan Consultative
Conference in Oudtshoorn between 29 March and 1 April 2001. Since
then, however, the movement has found scant support among the
mass of Coloured people, and there has been little evidence of formal

organization between various Khoisan groupings. Apart from the small number of people, largely in the Northern Cape, who have always regarded themselves as being of Khoisan descent, manifestations of Khoisan identity have been episodic and mainly in evidence on festive and symbolic occasions, such as Heritage Day celebrations and on the return of the remains of Sarah Baartman, the so-called Hottentot Venus, from the Musée de l'Homme in Paris where her remains had been on display for the greater part of two centuries.

Khoisan revivalism is a movement only in the broadest sense of the term, as a profusion of groups and individuals with a variety of agendas have claimed Khoisan identity since the mid-1990s. There also appears to be a good deal of mutual antagonism between various revivalist groups and self-proclaimed leaders, or "chiefs," who vie with each other for recognition and ascendancy. Khoisan revivalism is, in essence, both exclusionist and Coloured rejectionist. It is rejectionist in that Khoisan identity is proudly affirmed as an authentic culture of ancient pedigree in place of Colouredness, which is repudiated as the colonizer's perverted caricature of the colonized. It is exclusionist in that the Khoisans' claim to being the true indigenes of South Africa, even when not articulated as a demand for first-nation status, nevertheless represents a new argument for a position of relative privilege. It is exclusionist in another sense as well, in that at the Khoisan Consultative Conference, there was general agreement that Muslims and Malays did not qualify as being Khoisan.[57]

The overall sense one has regarding Coloured identity in the new South Africa is one of fragmentation, uncertainty, and confusion. For the greater part of its existence, Coloured identity was accepted as given by its bearers, and in the latter phases of the apartheid era, the emergence of a rejectionist movement created a schism between those who accepted and those who eschewed it. But the new South Africa has witnessed the emergence of a wide spectrum of positions on the nature of Colouredness and a plethora of initiatives to change or influence the ways in which it is expressed. Such attempts have thus far failed to have much of a popular impact because they lack resonance with the Coloured masses and are driven by small groups of intellectuals and community activists with limited influence. The evidence indicates that many people who have gone beyond simply accepting racial categories as given are wrestling with questions about the extent to which they should express their identity as black, as African, as South African, as Coloured, as Khoisan, as descendants of slaves or whether they should make a stand on the principle of nonracism. There is often confusion about whether Colouredness is inherent or imposed from outside, whether it is something negative to be discarded or something positive to be embraced and affirmed. Today, Coloured identity remains in flux and is experiencing a degree of change unparalleled since its emergence in the late nineteenth century.

Notes

Introduction

1. The main works are M. Hommel, *Capricorn Blues: The Struggle for Human Rights in South Africa* (Toronto: Culturama, 1981); R. van der Ross, *The Rise and Decline of Apartheid: A Study of Political Movements among the Coloured People of South Africa, 1880–1985* (Cape Town: Tafelberg, 1986); G. Lewis, *Between the Wire and the Wall: A History of South African "Coloured" Politics* (Cape Town: David Philip, 1987); I. Goldin, *Making Race: The Politics and Economics of Coloured Identity in South Africa* (Cape Town: Maskew Miller Longman, 1987); R. H. du Pre, *Separate but Unequal: The "Coloured" People of South Africa—A Political History* (Johannesburg: Jonathan Ball, 1994).

2. Z. Erasmus, *Coloured by History, Shaped by Place: New Perspectives on Coloured Identities in Cape Town* (Cape Town: Kwela Books, 2001).

3. It needs to be stressed that the argument is not for stasis but for stability and consistency of expression, which does not rule out change or fluidity.

4. For a discussion of the concept of the petite bourgeoisie in the South African context, see A. Cobley, *Class and Consciousness: The Black Petty Bourgeoisie in South Africa, 1924 to 1950* (Westport, CT: Greenwood Press, 1990), especially 2–12, 68–69, 225–33.

5. See N. Duncan, "'Listen Here, Just Because YOU Think I'm a Coloured . . . ': Responses to the Construction of Difference in Racist Discourses," in N. Duncan, P. D. Gqola, M. Hofmeyr, T. Schefer, F. Malunga, and M. Mashige, eds., *Discourses on Difference, Discourses on Oppression* (Cape Town: Centre for Advanced Studies of African Societies, 2002), 113–37.

6. Quoted in J. Crwys-Williams, ed., *The Penguin Dictionary of South African Quotations* (Sandton, SA: Penguin, 1999), 83.

Chapter 1: Continuity and Context

1. Comment from the floor by a young woman who identified herself as Coloured at a seminar, "The Predicament of Marginality: Coloured Identity and Politics in South Africa," presented by M. Adhikari at All Africa House, University of Cape Town, 12 October 2001.

2. *Cape Times*, 14 January 2002.

3. Cape slaves came mainly from Mozambique, Madagascar, India, Sri Lanka, and the Indonesian Archipelago.

4. The People of South Africa Population Census, 1996: Primary Tables—The Country as a Whole (Report No. 03-01-19), 6; *Statistics South Africa, 2000* (Pretoria: Government Publications Department, 2001), 1.1.

5. Before 1994 the term "western Cape" was a geographical expression and the lowercase "western" is used for such references. In 1994, however, the Western Cape became a province of the Republic of South Africa, and uppercase is used in such instances. The same applies to the eastern and northern Cape.

6. Compare statistics in Census of the Union of South Africa, 1911 (U.G.32-1912), Annexure 1, 7–11, with South Africa Census, 1996, 6.

7. M. Adhikari, "The Sons of Ham: Slavery and the Making of Coloured Identity," *South African Historical Journal* 27 (1992): 107–8; N. Worden, "Adjusting to Emancipation: Freed Slaves and Farmers in Mid-nineteenth Century Southwestern Cape," in W. James and M. Simons, eds., *The Angry Divide: Social and Economic History of the Western Cape* (Cape Town: David Philip, 1989), 33–34.

8. See M. Adhikari, *"Let Us Live for Our Children": The Teachers' League of South Africa, 1913–1940* (Cape Town: UCT Press, 1993), 11–18, and "Sons of Ham," 95–112, for a more detailed discussion of the origins of Coloured identity. For case studies of the process in Cape Town and Kimberley, respectively, see V. Bickford-Smith, *Ethnic Pride and Racial Prejudice in Victorian Cape Town, 1875–1902* (Cambridge: Cambridge University Press, 1995), 186–209, and P. Lawrence, "Class, Colour Consciousness and the Search for Identity at the Kimberley Diamond Diggings, 1867–1893" (master's thesis, University of Cape Town, 1994).

9. S. Trapido, "'The Friends of the Natives': Merchants, Peasants and the Political and Ideological Structure of Liberalism in the Cape," in S. Marks and A. Atmore, eds., *Economy and Society in Pre-industrial South Africa* (London: Longman, 1980), 266.

10. R. van der Ross, *The Rise and Decline of Apartheid: A Study of Political Movements among the Coloured People of South Africa, 1880–1985* (Cape

Town: Tafelberg, 1986), 43–55; G. Lewis, *Between the Wire and the Wall: A History of South African "Coloured" Politics* (Cape Town: David Philip, 1987), 30–39, 46–63.

11. This policy, implemented from the mid-1920s by the Hertzog government, sought to ameliorate the poor white problem by absorbing newly urbanized whites into industrial occupations and replacing black workers with whites at wages that would ensure a "civilized" standard of living. See T. Davenport and C. Saunders, *South Africa: A Modern History* (London: Macmillan, 2000), 636–37.

12. L. Thompson, *The Cape Coloured Franchise* (Johannesburg: South African Institute of Race Relations, 1949), 20–21, 55; G. Lewis, "The Reaction of the Cape 'Coloureds' to Segregation" (Ph.D. diss., Queens University, 1984), 330–31.

13. Van der Ross, *Rise and Decline of Apartheid*, chap. 16; Lewis, *Between Wire and Wall*, 261–70; R. H. du Pre, *Separate but Unequal: The "Coloured" People of South Africa—A Political History* (Johannesburg: Jonathan Ball, 1994), chaps. 4–8; V. Bickford-Smith, E. van Heyningen, and N. Worden, *Cape Town in the Twentieth Century: An Illustrated Social History* (Cape Town: David Philip, 1999), 143–96.

14. Lewis, *Between Wire and Wall*, 10–25; van der Ross, *Rise and Decline of Apartheid*, 1–30.

15. M. Adhikari, "Abdullah Abdurahman, 1872–1940," in *They Shaped Our Century: The Most Influential South Africans of the Twentieth Century* (Cape Town: Human and Rousseau, 1999), 438; Lewis, *Between Wire and Wall*, 124–33, 250–56.

16. M. Hommel, *Capricorn Blues: The Struggle for Human Rights in South Africa* (Toronto: Culturama, 1981), 65–72; Lewis, *Between Wire and Wall*, 179–98, 207–44; van der Ross, *Rise and Decline of Apartheid*, 209–16; A. Drew, *Discordant Comrades: Identities and Loyalties on the South African Left* (Aldershot, UK: Ashgate, 2000), 266–70.

17. SACPO was renamed the Coloured People's Congress (CPC) in December 1959.

18. Lewis, *Between Wire and Wall*, 263–71; Hommel, *Capricorn Blues*, 135–42, 157–59. The Congress Alliance was a popular, multiracial front formed in 1953 to oppose the apartheid state. Its main constituents were the ANC, SACPO, the South African Indian Congress, and the Congress of Democrats, representing sympathetic whites. In 1955, the South African Congress of Trade Unions and the Federation of South African Women joined the alliance.

19. The Black Consciousness Movement emerged in the late 1960s under the leadership of Steve Biko. Its main thrust was to promote black

assertiveness and self-esteem to overcome the psychological oppression of apartheid, a necessary step for overthrowing the system. Defining black inclusively as all those discriminated against on grounds of race, the movement included Coloureds and Indians but excluded whites. Black Consciousness ideology gained popularity within the Coloured community after the 1976 unrest spread to Coloured areas.

20. The United Democratic Front, founded in 1983, was the most important of the internal antiapartheid organizations of the 1980s. Aligned with the ANC, it stood for a nonracial, democratic order as envisioned by the Freedom Charter adopted by the ANC in 1955. The UDF was a federal organization that brought together over six hundred youth, worker, and communty bodies to coordinate resistance to P. W. Botha's ill-fated tricameral constitution of 1984. The Tricameral Parliament was one of Botha's most significant attempts to reform apartheid by introducing an element of power sharing with Coloureds and Indians. Because it excluded Africans and kept control of the state in white hands, it was justifiably condemned as a sham and widely boycotted by all but a few collaborationist black leaders.

21. For discussion of attitudes toward Coloured identity in the antiapartheid movement, see M. Adhikari, "'You Have the Right to Know': *South*, 1987–1994," 349–54, and I. Van Kessel, "*Grassroots:* From Washing Lines to Utopia," 308–10, both in L. Switzer and M. Adhikari, eds., *South Africa's Resistance Press: Alternative Voices in the Last Generation under Apartheid* (Athens: Ohio University Press, 2000).

22. See especially D. Caliguire, "Voices from the Communities," 9–15, and B. Williams, "The Power of Propaganda," 22–27, as well as the other eight chapters in sections 1–3 in W. James, D. Caliguire, and K. Cullinan, eds., *Now That We Are Free* (Boulder, CO: Lynne Rienner, 1996).

23. Adhikari, "*South*," 354; van Kessel, "*Grassroots*," 310; *South*, 13 June 1991.

24. Adhikari, *Teachers' League*, 14–17, 22–23, 150.

25. H. Giliomee, "The Non-racial Franchise and Afrikaner and Coloured Identities, 1910–1994," *African Affairs* 94, no. 375 (1995): 199–225; Lewis, *Between Wire and Wall*, 126–30.

26. Adhikari, *Teachers' League*, 14–15, 179–80.

27. See ibid., 17, 47–48, 157–60. The radical minority was clearly an exception.

28. See G. Watson, *Passing for White* (London: Tavistock, 1970), and B. Unterhalter, "Changing Attitudes to 'Passing for White' in an Urban Coloured Community," *Social Dynamics* 1, no. 1 (1975): 53–62, for case studies of the phenomenon.

29. Z. Erasmus, *Coloured by History, Shaped by Place: New Perspectives on Coloured Identities in Cape Town* (Cape Town: Kwela Books, 2001), emphasis in the original.

30. B. Kies, *The Background of Segregation* (Cape Town: Anti-CAD, 1943), 5.

31. See D. Bosman, I. van der Merwe, and L. Hiemstra, eds., *Tweetalige Woordeboek: Afrikaans-Engels/Engels-Afrikaans* (Cape Town: Tafelberg, 1967), 117, 1088: P. Grobbelaar, ed., *Readers' Digest Afrikaans-Engelse Woordeboek* (Cape Town: Readers' Digest Association of South Africa, 1987), 88–89; J. Branford and W. Branford, eds., *A Dictionary of South African English* (Cape Town: Oxford University Press, 1991), 51–52; P. Silva, ed., *A Dictionary of South African English on Historical Principles* (Oxford: Oxford University Press, 1996), 115–16.

32. N. van Wyk Louw, *"Voorwoord,"* in D. Botha, *Die Opkoms van Ons Derde Stand* (Cape Town: Human and Rousseau, 1960), vi.

33. C. Ziervogel, *Brown South Africa* (Cape Town: Maskew Miller, 1938); *Torch*, 19 June 1956; James, Caliguire, and Cullinan, *Now That We Are Free*, 60–61; G. Stone, "An Ethnographic and Socio-semantic Analysis of Lexis among Working-Class, Afrikaans-Speaking, Coloured Adolescents and Young Adult Males in the Cape Peninsula, 1963–1990" (master's thesis, University of Cape Town, 1991), 389–90.

34. C. Ziervogel, *The Coloured People and the Race Problem* (Ceres, SA: Weber, 1936), 5; Adhikari, *Teachers' League*, 13–18, 149–50, 162–64.

35. *Educational Journal*, November 1920.

36. H. Villa-Vicencio, "Colour, Citizenship and Constitutionalism: An Oral History of Political Identity among Middle Class Coloured People with Special Reference to the Formation of the Coloured Advisory Council in 1943 and the Removal of the Male Franchise in 1956" (master's thesis, University of Cape Town, 1995), 140.

37. S. Field, "Fragile Identities: Memory, Emotion and Coloured Residents of Windermere," in Erasmus, *Coloured by History*, 105. Translated from Afrikaans. *Masala* is a general term for a blend of spices.

38. Organizations within the radical tradition are obvious exceptions. Although, for example, the Anti-CAD was effectively and SACPO was exclusively Coloured in membership, their ultimate goals were broadly socialist.

39. J. Cell, *The Highest Stage of White Supremacy: The Origins of Segregation in South Africa and the American South* (Cambridge: Cambridge University Press, 1982), 19.

40. For discussion of official definitions of the term *Coloured*, see A. Venter, *Coloured: A Profile of Two Million South Africans* (Cape Town: Human and Rousseau, 1974), 1–2; Lewis, *Between Wire and Wall*, 3; S.

Patterson, *Colour and Culture in South Africa: A Study of the Status of Cape Coloured People in the Union of South Africa* (London: Routledge and Keegan Paul, 1953), 361–63.

41. Erasmus, *Coloured by History*, 17.

42. *Sunday Tribune*, 5 February 1983.

43. Unrecorded conversation with a middle-aged, working-class Coloured man, translated from Cape Vernacular Afrikaans.

44. See Z. Erasmus, "Some Kind of White, Some Kind of Black," in B. Hesse, ed., *Un/settled Multiculturalisms* (London: Zed Books, 2000), 199, and K. Jachoutek, "Mixed Bredie in the Creole Cuisine: Cultural Drivers in the Search for 'Coloured' Identity at the Cape," seminar paper, University of Cape Town, 2003.

45. J. Lelyveld, *Move Your Shadow: South Africa Black and White* (London: Michael Joseph, 1985), 173–74.

46. See Patterson, *Colour and Culture*, 199; Lewis, *Between Wire and Wall*, 9–10, 128, 131; Venter, *Two Million South Africans*, 2, 14.

47. M. Horrell, *Legislation and Race Relations: A Summary of the Main South African Laws Which Affect Race Relations* (Johannesburg: South African Institute of Race Relations, 1971), 9–12.

48. For further discussion of Colouredness associated with shame, see Z. Wicomb, "Shame and Identity: The Case of the Coloured in South Africa," in D. Attridge and R. Jolly, eds., *Writing South Africa: Literature, Apartheid and Democracy, 1970–1995* (Cambridge: Cambridge University Press, 1998), 91–107.

49. Erasmus, *Coloured by History*, 17.

50. Ibid., 13.

51. C. Hendricks, "'Ominous' Liaisons: Tracing the Interface between 'Race' and 'Sex' at the Cape," in Erasmus, *Coloured by History*, 35.

52. Allan Boesak, interview by Shaheen Ariefdien, September 2003.

53. S. G. Millin, *The South Africans* (London: Constable, 1926), 276.

54. This incident was related to me on an understanding of anonymity by a confidant of the politician who accompanied him on the tour sometime during the course of 2000. Genadendal in the Western Cape was the site of the first mission station in the Cape Colony and was established in 1737 by the Moravian Missionary Society to serve the Khoi. It was forced to close down after six years as a result of hostility from white colonists and the Dutch Reformed Church. Christianity nevertheless survived among a few of the converts, and the mission station thrived after it was reopened in 1792. To many Genadendal thus serves as a symbol of the resilience of the Coloured people and their irrepressible drive for self-improvement in the face of adversity and white oppression.

55. Unrecorded casual conversation with a Coloured businessman.

56. The year was 1976, and I was teaching at Bonteheuwel High School in the working-class suburb of Bonteheuwel, Cape Town. The name of the inspector has long since escaped me.

57. See M. Adhikari, "Hope, Fear, Shame, Frustration: Continuity and Change in the Expression of Coloured Identity in White Supremacist South Africa, 1910–1994" (Ph.D. diss., University of Cape Town, 2002), 39 n. 65, for detailed references.

58. A. Drew, "Social Mobilization and Racial Capitalism in South Africa" (Ph.D. diss., University of California, 1991), 476–77; van der Ross, *Rise and Decline of Apartheid*, 211–15.

59. For a study of marginality within the Coloured community of Durban, see H. Dickie-Clark, *The Marginal Situation: A Sociological Study of a Coloured Group* (New York: Routledge and Kegan Paul, 1996).

60. Compare figures provided in *Statistics South Africa, 2000*, 1.4, which summarizes basic population census data from 1904 onward.

61. South Africa Census, 1996, 6.

62. Lewis, *Between Wire and Wall*, 46–63; Adhikari, *Teachers' League*, 23–24.

63. See Adhikari, *Teachers' League*, chap. 4, for a detailed case study of this strategy in operation.

64. This expression appears to be a version of the more conventional "ham in the sandwich," which is also meant to convey the idea of being caught between two more powerful forces.

65. L. Witz, "Beyond van Riebeeck," in S. Nuttal and C. Michael, eds., *Senses of Culture: South African Culture Studies* (Oxford: Oxford University Press, 2000), 318–43, discusses the ways in which van Riebeeck was presented in school history texts under apartheid.

66. See L. Witz, "Commemorations and Conflicts in the Production of South African National Pasts: The 1952 Jan van Riebeeck Tercentenary Festival" (Ph.D. diss., University of Cape Town, 1997).

67. "Kaffir" is a highly offensive reference to an African person, which has, in recent times, become an actionable insult.

68. Although I can never recall having seen it in print, I have heard this joke told on countless occasions since the early 1960s.

69. *Cape Argus*, 5 November 1988. The substitution of *colourful folk* for *Coloured people* is a pointed reference to the stereotype of working-class Coloured people as happy-go-lucky, "colourful" people.

70. K. Jordaan, "Jan van Riebeeck: His Place in South African History," *Discussion* 1, no. 5 (1952): 34.

71. *Torch*, 3 March 1947.

72. *Mail and Guardian*, 2 July 1999.

73. Ibid., 26 October 2001.

74. Du Pre, *Separate but Unequal*, viii, refers to this joke.

75. Wicomb, "Shame and Identity," 93.

76. There appears to be no academic writing on the *goffel* stereotype, and all dictionaries and reference works consulted, bar one, fail to mention the term. My own experience and initial investigations, however, indicate that the term has currency over a broad spectrum of South African society and is also commonly used in Zimbabwe. As Silva, *Dictionary of South African English*, 257–58, attests, the term is also used to refer to Coloured people generally.

77. Erasmus, *Coloured by History*, 14.

78. See, for example, Cell, *White Supremacy*, 195–96; S. Dubow, *Illicit Union: Scientific Racism in Modern South Africa* (Johannesburg: Witwatersrand University Press, 1995), 180–81; R. Young, *Colonial Desire: Hybridity in Theory, Culture and Race* (London: Routledge, 1995), especially 100–118.

79. J. Marais, *The Cape Coloured People* (Johannesburg: Witwatersrand University Press, 1968), 282.

80. Prohibition of Mixed Marriages Act, No. 55 of 1949, and the Immorality Amendment Act, No. 21 of 1950. The latter extended the ban on sexual intercourse between whites and Africans, introduced by the Immorality Act of 1927, to all black people.

81. J. Gordon, *Under the Harrow: Lives of White South Africans Today* (London: Heinemann, 1988), 171.

82. Undated quote from J. Crwys-Williams, ed., *The Penguin Dictionary of South African Quotations* (Sandton, SA: Penguin, 1999), 83.

83. For further elaboration on this topic, see Young, *Colonial Desire*, especially chap. 6; J. Coetzee, "Blood, Taint, Flaw, Degeneration: The Novels of Sarah Gertrude Millin," in J. Coetzee, *White Writing: On the Culture and Letters of South Africa* (Sandton, SA: Radix, 1988), 136–62. Erasmus, *Coloured by History*, 17.

84. *Malau* is derived from the Xhosa *amalawu* or *ilawu*, which is usually defined as "Hottentot" in Xhosa dictionaries. M. Wilson and A. Mafeje, *Langa: A Study of Social Groups in an African Township* (London: Oxford University Press, 1963), 13, explain that *malau* refers to Coloured people and is generally taken to signify "a rogue, someone without customs and tradition . . . who drinks excessively." Stone's knowledgeable "Socio-semantic Analysis," 354, interprets the term as referring to people who are "acultural, bastardized and authentic in neither blackness or whiteness."

85. S. Plaatje, *Mhudi* (Cape Town: Francolin Publishers, 1996), 147.

86. *Mail and Guardian*, 17 November 2000.

87. Du Pre, *Separate but Unequal*, 225.

88. In my personal recollections, which date back to the late 1950s, these perceptions of Coloured people were very common among Indians and whites and sometimes shared by middle-class Coloureds as well. See Hendricks, "'Ominous' Liaisons," 41, and D. Lewis, "Writing Hybrid Selves: Richard Rive and Zoë Wicomb," in Erasmus, *Coloured by History*, 133, for further discussion of these issues.

89. An example of this perception expressed as a joke, told to me by an African student in 2002, has the white man stirring his tea in a clockwise direction, the African stirring in a counter-clockwise direction, and the Coloured man stirring his tea in an erratic, haphazard way because he was *deurmekaar* (confused).

90. I have, on occasion, heard such children jokingly referred to as "zebras," that is, having black and white stripes.

91. See Jordaan, "Jan van Riebeeck," 34; Ziervogel, *Brown South Africa*, 6; Hommel, *Capricorn Blues*, 10; S. Field, "Remembering Experience, Interpreting Memory: Life Stories from Windermere," *African Studies* 60, no. 1 (2001): 122, for evidence that Jan van Riebeeck was generally accepted as their symbolic father within the Coloured community itself.

92. For a discussion of meanings and subtexts attached to the term *mixed race*, refer to K. Ratele, "'Mixed' Relations," in K. Ratele and N. Duncan, eds., *Social Psychology: Identities and Relationships* (Cape Town: University of Cape Town Press, 2003), 241–65.

93. See chapter 2.

94. See, for example, G. Jahoda, *Images of Savages: Ancient Roots of Modern Prejudice in Western Culture* (London: Routledge, 1999), chaps. 5–7; J. Nederveen Pieterse, *White on Black: Images of Africa and Blacks in Western Popular Culture* (New Haven, CT: Yale University Press, 1992), 47–49; N. Stepan, *The Idea of Race in Science: Great Britain, 1800–1960* (London: Macmillan, 1982), chap. 3; Dubow, *Illicit Union*, 67–74.

95. A weakness for wine is one of the most common aspects of the racial stereotyping of Coloured people, as demonstrated by the popular joke: What is the Coloured people's contribution to philosophy? "I drink therefore I am!" A similar apartheid era joke was to pose the question, "As drunk as . . . ?" for completion. The answer "a Coloured teacher" was meant, among other things, to signify that even "respectable" Coloureds could not escape their racial destiny.

96. Lelyveld, *Move your Shadow*, 261.

97. Field, "Remembering Experience," 122.

98. Marais, *Cape Coloured People*, 9–10, 31, and P. Maylam, *South Africa's Racial Past: The History and Historiography of Racism, Segregation and Apartheid* (Aldershot, UK: Ashgate, 2001), 42.

99. C. Dover, *Half-Caste* (London: Secker and Warburg, 1937), 13.

100. Caliguire, "Voices from the Communities," 11.

101. *Cape Times*, 30 April 1991.

102. S. Millin, *God's Stepchildren* (Cape Town: A. D. Donker, 1924).

103. I recall that in the 1960s and 1970s this joke was one of the favorites of a well-to-do Coloured businessman and former member of the Union Council of Coloured Affairs (UCCA), who used it to denounce the supposedly improvident habits of the Coloured working class.

104. Stone, "Socio-semantic Analysis," 386–87, 391; Branford, *Dictionary*, 56;

105. *S. A. Clarion*, 26 April 1919.

106. Stone, "Socio-semantic Analysis," 386–87.

107. For an analysis of the negative stereotyping of Khoisan peoples in school history texts, see A. Smith, "The Hotnot Syndrome: Myth-Making in South African School Textbooks," *Social Dynamics* 9, no. 2 (1983): 37–49.

108. *Cape Times*, 16 November 1987.

109. I have heard versions of this saying applied to Africans along the lines of "You can take the Kaffir out of the bush but you can't take the bush out of the Kaffir." See Field, "Fragile Identities," 105, for an example of a Coloured man using this expression to denigrate Africans.

110. N. Worden, *Slavery in Dutch South Africa* (Cambridge: Cambridge University Press, 1985), 93–100; Adhikari, "Sons of Ham," 99–102.

111. Malay identity, of which the profession of Islam is the main feature, though popularly associated with a slave past, was dependent for survival on free blacks, who had the personal freedom to maintain a culturally distinct lifestyle.

112. *Gam*, Afrikaans for "Ham," is a reference to the biblically derived "Curse of Ham" justification for the enslavement of Africans. See Adhikari, "Sons of Ham," 95–96. As Stone, "Socio-semantic Analysis," 407, confirms, few Coloured people who use the term do so with any knowledge of its origins.

113. Not only does the use of such language run contrary to the sense of decorum—and more recently, the dictates of political correctness—of the Coloured middle class but Khoisan physical features are also conspicuously less common within this social group. This is due to the Khoisan being assimilated into colonial society largely as farm laborers in the more remote rural areas. Their descendants thus tend to be poorer and relatively recent migrants to urban areas.

114. Among Afrikaans-speakers, both black and white, expressions such as *my Hotnotjie* (my little Hottentot) or *my Boesmantjie* (my little Bushman) are used as terms of endearment, equivalent to "my little darling" or "my dear boy." Bosman, Van der Merwe, and Hiemstra, *Woordeboek*, 103, 300; Grobbelaar, *Woordeboek*, 80, 211.

115. "Gammatjie" and "Abdoltjie," contracted, diminutive, Afrikaans forms of "Mohamed" and "Abdullah," are stereotypes of the stupid Malay. "Raj" is the stereotype of the stupid Tamil-speaking Indian. The former have predominated in the western Cape and the latter in Natal.

116. *Cape Times*, 28 September 1988.

117. See ibid., 30 November 2001, for controversy over whether the 350th anniversary of the landing of van Riebeeck should be celebrated.

118. *Cape Argus*, 4 November 2000.

119. See, for example, A. Dundas, *Cracking Jokes: Studies of Sick Humour Cycles and Stereotypes* (New York: Ten Speed Press, 1987), vi–vii.

Chapter 2: History from the Margins

1. For more detail and examples, see M. Adhikari, "Hope, Fear, Shame, Frustration: Continuity and Change in the Expression of Coloured Identity in White Supremacist South Africa, 1910–1994" (Ph.D. diss., University of Cape Town, 2002), 63 n. 1.

2. *Cape Argus*, 22 March 1913; *Cape Times*, 22 March 1913.

3. L. Switzer, "Reviews," *Journal of African History* 36, no. 2 (1995): 338.

4. See, for example, H. Cruse, *Die Opheffing van die Kleurlingbevolking: Deel I; Aanvangsjare, 1652–1795* (Stellenbosch, SA: Christen Studentevereniging, 1947), and W. M. MacMillan, *The Cape Colour Question: A Historical Survey* (Cape Town: Balkema, 1968), first published in London by Faber and Gwyer, 1927.

5. J. Marais, *The Cape Coloured People* (Johannesburg: Witwatersrand University Press), and R. van der Ross, *The Rise and Decline of Apartheid: A Study of Political Movements among the Coloured People of South Africa, 1880–1985* (Cape Town: Tafelberg, 1986), are leading examples.

6. See Adhikari, "Continuity and Change," 63 n. 1, and 65 n. 10, for further detail and examples.

7. Examples include M. Hommel, *Capricorn Blues: The Struggle for Human Rights in South Africa* (Toronto: Culturama, 1981), and G. Lewis, *Between the Wire and the Wall: A History of South African "Coloured" Politics* (Cape Town: David Philip, 1987).

8. R. H. du Pre, *Separate but Unequal: The "Coloured" People of South Africa—A Political History* (Johannesburg: Jonathan Ball, 1994), and I.

Goldin, *Making Race: The Politics and Economics of Coloured Identity in South Africa* (Cape Town: Maskew Miller Longman, 1987), respectively represent these two standpoints.

9. There were many people who took this line in public but privately acknowledged the salience of Coloured identity.

10. For examples, see Adhikari, "Continuity and Change," 66–67 nn. 13–15.

11. Lewis, *Between Wire and Wall*, 4.

12. See Adhikari, "Continuity and Change," 69 nn. 19 and 20, for examples.

13. Refer to M. Adhikari, *"Let Us Live for Our Children": The Teachers' League of South Africa, 1913–1940* (Cape Town: UCT Press, 1993), 14–15, for further discussion of the issue.

14. See chapter 3 for detailed information on Abdurahman and the APO.

15. *APO*, 24 May 1909, 21 April 1923, and 19 May 1923; R. van der Ross, *"Say It Out Loud": The APO Presidential Addresses and Other Major Political Speeches, 1906–1940, of Dr. Abdullah Abdurahman* (Bellville, SA: University of the Western Cape Institute for Historical Research, 1990), 75, 106–17.

16. Adhikari, *Teachers' League*, 66, 185. The TLSA was an explicitly Coloured teachers' association and the leading professional organization within the Coloured community.

17 The South African history section is covered by pp. 150–251 whereas the subsections relevant to Coloured history are on pp. 157–61, 169–70, 192–99, 240–41.

18. D. Hendricks and C. Viljoen, *Student Teacher's History Course: For the Use in Coloured Training Colleges* (Paarl, SA: Huguenot Drukkery, 1936), 158–60, 169–70, 192.

19. Ibid., 199, 240–41.

20. See Adhikari, *Teachers' League*, 116–28.

21. R. Edgar, ed., *An African American in South Africa: The Travel Notes of Ralphe Bunche* (Johannesburg: Witwatersrand University Press, 1992), 96.

22. For further elaboration, consult Adhikari, "Continuity and Change," 77.

23. For biographical information and references relating to Ziervogel, see Adhikari, "Continuity and Change," 77–78, 82 n. 66.

24. M. Adhikari, ed., *Jimmy La Guma: A Biography by Alex La Guma* (Cape Town: Friends of the South African Library, 1997), 58; *Liberator*, February–March 1937.

25. Edgar, *Ralphe Bunche*, 78–79.

26. C. Ziervogel, *Brown South Africa* (Cape Town: Maskew Miller, 1938), 19–22, 86, 29.

27. Ibid., 22.

28. Ibid., 6, 10, 15, 22–23, 32.

29. Ibid., 49; see also C. Ziervogel, *Who Are the Coloured People* (Cape Town: African Bookman, 1944), 12–13.

30. Ziervogel, *Brown South Africa*, 18, 21, 24–26, 59–60, 73–80; C. Ziervogel, *The Coloured People and the Race Problem* (Ceres, SA: Weber, 1936), 8.

31. Ziervogel, *Race Problem*, 5.

32. Ibid., 6. Consult Adhikari, "Continuity and Change," 83, for subsequent changes in Ziervogel's outlook.

33. See Adhikari, "Continuity and Change," 84 n. 74, for references relating to the Trotskyist movement in South Africa.

34. K. Jordaan, *"The Origin and Development of Segregation in South Africa*—by W. P. van Schoor: A Critique," *Discussion* 1, no. 3 (1951): 13.

35. See W. van Schoor, *The Origin and Development of Segregation in South Africa* (Cape Town: Teachers' League of South Africa, 1951), and Jordaan, "A Critique." Jordaan's "Jan van Riebeeck" article is also a critique of aspects of NEUM interpretations of South African history; see K. Jordaan, "Jan van Riebeeck: His Place in South African History," *Discussion* 1, no. 5 (1952): 34.

36. Good examples are provided by B. Kies, *The Contribution of the Non-European Peoples to World Civilization* (Cape Town: Teachers' League of South Africa, 1953), and E. Maurice, *The Colour Bar in Education* (Cape Town: Teachers' League of South Africa, 1957).

37. Van Schoor, *Development of Segregation*, 7, 32.

38. Maurice, "The Colour Bar in Education," reproduced in M. Hommel, ed., *The Contribution of the Non-European Peoples to World Civilization* (Johannesburg: Skotaville, 1989), 82.

39. Van Schoor, *Development of Segregation*, 20.

40. Jordaan, "A Critique," 19.

41. Jordaan, "Jan van Riebeeck," 21–35.

42. Jordaan identifies four social systems, apart from the "primitive tribalism" of precapitalist African societies, in South Africa, each with distinctive social and political orders and methods of production, exchange, and distribution. By "social system," Jordaan meant something akin to the concept of mode of production elaborated by left-wing scholars in the 1970s.

43. Jordaan, "Jan van Riebeeck," 23–24.

44. For further biographical information on Jordaan, refer to Adhikari, "Continuity and Change," 89 n. 87.

45. Jordaan, "Jan van Riebeeck," 23, 34.

46. Ibid., 23.

47. Ibid., 24.

48. For comment on the progressionism of the socialist movement generally, see A. Drew, *Discordant Comrades: Identities and Loyalties on the South African Left* (Aldershot, UK: Ashgate, 2000), 1.

49. See Adhikari, "Continuity and Change," 98–99, for further discussion and examples.

50. For biographical information on Professor Hommel, consult Adhikari, "Continuity and Change," 91–92.

51. M. Hommel, "The Organization and Evolution of Coloured Political Movements in South Africa" (Ph.D. diss., York University, 1978).

52. Hommel, *Capricorn Blues*, abstract, 1.

53. See Adhikari, "Continuity and Change," 92 n. 97, for details.

54. See ibid., 93, for discussion on the influence of *Capricorn Blues* on subsequent writing on Coloured identity.

55. Hommel, *Capricorn Blues*, 2.

56. Ibid., abstract, 1.

57. Ibid., 8, 10.

58. Ibid., 16–22, chap. 2, 56–59, 73–106.

59. Ibid., 90–101, chap. 6.

60. Lewis, *Between Wire and Wall*, chaps. 1–6; van der Ross, *Rise and Decline of Apartheid*, chaps. 1–9.

61. Jordaan, "Jan Van Riebeeck"; H. Simons and R. Simons, *Class and Colour in South Africa, 1850–1950* (London: Penguin, 1969), and I. Tabata, *The Awakening of a People* (London: Spokesman Books, 1974).

62. Access to South African material appears not to have been a problem, as Hommel was able to go to South Africa to conduct research. Hommel, *Capricorn Blues*, "Acknowledgements."

63. Van der Ross, *Rise and Decline of Apartheid*, xi.

64. For biographical information on van der Ross and a recent assessment of his career, refer to P. Kapp, "Richard van der Ross," in *They Shaped Our Century: The Most Influential South Africans of the Twentieth Century* (Cape Town: Human and Rousseau, 1999), 377–81.

65. Van der Ross, *Rise and Decline of Apartheid*, "Preface."

66. This consciousness comes through most clearly in a previous book he had written. See R. van der Ross, *Myths and Attitudes: An Inside Look at the Coloured People* (Cape Town: Tafelberg, 1979).

67. Van der Ross, *Rise and Decline of Apartheid*, xi.

68. Ibid., xii, 1–2.

69. Van der Ross, *Myths and Attitudes*.

70. Van der Ross, *Rise and Decline of Apartheid*, 2.

71. Ibid., xii.

72. For some examples, see van der Ross, *Rise and Decline of Apartheid*, 23, 29, 47, 49–51, 56, 69, 85, 127, 149–50, 185, 202–4, 206, 229–32, 239–41, 250–51, 291, 299–301.

73. Some of these documents are reproduced in R. van der Ross, "A Political and Social History of the Cape Coloured People" (manuscript, University of Cape Town Manuscript and Archives Division, 1973), iv.

74. Consult van der Ross, *Rise and Decline of Apartheid*, 398–403, chaps. 10 and 16, for the extent to which van der Ross can be dependent on a single source.

75. See ibid., 286–96.

76. Compare, for example, ibid., 205–8 and 250–55 with 233–47.

77. See ibid., 167, 185, 191, 239, for some examples, and *Educational Journal*, July–August 1965, for an example of NEUM comment on van der Ross.

78. For an extended evaluation of the book, see M. Adhikari, "Blinded by Anger: Coloured Experience under Apartheid," *South African Historical Journal* 35 (1996): 169–82. Consult Adhikari, "Continuity and Change," 106, for discussion of du Pre's other publications.

79. R. du Pre, "Confrontation, Co-optation and Collaboration: The Response and Reaction of the Labour Party to Government Policy, 1965–1984" (Ph.D. diss., Rhodes University, 1994).

80. Du Pre, *Separate but Unequal*, xii–xiv.

81. Ibid., vii.

82. Ibid., 253.

83. *Sunday Times*, 21 August 1994.

84. Refer to Adhikari, "Blinded by Anger," 172, for further detail.

85. For further elaboration of this point, see ibid., 172–73.

86. Du Pre, *Separate but Unequal*, vii, 7–8, 22, 44, 46, 49, 62, 92, 106, 130, 137, 141, 234, 248, 262.

87. Ibid., xiii.

88. See ibid., xv, for an indication that du Pre was aware of this.

89. Ibid., 105.

90. For detailed elaboration of this point, consult Adhikari, "Continuity and Change," 110–11.

91. Du Pre, *Separate but Unequal*, 89, 95–96, 103.

92. Ibid., 17. See Adhikari, "Continuity and Change," 110–13, for detailed elaboration of these issues.

93. Du Pre, *Separate but Unequal*, vii, xii, 4, 13, 16, 17–18, 36–37.

94. Presumably, du Pre meant Canaan rather than Cain. Canaan, the son of Ham, would have been the first one on whom Noah's curse would have been visited.

95. Du Pre, *Separate but Unequal*, 260–62.

96. Ibid., xvii is correct when he states that "Much of what appears in this book has been expressed in countless houses, schools, church gatherings, conversations."

97. See Adhikari, "Blinded by Anger," 176, for some examples.

98. This refers to the idealized vision of a multicultural postapartheid South Africa or "rainbow nation" in which all cultures are respected and people of all racial and ethnic backgrounds live in harmony.

99. One possible exception, Hommel, is a political scientist by training. He was able to become an academic only because he left the country and studied overseas. Another, Richard van der Ross, had no professional training in the discipline and did not regard himself as a professional historian.

100. Consult Adhikari, "Continuity and Change," 116–17, for an explanation of why the work of Neville Alexander and Bill Nasson falls beyond the scope of this enquiry.

101. Jordaan, "Jan van Riebeeck," 34.

102. The radical analyses are an exception in that they sought formulations for overthrowing the system.

Chapter 3: The Predicament of Marginality

1. The Treaty of Vereeniging, which brought the Anglo-Boer War (1899–1902) to a close, stipulated that the question of black voting rights would only be settled once the former Boer republics gained self-government, effectively disfranchising blacks.

2. See M. Adhikari, "Hope, Fear, Shame, Frustration: Continuity and Change in the Expression of Coloured Identity in White Supremacist South Africa, 1910–1994" (Ph.D. diss., University of Cape Town, 2002), 122 n. 2, for discussion about the size of the APO's membership.

3. G. Lewis, *Between the Wire and the Wall: A History of South African "Coloured" Politics* (Cape Town: David Philip, 1987), 50–52; R. van der Ross, *The Rise and Decline of Apartheid: A Study of Political Movements among the Coloured People of South Africa, 1880–1985* (Cape Town: Tafelberg, 1986), 43–44; L. Thompson, *The Unification of South Africa, 1902–1910* (London: Oxford University Press, 1960), 305–6, 340–41.

4. The APO defined its objectives in its constitution as (1) the promotion of unity between the Coloured races of British South Africa, (2) the attainment of better and higher education for the children of these races, (3) the registration of the names of all the Coloured men who have the necessary qualifications as Parliamentary voters on the Voters' List, (4)

the defence of the social, political and civil rights of the Coloured races, (5) the general advancement of the Coloured races in British South Africa. See *APO*, 25 February 1911.

5. *APO*, 4 June 1910.

6. See Adhikari, "Continuity and Change," 123–24 nn. 7–8, for biographical information on Matt Fredericks.

7. For details of these organizations, see Lewis, *Between Wire and Wall*, 34–39, 49–53, 81–82, 122–26, 129–30.

8. Van der Ross, *Rise and Decline of Apartheid*, 75; Lewis, *Between Wire and Wall*, 128; *Cape Standard*, 27 February 1940; G. Pretorius, *Man van die Daad: 'n Biografie van Bruckner de Villiers* (Cape Town: HAUM, 1959), 116.

9. *Census of the Union of South Africa, 1911* (U.G.32-1912), Annexures to the general report, 10–11, 24, numbered the Coloured population at just over half a million out of a total of six million.

10. M. Adhikari, *"Let Us Live for Our Children": The Teachers' League of South Africa, 1913–1940* (Cape Town: UCT Press, 1993), 6–7, 148–74.

11. M. Adhikari, "'Wanner Gaat ons tog en Eksampel Neem Uit die Wit Man s'Boek': Resistance, Protest and Accommodation in Piet Uithalder's 'Straatpraatjes' Column, 1909–1922," *Stilet* 8, no .2 (1996): 5–6.

12. See Adhikari, "Continuity and Change," 127 nn. 20–21, for further detail and references relating to Abdurahman.

13. *APO* 8 April 1911.

14. *APO*, 13 August 1910, and 10 August 1912; E. Maurice, "The Development of Policy in Regard to the Education of Coloured Pupils at the Cape, 1880–1940" (Ph.D. diss., University of Cape Town, 1966), 332–34.

15. *APO*, 13 August 1910.

16. The language in this section of the newspaper ranged from formal Dutch, through Dutchified Afrikaans, to vernacular Afrikaans.

17. See *APO*, 24 May 1909, 11 September 1909, and 9 April 1910 for some examples.

18. Ibid., 7 May 1910 and 4 June 1910.

19. *Cape Times*, 9 January 1901; *Cape Mercury*, 8 January 1901; *South African Spectator*, 20 April 1902; J. Marais, *The Cape Coloured People* (Johannesburg: Witwatersrand University Press, 1968), 275–76.

20. Nasson, *Abraham Esau's War: A Black South African War in the Cape, 1899–1902* (Cambridge: Cambridge University Press, 1991), 39; Marais, *Cape Coloured People*, 275–77; S. Trapido, "'The Friends of the Natives': Merchants, Peasants and the Political and Ideological Structure of Liberalism in the Cape," in S. Marks and A. Atmore, eds., *Economy and Society in Pre-industrial South Africa* (London: Longman, 1980), 256.

21. In 1917, the School Board Act was amended to extend compulsory schooling for whites to the age of fifteen, or standard V (grade 7), and in 1919 to sixteen, or standard VI (grade 8).

22. Maurice, "Coloured Education," 13–14; *The Owl*, 17 March 1905; *South African News*, 17 August 1904, 25 February 1905, and 6 March 1905; *Cape Times*, 26 August 1904; Adhikari, *Teachers' League*, 21–22.

23. *Cape Times*, 1 October 1906; *South African News*, 13 June 1906; *APO*, 19 June 1909; Thompson, *Unification*, 23–27.

24. Lewis, *Between Wire and Wall*, 70–74.

25. Adhikari, *Teachers' League*, 14.

26. Ibid., 145, 152–53.

27. Ibid., 162–63.

28. *APO*, 4 November 1911; S. Trapido, "The Origin and Development of the African Political Organization," *Institute of Commonwealth Studies Collected Seminar Papers on Southern Africa*, University of London 1 (1969–70), 100–101.

29. The term *African* in this instance was meant to denote the geographic location of the organization and to imply international solidarity with black people. At that time, Africans were generally referred to as "Natives," or more disparagingly as "Kaffirs," a term occasionally used by the *APO*.

30. *APO*, 9 April 1910.

31. Ibid., 24 May 1909.

32. See ibid., 24 December 1910, 6 December 1913, and 30 October 1920 for a few examples.

33. *APO*, 24 February 1912.

34. Ibid., 23 March 1912.

35. The Non-European Conferences consisted of a series of four symposia held between 1927 and 1934 convened by Abdurahman with a view to fostering cooperation between Coloured, Indian, and African political organizations. The movement had very limited success. Lewis, *Between Wire and Wall*, 79, 121, 141–42.

36. Washington argued that African Americans should temporarily accept their inferior status instead of protesting against the injustices they suffered. They should rather endeavor to elevate themselves through hard work, educational improvement, and strict observance of the Christian moral code. He reasoned that by achieving economic self-sufficiency and by demonstrating that they were responsible citizens, blacks would win the respect of whites who, through self-interest and their innate sense of justice, would accord African Americans full civil rights. See L. Harlan, *Booker T. Washington: The Making of a Black Leader* (New York:

Oxford University Press, 1972), chap. 11; A. Meier, *Negro Thought in America* (Ann Arbor: Michigan University Press, 1966), chap. 7.

37. See, for example, *APO*, 31 July 1909, 12 February 1910, 5 November 1910, 19 October 1912, and 8 August 1914.

38. Ibid., 8 April 1911 and 6 December 1913.

39. Ibid., 24 May 1912; *Educational Journal*, December 1917; Adhikari, *Teachers' League*, 39–40.

40. *APO*, 31 July 1909.

41. Ibid., 3 December 1910.

42. See M. Marable, *W. E. B. Du Bois: Black Radical Democrat* (Boston: Twayne, 1986), 75–80; M. Weinberg, *W. E. B. du Bois: A Reader* (New York: Harper and Row, 1970), xi–xvii; Meier, *Negro Thought*, chap. 9.

43. Consult *APO*, 8 October 1910, 26 August 1911, 1 June 1912, and 8 August 1914 for some examples.

44. For biographical detail on Cressy, refer to M. Adhikari, *"Against the Current": A Biography of Harold Cressy, 1889–1916* (Cape Town: Harold Cressy High School, 2000).

45. *APO*, 25 March 1911.

46. See ibid., 26 March 1910, 17 June 1911, 13 January 1912, 7 November 1919, and 2 October 1920 for a few examples.

47. Ibid., 12 February 1910. See also *Educational Journal*, June 1918.

48. *APO*, 17 October 1914 and 31 October 1914.

49. Ibid., 5 September 1914 and 19 September 1914.

50. A. Desmore, *With the Second Cape Corps through Central Africa* (Cape Town: Citadel, 1920), 5.

51. *APO*, 1 August 1919.

52. Adhikari, *Teachers' League*, 7, 39.

53. The black vote had grown from 15 percent of the Cape electorate at the time of Union to 21 percent by 1921, whereas the Coloured share of the electorate had grown from 9.5 percent to 14 percent over the same period. L. Thompson, *The Cape Coloured Franchise* (Johannesburg: South African Institute of Race Relations, 1949), 55.

54. The decision by the South African government to invade South West Africa during World War I triggered a rebellion among Afrikaners in the Orange Free State and Transvaal. The rebels, mainly poorer farmers under the leadership of former Boer generals, hoped to regain their lost republican independence. The revolt was easily suppressed, and rebels were, on the whole, treated leniently.

55. Starting as a strike against the decision of the Chamber of Mines to cut costs by replacing white workers with blacks who were able to perform the same semiskilled jobs at a fraction of their wage, this episode

quickly escalated into a large-scale armed insurrection. Prime Minister Smuts proclaimed martial law and used the full might of the state to suppress the revolt. Nearly two hundred rebels were killed, and nearly a thousand were wounded.

56. *APO*, 28 January 1922 and 25 March 1922; *Educational Journal*, April 1922.

57. *Cape Times*, 24 June 1913; *APO*, 28 June 1913; *Educational Journal*, May 1915.

58. Adhikari, *Teachers' League*, 49–53, 60–62.

59. Ibid., especially "Introduction" and chap. 3.

60. *Rules and Bye-laws of the Teachers' League of South Africa* (Cape Town: Teachers' League of South Africa 1913), 1; *Rules and Bye-laws of the Teachers' League of South Africa* (Cape Town: Teachers' League of South Africa, 1916), 1; see *Educational Journal*, June 1931, June 1933, and February 1936 for updated versions of the *Rules and Bye-Laws*.

61. Adhikari, *Teachers' League*, chaps. 4, 5; van der Ross, *Rise and Decline of Apartheid*, 71–89; Goldin, *Making Race*, 29–52; Lewis, *Between Wire and Wall*, 2–4, 60.

62. For an extended discussion of league experience in this regard, consult Adhikari, *Teachers' League*, 116–28.

63. See *Educational Journal*, May 1915, June 1917, May 1922, October 1932, and August 1937 for some examples.

64. Sampson's speech was serialized over three editions of the *Educational Journal*, namely, August 1916, September 1916, and October 1916.

65. Ibid., September 1916.

66. Ibid., October 1916.

67. Ibid.

68. *Report of the Commission of Enquiry Regarding the Cape Coloured Population of the Union, 1937* (U.G.54-1937), 13–16.

69. *Educational Journal*, January 1917, January 1931, January 1933, and October 1936; *Sun*, 27 June 1941.

70. *APO*, 28 January 1922.

71. *Educational Journal*, August 1916. For other examples, see May 1923 and January 1931 issues.

72. Ibid., August 1915, July 1917, March 1922, July 1923, January 1925, and October 1931; *APO*, 15 July 1912.

73. *Educational Journal*, October 1917.

74. Ibid., February 1936.

75. Ibid., September 1921.

76. Ibid., March 1929; J. Rhoda, "A Contribution toward the Study of Education among the Cape Coloured People" (B. Ed. thesis, University of

Cape Town, 1929), 44; "Evidence of a Coloured Deputation from Beaufort West before the Cape Coloured Commission, 13 May 1936," Abdurahman Family Papers, Manuscripts and Archives Division, University of Cape Town.

77. *Educational Journal,* April 1917, March 1922, July 1926, September 1928, August 1934, and February 1938.

78. Ibid., August 1932.

79. Ibid., August 1937.

80. Ibid., March 1929.

81. Ibid., August 1937.

82. Ibid., August 1934.

83. *Cape Standard,* 5 July 1938.

84. Lewis, *Between Wire and Wall,* 119–49; Goldin, *Making Race,* 33–40; *Cape Standard,* 27 June 1939.

85. A small group of radicals worked outside of this framework.

86. *Educational Journal,* July 1927.

87. Ibid., April 1923.

88. Ibid., April 1925.

89. Ibid., April 1925 and July 1926.

90. The War Bonus was a temporary salary supplement paid to teachers between 1916 and 1921 to compensate them for the erosion of the purchasing power of their salaries as a result of high wartime inflation.

91. *APO,* 30 October 1920; *Educational Journal,* November 1920 and December 1920.

92. C. E. Z. Watermeyer, "Report on Coloured Education," 15 March 1920, in *Superintendent General of Education (SGE) Report, 1919.*

93. For a discussion of Coloured teachers' salaries during this period, see M. Adhikari, *Teachers' League,* 28–29, 120–27.

94. *Educational Journal,* September 1920, October 1920, and April 1922.

95. For a discussion of the league's relationship with the Cape Education Department in this regard, see Adhikari, *Teachers' League,* 113–14, 116–28.

96. In March 1938, Smuts caused consternation within the Coloured community when he announced the government's intention of implementing residential segregation for Coloureds. He claimed that £15m had already been set aside for the project and that it would be completed within ten to twelve years. Moving swiftly, J. H. Conradie, the administrator of the Cape Province, published a draft ordinance the following month allowing local authorities to segregate residential areas and public facilities.

97. *Educational Journal*, April 1939. For further examples, see the April and May issues of 1922. The "five fingers make one hand" metaphor was a favorite of Booker T. Washington's.

98. Ibid., April 1939. See also *Cape Argus*, 29 June 1938.

99. For some examples see *Educational Journal*, April 1917, June 1918, July 1921, January 1922, April 1922, July 1927, November 1928, and August 1938.

100. Ibid., April 1939.

101. Ibid., April 1916.

102. Ibid., June 1916, March 1917, November 1920, June 1922, June 1929, August 1932, May 1934, May 1935, and August 1938.

103. Ibid., June 1918 and August 1938.

104. Ibid., June 1918.

105. Ibid., October 1920.

106. Ibid., January 1921.

107. Ibid., August 1938.

108. See, for example, *APO*, 26 March 1910 and 1 June 1912; *Educational Journal*, August 1916, January 1917, November 1917, June 1918, and March 1922.

109. *Educational Journal*, March 1922.

110. Ibid., December 1917. Beattie was about to become the first principal of the University of Cape Town.

111. Ibid., May 1915, April 1916, March 1917, April 1921, and June 1923; *Report of the Commission of Enquiry Regarding the Cape Coloured People of the Union of South Africa, 1937* (U.G.54-1937), 14–15; Maurice, "Coloured Education," 328.

112. *Educational Journal*, April 1939.

113. Ibid., August 1922 and September 1922.

114. See, for example, *SGE Report, 1918*, 15; Cape Archives Depot, Cape Town (hereafter CAD), Provincial Administration of Education (hereafter PAE), vol. 250, SF/A2/6, SGE. to Administrator of the Cape, 21 January 1920; PAE, vol. 1882, EM/372, correspondence spanning 2 September 1919–10 February 1920; *Education Gazette*, 17 November 1938, 27 July 1939, and 10 August 1939; Maurice, "Coloured Education," 384–85.

115. *Educational Journal*, July 1917.

116. *Cape Coloured Commission*, 14–15.

117. *Educational Journal*, July 1921, July 1926, August 1932, August 1939, and August 1943; *Cape Times*, 11 April 1923; *Sun*, 5 May 1933.

118. *Educational Journal*, July 1926.

119. Ibid. See also, for example, CAD, PAE, vol. 1862, EM/62, Gen-

eral Secretary of the Cape Malay Association to the Administrator of the Cape, 23 November 1928.

120. *Educational Journal*, September 1923 and December 1923.

121. Whereas the 1913 and 1916 versions of the *Rules and Bye-laws* did not contain explicit racial bars, the next available version, dated 1931, did.

122. *APO*, 30 October 1920; *Educational Journal*, December 1920.

123. *Sun*, 29 June 1934, 6 July 1934, and 13 July 1934.

124. *Educational Journal*, November 1920.

125. *Cape Times*, 25 June 1913; *Cape Argus*, 25 June 1913.

126. *Educational Journal*, July 1923.

127. S. Marks, *The Ambiguities of Dependence in South Africa: Class, Nationalism and State in Twentieth Century Natal* (Johannesburg: Ravan, 1986), 14.

Chapter 4: The Hegemony of Race

1. For references relating to the history of the Trotskyist movement in South Africa, see M. Adhikari, "Hope, Fear, Shame, Frustration: Continuity and Change in the Expression of Coloured Identity in White Supremacist South Africa, 1910–1994" (Ph.D. diss., University of Cape Town, 2002), 180 n. 1.

2. A. La Guma, *A Walk in the Night and Other Stories* (London: Heinemann, 1967).

3. For information on and references relating to the NLL and radical precursors to the NEUM, refer to Adhikari, "Continuity and Change," 180–82.

4. For information on the NEUM's political philosophy, consult R. Davies, D. O'Meara, and S. Dlamini, comps., *The Struggle for South Africa: A Reference Guide* (London: Zed Books, 1984), 310–14; A. Drew, *South Africa's Radical Tradition: A Documentary History*, vol. 2 (Cape Town: Buchu Books, Mayebuye Books, UCT Press, 1997), 14–16.

5. R. Kayser, "Land and Liberty: The Non-European Unity Movement and the Agrarian Question, 1933–75" (master's thesis, University of Cape Town, 2002), 14; S. Bhana, *Gandhi's Legacy: The Natal Indian Congress, 1894–1994* (Pietermaritzburg, SA: Natal University Press, 1997), 52.

6. B. Nasson, "The Unity Movement: Its Legacy in Historical Consciousness," *Radical History Review* 46/47 (1990): 192.

7. C. Soudien, "Social Conditions, Cultural and Political Life in Working Class Cape Town, 1950 to 1990," in H. Willemse, ed., *More Than Brothers: Peter Clarke and James Matthews at Seventy* (Cape Town: Kwela Books, 2000), 35.

8. S. Viljoen, "Non-Racialism Remains a Fiction: From Richard Rive's *Buckingham Palace, District Six* to K. Sello Duiker's *The Quiet Violence of Dreams*," paper presented at the "Burden of Race" conference, University of the Witwatersrand, July 2001, 2.

9. See M. Adhikari, *"Let Us Live for Our Children": The Teachers' League of South Africa, 1913–1940* (Cape Town: UCT Press, 1993), 180–81. Neville Alexander, *One Azania, One Nation: The National Question in South Africa* (London: Zed Books, 1979), 111, notes a degree of confusion in the NEUM regarding the concepts of race and nation.

10. A distinction needs to be drawn between the terms *racist* and *racial* as used in this study. Whereas the former always involves a judgment about the supposed inferiority or superiority of one or another racial group, the latter refers to distinctions made between groups of people on the basis of racial characteristics but does not necessarily contain inferences of superiority or inferiority. Such recognition of racial differences are, indeed, often accompanied by explicit assertions of racial equality.

11. B. Kies, *The Background of Segregation* (Cape Town: Anti-CAD, 1943), 13–14. Emphasis in the original.

12. *Herrenvolk*, German for master race, was one of the NEUM's trademark terms and was used to refer to white supremacists and the racist power structure in South Africa. An effective piece of invective during and in the aftermath of World War II, its usage became a quaint reminder of an outdated analysis in later decades. *Quisling*, used to refer to collaborators, is another term emblematic of the NEUM in the context of South African liberatory politics.

13. Kies, *Background of Segregation*, 5; *A Declaration to the People of South Africa from the Non-European Unity Movement* (Cape Town: NEUM, 1951), 4–5; I. Tabata, *The Awakening of a People* (London: Spokesman Books, 1974), 4–5; *Torch*, 18 April 1949, 15 July 1952, 17 August 1952, and 2 September 1952.

14. Kies, *Background of Segregation*, 5. See also *Torch*, 15 April 1946.

15. *Declaration to the People of South Africa*, 2.

16. Tabata, *Awakening*, 4.

17. Ibid., 35.

18. See *Torch*, 26 December 1950, for a report of Tsotsi's address.

19. Alexander, *One Azania, One Nation*, 112–13.

20. *Iskra* translates into English as "spark." Since the Workers Party had already claimed that name for its paper, the NEUM settled for *Torch*. Richard Dudley, interviewed by Robin Kayser, 30 September 1999, 10.

21. For more information on the *Torch* and the way it functioned, see Adhikari, "Continuity and Change," 195–97.

22. For examples and relevant references, see ibid., 197–98 nn. 64–66. "A History of Despotism" was written by NEUM stalwart Hosea Jaffe and was later published as *Three Hundred Years* (Cape Town: New Era Fellowship, 1952).

23. *Torch*, 25 February 1946 and 26 June 1949.

24. Ibid., 25 February 1946.

25. Ibid., 18 April 1949 and 20 January 1953.

26. Ibid., 2 December 1946. Emphasis in the original. See also ibid., 14 October 1946.

27. Although the term *politically correct* became current some two decades later and today might carry connotations that were not applicable at the time, the *Torch*'s approach to race was politically correct in the sense that it developed a set of conventions that served to distance itself from racist values when discussing issues of race.

28. Kies, *Background of Segregation*, 13–14.

29. *Torch*, 19 August 1952.

30. For some examples, see ibid., 1 April 1946, 13 March 1947, 18 September 1951, 30 June 1953, 12 January 1954, 13 March 1956, and 7 September 1960.

31. Ibid., 15 July 1952 and 29 July 1952, respectively.

32. Ibid., 3 April 1950, 1 January 1952, and 12 April 1955.

33. Ibid., 16 January 1950 and 8 July 1952.

34. Ibid., 11 July 1949 and 21 June 1961, respectively.

35. Derived from *pang*, a Malay word meaning "man" that had entered Cape Vernacular Afrikaans; *Pankie*, a diminutive form, is mildly derogatory slang for a Malay person, usually male.

36. *Torch*, 1 November 1948.

37. Ibid., 17 March 1947. The use of *Afrikaan* was also meant to assert the prior claim of Africans both to the land and to Africa as homeland.

38. Ibid., 14 October 1946.

39. See, for example, ibid., 5 January 1948, 7 August 1951, and 6 January 1953.

40. Ibid., 27 February 1951. See ibid., 8 July 1952, for the similar "Boycott call to the Coloured people."

41. Ibid., 12 January 1954.

42. Ibid., 30 June 1953. For a similar example, see ibid., 3 July 1956.

43. See Adhikari, "Continuity and Change," 206, for examples.

44. See *Torch*, 27 March 1956, 27 October 1953, and 8 September 1947, respectively. *Skolly* is a South African colloquialism for a hoodlum or petty gangster.

45. For some examples of the use of *Bantu*, see ibid., 25 October 1948, 16 October 1950, and 19 February 1957; for *Ampies*, see ibid., 4 September

1951 and 7 October 1952; for *Negro*, see ibid., 22 July 1946, 13 June 1949, 16 August 1955, 13 March 1956, 12 February 1957, and 4 December 1963; for *Yanks*, see ibid., 4 November 1946, 20 December 1948, and 26 April 1961. On one occasion, the term *Native* was also used in its normative sense. See ibid., 25 February 1946.

46. See ibid., 17 March 1947, 18 July 1949, and 30 January 1950, respectively.

47. For a few examples, consult Adhikari, "Continuity and Change," 208 n. 102.

48. *Torch*, 4 March 1946, 5 August 1946, 16 October 1950, and 25 September 1951.

49. Ibid., 28 October 1946.

50. Ibid., 13 May 1946, 16 June 1947, 11 October 1948, 9 January 1950, 30 January 1950, 20 February 1950, and 10 March 1953 for examples.

51. Ibid., 25 February 1946. The 1 April 1946 edition reported the play was "a thrilling success."

52. Ibid., 29 July 1946.

53. This claim was probably based on Theal's mistaken observation that Simon van der Stel's mother was an Indian woman. It seems more likely that his maternal grandmother was of Indian or possibly slave origin. See G. M. Theal, *Willem Adriaan van der Stel and Other Historical Sketches* (Cape Town: Maskew Miller, 1913), 172; Adhikari, "Continuity and Change," 210 n. 109.

54. *Torch*, 22 April 1946. Emphasis added.

55. Ibid., 18 October 1948. At the time Meyer Fortes, reader in social anthropology at Oxford University, occupied a temporary professorial post in anthropology at the University of Cape Town.

56. Ibid., 23 October 1951.

57. Ibid., 16 April 1957.

58. See ibid., 13 May 1952–28 October 1952. Stella Jacobs was most likely the author of this series.

59. Ibid., 13 May 1952.

60. Ibid., 20 May 1952, 27 May 1952, 3 June 1952, and 10 June 1952.

61. Ibid., 17 June 1952, 19 August 1952, 26 August 1952, 2 September 1952, 9 September 1952, 23 September 1952, 30 September 1952, 7 October 1952, and 14 October 1952.

62. Ibid., 19 August 1952.

63. For some examples, see ibid., 29 January 1957, 4 November 1958, 21 April 1959, 20 October 1959, 23 February 1960, 26 April 1961, and 27 February 1963.

64. Ibid., 21 February 1956 and 13 March 1956. A typical banning order issued under the Suppression of Communism Act of 1950 was im-

posed for five years and was often renewed. Banning usually restricted individuals to a magisterial district; prevented them from being quoted or published; excluded them from entering places such as educational institutions, factories, or harbors; precluded them from meeting socially with more than one person at a time; and required them to report to a police station at regular intervals. Banning sometimes entailed banishment to remote areas or house arrest. Banned persons were often under constant police surveillance and both they and their families were harassed by security police. Meetings, publications, and organizations could also be banned under this legislation.

65. For further detail and references relating to these banning orders, refer to Adhikari, "Continuity and Change," 218.

66. C. Abrahams, *Alex La Guma* (Boston: Twayne Publishers, 1985), 69.

67. District Six was a commercial and residential area adjacent to Cape Town's central business district. Although highly cosmopolitan in the earlier part of the century, its population was largely Coloured and working class in character by the time of La Guma's portrayal. V. Bickford-Smith, "The Origins and Early History of District Six to 1910," in S. Jeppie and C. Soudien, *The Struggle for District Six: Past and Present* (Cape Town: Buchu Books, 1990), 35–43; N. Worden, E. van Heyningen, and V. Bickford-Smith, *Cape Town: The Making of a City* (Cape Town: David Philip, 1998), 250–51.

68. For further biographical detail on Jimmy La Guma, see M. Adhikari, "James Arnold La Guma," in E. Verwey, ed., *New Dictionary of South African Biography* (Pretoria: HSRC Publishers, 1995), 123–27; M. Adhikari, ed., *Jimmy La Guma: A Biography by Alex La Guma* (Cape Town: Friends of the South African Library, 1997).

69. For further biographical detail on Alex La Guma and his life in exile, see Abrahams, *Alex La Guma*, 1–20, and K. Balutansky, *Alex La Guma: The Representation of a Political Conflict* (Washington, DC: Three Continents Press, 1989), 1–12.

70. For several examples, consult Adhikari, "Continuity and Change," 222 n. 140.

71. La Guma, *Walk in the Night*, 4.

72. Abrahams, *Alex la Guma*, 48, 51.

73. La Guma, *Walk in the Night*, 21.

74. G. Cornwell, "Justin Alexander La Guma," in Verwey, *Dictionary of South African Biography*, 128.

75. L. Nkosi, *Tasks and Masks: Themes and Styles of African Literature* (London: Longman, 1981), 86.

76. See Alex La Guma, *And a Threefold Cord* (London: Kliptown Books; 1988); La Guma, *The Stone Country* (London: Heinemann, 1974); La Guma,

In the Fog of the Season's End (London: Heinemann, 1972); La Guma, *Time of the Butcherbird* (London: Heinemann, 1979).

77. See La Guma, *Walk in the Night*, 4, 16.

78. A. JanMohamed, *Manichean Aesthetics: The Politics of Literature in Colonial Africa* (Amherst: University of Massachusetts Press, 1983), 225. Emphasis in the original.

79. Balutansky, *Alex La Guma*, 9, 10, 16, 29

80. Abrahams, *Alex La Guma*, 46–68.

81. See J. Coetzee, "Man's Fate in the Novels of Alex La Guma," in D. Attwell, ed., *Doubling the Point: Essays and Interviews* (London: Harvard University Press, 1992), 345, and M. Wade, "Art and Morality in Alex La Guma's *A Walk in the Night*," in K. Parker, ed., *The South African Novel in English: Essays in Criticism and Society* (New York: African Publishing, 1978), 164–91.

82. N. Yousaf, *Alex La Guma: Politics and Resistance* (Portsmouth, UK: Heinemann, 2001), 25–46.

83. B. Chandramohan, *Trans-Ethnicity in Modern South Africa: The Writings of Alex La Guma* (Lampeter, UK: Mellen Research University Press, 1992), 7.

84. Ibid., 29.

85. See La Guma, *Walk in the Night*, 11–12, 131–36. "The Lemon Orchard" is based on a true story of a teacher in Calvinia. See Abrahams, *Alex La Guma*, 26.

86. See JanMohamed, *Manichean Aesthetics*, 225, and Chandramohan, *Trans-Ethnicity*, 29.

87. Abrahams, *Alex La Guma*, 48.

88. La Guma, *Walk in the Night*, 3. Castle Bridge, situated at the city end of Hanover Street, the main thoroughfare through District Six, was generally regarded as the entrance to District Six.

89. Balutansky, *Alex La Guma*, 22.

90. Abrahams, *Alex La Guma*, 49.

91. For details, see A. Odendaal and R. Field, *Liberation Chabalala: The World of Alex La Guma* (Bellville, SA: Mayebuye Books, 1993), ix–xv.

92. *New Age*, 23 June 1955.

93. *New Age*, formerly the *Guardian*, was the mouthpiece of the Communist Party of South Africa. Odendaal and Field, *Liberation Chabalala*, xi, characterize *New Age* as the "semi-official mouthpiece of the ANC."

94. *New Age*, 8 September 1960.

95. Ibid., 30 August 1956.

96. La Guma, *Walk in the Night*, 114.

97. Ibid., 114–20.

98. Odendaal and Field, *Liberation Chabalala*, ix.

99. G. Lewis, *Between the Wire and the Wall: A History of South African "Coloured" Politics* (Cape Town: David Philip, 1987), 221, 227; R. van der Ross, *The Rise and Decline of Apartheid: A Study of Political Movements among the Coloured People of South Africa, 1880–1985* (Cape Town: Tafelberg, 1986), 170–71.

100. H. Jaffe, *European Colonial Despotism: A History of Oppression and Resistance in South Africa* (London: Kamak House, 1994).

101. La Guma, *Walk in the Night*, 2–5, 6, 12, 14, 22–23, 31, 33, 35–36, 39, 41, 50–51, 63, 65, 79–80, 86, 88, 91, 114–15, 117, 119, 122–23, 125, 127, 132–34.

102. Ibid., 4, 16, 27, 29, 43–44, 54.

103. The name entered the Afrikaans lexicon in a similarly ironic fashion, so that the word *adoons* today means "ugly" or "apelike."

104. See Stone, "Identity among Lower Class Coloured People," 35, for some comment on the significance of such nicknames.

105. For some examples, see La Guma, *Walk in the Night*, 4–5, 14–19, 27, 31–33, 44–46, 52, 59, 63, 69, 72, 80, 84, 87–88, 102, 111, 116–17, 128.

106. Ibid., 4, 6, 13, 17, 19, 37, 50, 54, 58–59, 63, 68, 73, 84, 87, 101, 114–16, 126–27. See Adhikari, "Continuity and Change," 238–39, for an assessment of La Guma's success in substituting colloquial English for colloquial Afrikaans in characters' speech.

Chapter 5: The Emperor's New Clothes

1. For studies of the Black Consciousness movement in the Coloured community, see E. Messina, "Swartbewustheid in die Wes-Kaap, 1970–1984" (Ph.D. diss., University of the Western Cape, 1995), and E. Messina, "Kleurlinge is ook Swart: Swartbewustheid in die Wes-Kaap," *Kronos* 22 (1995).

2. For a more detailed study of *South* newspaper, see M. Adhikari, "'You Have the Right to Know': *South*, 1987–94," in Switzer and Adhikari, *Resistance Press*, 327–77.

3. L. Chisolm, "Making the Pedagogical More Political, and the Political More Pedagogical: Educational Traditions and Legacies of the Non-European Unity Movement, 1943–1985," in W. Flanagan, C. Hemson, J. Muller, and N. Taylor, comps., *Vintage Kenton: A Kenton Education Association Commemoration* (Cape Town: Maskew Miller Longman, 1994), 243; B. Nasson, "The Unity Movement: Its Legacy in Historical Consciousness," *Radical History Review* 46/47 (1990): 192; C. Soudien, "Social Conditions, Cultural and Political Life in Working Class Cape Town, 1950 to

1990," in H. Willemse, ed., *More Than Brothers*, 35; N. Alexander, "Noncollaboration in the Western Cape, 1943–1963," in W. James and M. Simons, eds., *The Angry Divide: Social and Economic History of the Western Cape* (Cape Town: David Philip, 1989), 183.

4. The acceptance in 1943 of seats on the Coloured Advisory Council by five moderate TLSA leaders led to an irreparable split in the organization. The radicals instigated a campaign of ostracizing these "quislings" and unsuccessfully tried to capture the executive at the TLSA's June 1943 conference. The majority moderate faction felt that the TLSA had been so badly compromised by the radicals' behavior that they preferred hiving off and forming their own organization, the Teachers' Educational and Professional Association. See M. Adhikari, "*Let Us Live for Our Children*": *The Teachers' League of South Africa, 1913–1940* (Cape Town: UCT Press, 1993), 67–71, for details.

5. For a study of *Grassroots*, see I. van Kessel, "*Grassroots:* From Washing Lines to Utopia," in Switzer and Adhikari, *Resistance Press*, 283–326.

6. For some examples, see *Educational Journal*, July 1958, May 1959, January 1960, January 1961, and October 1962.

7. Ibid., March 1958.

8. When Kies's banning order prevented him from filling this post, his wife, Helen, took on the mantle.

9. *Educational Journal*, April 1962, emphases in the original. P. W. Botha was minister of the Department of Coloured Affairs, constituted as a separate department in 1959, and I. D. du Plessis was secretary of Coloured Affairs. "Outa Tom and his *handlangers*" was a reference to Tom Swarts and the Union Council of Coloured Affairs.

10. *Educational Journal*, April 1962.

11. For some examples, see M. Adhikari, "Hope, Fear, Shame, Frustration: Continuity and Change in the Expression of Coloured Identity in White Supremacist South Africa, 1910–1994" (Ph.D. diss., University of Cape Town, 2002), 246.

12. *Educational Journal*, April 1965.

13. Ibid., January 1967.

14. Chisolm, "Making the Pedagogical More Political," 242, 256–57. The fellowships, of which there were no more than half a dozen operating at any one time, met monthly to discuss issues of political, social, and cultural interest, with meetings usually drawing between twenty and fifty people.

15. *Educational Journal*, September 1971. See also the March and April 1976 issues for the article "Black Consciousness: A Reactionary Tendency: Origins, Nature and Fallacies of a Dogma."

16. Rashid Seria, interviewed by Mohamed Adhikari, 16 January 1998.

17. *South*, 25 April 1992.

18. James Matthews, interviewed by Mohamed Adhikari, 18 June 2002.

19. H. Willemse, "More Than Brothers: Peter Clarke and James Matthews at Seventy," in Willemse, *More Than Brothers*, 7, 12–13; "Living through a Chunk of the Century: Peter Clarke and James Matthews in Conversation with Kayzuran Jaffer and Hein Willemse, 2 May 1999," in Willemse, *More Than Brothers*, 41–43.

20. *New Age*, published between 1954 and 1962, was the successor to the *Guardian*. It was the unofficial mouthpiece of the Congress Movement and the banned Communist Party.

21. J. Matthews, "The Pictures Swirling in My Mind," in Willemse, *More Than Brothers*, 104.

22. James Matthews, interviewed 18 June 2002.

23. M. Mzamane and D. Howarth, "Representing Blackness: Steve Biko and the Black Consciousness Movement," in Adhikari and Switzer, *Resistance Press*, 186.

24. James Matthews, interviewed by Paul Boobyer, 8 November 1988, 1.

25. See Adhikari, "Continuity and Change" 250 n. 28, for a list of the main anthologies.

26. For a comprehensive list of Matthews's output, see Willemse, *More Than Brothers*, 133–37.

27. Willemse, "More Than Brothers," 13, 16; "Living through a Chunk of the Century," 40. Matthews attests that by the mid-1980s, "BLAC produced nine books and three broadsheets before it was forced to close through lack of funds and pressure from the state." See Matthews, "Pictures Swirling," 107.

28. Matthews, "Pictures Swirling," 107; K. Jaffer, "'Being Coloured Is a State of Mind' or the Complexities of Identity, Selfhood and Freedom in the Writing of James Matthews," in Willemse, *More Than Brothers*, 117; Willemse, "More Than Brothers," 13; James Matthews, interviewed 18 June 2002. The apartheid government refused to renew the passport after it had expired.

29. Matthews, "Pictures Swirling," 102; Willemse, "More Than Brothers" 14–15.

30. R. Rive, *Writing Black* (Cape Town: David Philip, 1981), 11.

31. James Matthews, interviewed 8 October 1988, 3.

32. See Adhikari, "Continuity and Change," 252–53, for the reasons for this shift.

33. G. Cornwell, "James Matthews' 'Protest Songs': The Problem of Evaluation," in M. Chapman, ed., *Soweto Poetry* (Johannesburg: McGraw-Hill, 1982), 184.

34. M. Serote, "Panel on Contemporary South African Poetry," *Issue* 6, no. 1 (1976): 25.

35. M. Mzamane, "Cultivating a People's Voice in the Criticism of South African Literature," *Staffrider* 9, no. 3 (1991): 68.

36. Willemse, "More Than Brothers," 7. In 1982, Cornwell, "Protest Songs," 184, still regarded Matthews's poetry as "yet unmatched in polemical intensity."

37. J. Matthews, ed., *Black Voices Shout! An Anthology of Poetry* (Cape Town: BLAC, 1974), was banned within three weeks of its appearance, leaving the straitened Matthews with a large printer's account and no means of recouping his outlay. The volume was republished under the same title by Troubadour Books, Austin, TX, in 1975.

38. See Willemse, *More Than Brothers*, 134, for a list of such poems.

39. Matthews, "Pictures Swirling," 106; "Living through a Chunk of the Century," 40.

40. Cornwell, "Protest Songs," 184.

41. Matthews used this as the subtitle of his next volume of poetry, *Pass Me a Meatball, Jones: A Gathering of Feelings* (Cape Town: BLAC, 1977). See also James Matthews, interviewed 8 November 1988, 6; J. Matthews, *No Time for Dreams* (Cape Town: BLAC, 1981), back cover, and Jaffer, "Being Coloured," 114.

42. Matthews, *Black Voices Shout!* 64; J. Matthews and G. Thomas, *Cry Rage!* (Johannesburg: Spro-cas Publications, 1972), 9, 12.

43. Matthews and Thomas, *Cry Rage!* 5, 7, 55.

44. Ibid., introduction and also 5, 14, 28, 40, 65; Matthews, *Black Voices Shout!* 19.

45. Matthews and Thomas, *Cry Rage!* 64. See also 6–7, 50, and the poem "Liberal Student Crap!" 33 in the same volume.

46. Matthews and Thomas, *Cry Rage!* 31, 35. On 19 August 1971, Wrankmore, an Anglican chaplain, started a forty-day fast at the Muslim shrine, or *kramat*, on Signal Hill to publicize his call for a judicial inquiry into the death in detention of Imam Haron two years earlier. By the time he broke his fast sixty-seven days later, the National Party government still refused to consider his demand, but Wrankmore had succeeded in attracting international attention to the abuse and torture of political prisoners in South African jails.

47. Matthews, *Black Voices Shout!* 29; Matthews and Thomas, *Cry Rage!* 51; Willemse, "More Than Brothers," 15. Matthews explains that he had

in the meantime become much more politicized. James Matthews, interviewed 18 June 2002.

48. See Matthews and Thomas, *Cry Rage!* 52, for the one example where he uses *black* and *brown*, and 51 and 59 for the two instances in which he used the term *Coloured*.

49. These were rural resettlement camps set up by the apartheid government for those Africans "endorsed out" of white South Africa under influx control laws.

50. Matthews and Thomas, *Cry Rage!* 6–9, 16–19, 23–24, 58–59.

51. *SASO Newsletter,* September 1970.

52. James Matthews, interviewed 18 June 2002.

53. J. Matthews, *The Party Is Over* (Cape Town: Kwela, 1997).

54. Ibid., 62.

55. J. Matthews, "An Autumn Afternoon: An Excerpt from an Unpublished Novel," *Realities* (Cape Town: BLAC, 1985), 7.

56. "Living through a Chunk of the Century," 45.

57. *Cape Argus,* 16 February 1998.

58. Messina, "Kleurlinge Is Ook Swart," 124–25, 130–31; B. Hirson, *Year of Fire, Year of Ash: The Soweto Revolt—Roots of a Revolution?* (London: Zed Press, 1979), 221–22.

59. The title derives from an "in-joke" between Matthews and fellow detainee Peter Jones. Inmates, who had recently won a legal battle for the right to buy foodstuff from outside, pooled their money to buy essentials. Jones used this opportunity to indulge his predilection for meatballs. James Matthews, interviewed 18 June 2002. This volume was later republished as *Poems from a Prison Cell* (Cape Town: Realities, 2001).

60. Matthews, *No Time for Dreams,* 62.

61. Van Kessel, "*Grassroots,*" 324.

62. See Switzer and Adhikari, *Resistance Press,* for detailed treatment of this development.

63. Van Kessel, "*Grassroots,*" 283.

64. Rehana Rossouw, telephone interview with author, 12 October 1998; See, in addition, D. Pinnock, "Popularize, Organize, Educate and Mobilize: Culture and Communication in the 1980s," in K. Tomaselli and P. Louw, eds., *The Alternative Press in South Africa* (Bellville, SA: Anthropos, 1991), 133–54, who used the acronym as the title of his chapter.

65. Among these victories were getting the Cape Town City Council to change the due dates for electricity payments, to repair washing lines in the courtyards of council flats in Lavender Hill, and allowing people who had built penthouse roofs (*afdakkies*) without having the necessary

building plans passed to keep these structures. See van Kessel, "*Grass-roots*," 284–85, 292–93, 302.

66. R. Abel, *Politics by Other Means: Law in the Struggle against Apart-heid, 1980–1994* (New York: Routledge, 1995), 264, 300; *South*, 16 March 1989 and 26 October 1989; *Cape Times*, 14 July 1998; Van Kessel, "*Grass-roots*," 315.

67. Van Kessel, "*Grassroots*," 319.

68. By the mid-1980s, the UDF leadership started exercising direct control over editorial policy. Van Kessel, "*Grassroots*," 308.

69. *Saamstaan* (meaning "stand together"), an Afrikaans community newspaper in Oudtshoorn that serviced the southern Cape and Karoo re-gions, was a highly successful venture set up in early 1984 by *Grassroots*. G. Claassen, "Breaking the Mould of Political Subservience: *Vrye Week-blad* and the Afrikaans Alternative Press," in Switzer and Adhikari, *Resis-tance Press*, 442–47.

70. The paper adopted a five-week publishing cycle to avoid having to register as a newspaper and hence having to make a R40,000 (US$13,500–20,000) security deposit. See note 80 to this chapter.

71. Moegsien Williams, interviewed by Mohamed Adhikari, 15 July 1988; South Press Services, *Free the Press* (Cape Town: South Press Ser-vices, 1988), 7; *South* Newspaper Collection (hereafter SNC), University of Cape Town Manuscripts and Archives Division, Seria, Weekly News-paper Project Feasibility Report, 4.

72. K. Tomaselli and P. Louw, "The Struggle for Legitimacy: State Pres-sures on the Media, 1950–1991," in Tomaselli and Louw, *Alternative Press*, 81, 89; Abel, *Politics by Other Means*, 259; G. Jackson, *Breaking Story: The South African Press* (Boulder, CO: Westview Press, 1993), 10, 152, 160–61.

73. SNC, Seria, Feasibility Report, 1986, Summary, 1, 6; SNC, Adden-dum on consultations, 2–3; S. Johnson, "Resistance in Print I: *Grassroots* and Alternative Publishing," in Tomaselli and Louw, *Alternative Press*, 199.

74. For detailed discussion of the media curbs introduced by the vari-ous states of emergency, see Jackson, *Breaking Story*, 128–57, and Abel, *Politics by Other Means*, 259–310.

75. *Grassroots* and other community papers were newsletters rather than newspapers.

76. SNC, R. Seria, Feasibility Report, Introduction, 1–2; Rashid Seria, interviewed by Mohamed Adhikari, 16 January 1998; Moegsien Williams, interviewed, 15 July 1998.

77. SNC, Seria, Feasibility Report, 2–3; SNC, M. Brey and R. Seria, "Memorandum for the Private Placing of Shares in South Press Services Limited" (Cape Town, nd), 4. See also A. Akhalwaya, "The Role of the Al-ternative Press," *Nieman Reports* 42 (1988): 14–18.

78. For biographical information on Seria and Williams, see Adhikari, "Continuity and Change," 271–72.

79. SNC, Seria, Feasibility Report; Rashid Seria, interviewed, 16 January 1998; Rashid Seria, interviewed by Mohamed Adhikari, 11 October 1998; Moegsien Williams, interviewed, 15 July 1998.

80. Rashid Seria, interviewed, 16 January 1998; Moegsien Williams, interviewed, 15 July 1998. A number of documents relating to the consultation process are in the private possession of Rashid Seria, henceforth referred to as the Seria Private Collection (SPC). A precise value cannot be provided here because the Rand-US Dollar exchange rate was particularly volatile during this period and fluctuated wildly between R2.00 and R3.00 to the Dollar.

81. SNC, Seria, Feasibility Report, summary, 3.

82. Ibid.; SNC, G. Berger, Memorandum to *South* Directors, 4 September 1993; Moegsien Williams, interviewed, 15 July 1998.

83. This message was carried in *South's* appearances panel.

84. *South,* 19 September 1987.

85. Moegsien Williams, interviewed, 15 July 1998.

86. SNC, Minutes of meeting of trustees of South Press Services, 30 July 1987; Minutes of meeting of trustees and board of directors of South Press Services, 1 October 1987; Rashid Seria, interviewed, 16 January 1998; Moegsien Williams, interviewed, 15 July 1998; Derek Carelse, interviewed by Mohamed Adhikari, 13 October 1998; Rehana Rossouw, e-mail communication with author, 20 July 1998.

87. *South,* 2 April 1987.

88. Rashid Seria, interviewed, 16 January 1998.

89. K. Tomaselli and P. Louw, "The South African Progressive Press under Emergency, 1986–1989," in Tomaselli and Louw, *Alternative Press,* 186; SPC, Letter from R. Seria to W. Minnaard, ICCO, Netherlands, 19 May 1988.

90. The dour, reserved Stoffel Botha was known as *dom* (stupid) Stoffel in antiapartheid circles, in contrast to his more adroit and engaging colleague Stoffel van der Merwe, minister of information, referred to as *slim* (smart) Stoffel. Anton Harber, former editor of the *Weekly Mail,* coined the term *to stoffel* (meaning "to snuff out") to ridicule *dom* Stoffel's banning of newspapers, including the month-long banning of the *Weekly Mail. Mail and Guardian,* 24 April 1998.

91. For detailed discussion of state harassment of the alternative press during this period, see Abel, *Politics by Other Means,* 259–72.

92. For more detailed discussion of this harassment and victimization of *South* staff by the state's security apparatus, see Adhikari, "*South,*" in Switzer and Adhikari, *Resistance Press,* 344–47.

93. Moegsien Williams, interviewed, 15 July 1998; Rashid Seria, interviewed, 16 January 1998, 11 October 1998; SNC, "Report of the Chairperson," August 1988; *Mail and Guardian*, 24 April 1998.

94. For details, see Adhikari, "*South*," in Switzer and Adhikari, *Resistance Press*, 346–47.

95. Rashid Seria, interviewed, 16 January 1998, 11 October 1998; Moegsien Williams, interviewed, 15 July 1998; Derek Carelse, interviewed, 13 October 1998; SNC, Annual Report, 1988, 14; SNC, Minutes of Meeting of the Trustees and Board of Directors of South Press Services, 30 July 1987.

96. Moegsien Williams, interviewed, 15 July 1998; Rashid Seria, interviewed, 16 January 1998, 11 October 1998.

97. See *South*, 27 August 1987, for a cartoon that explicitly does this. The cartoon is reproduced in Adhikari, "*South*," in Switzer and Adhikari, *Resistance Press*, 350.

98. See *Grassroots*, April 1980, for the only time the paper used the term *black*.

99. See Adhikari, "Continuity and Change," 282, for examples.

100. *Grassroots*, June 1981 and July–August 1982.

101. Ibid., April 1983.

102. Ibid., August 1984. See also van Kessel, "*Grassroots*," 305–6.

103. *Grassroots*, August 1984.

104. Ibid., February 1985.

105. Van Kessel, "*Grassroots*," 308.

106. See *Grassroots*, August 1983 and December 1985, for examples.

107. *South*, 9 February 1988.

108. For some examples, see ibid., 25 June 1986, 6 August 1987, 24 September 1987, 4 February 1988, 21 July 1988, 26 February 1989, 4 April 1990, and 18 April 1991.

109. Ibid., 7 July 1988.

110. The *Cape Herald*, published from the late 1960s, was a white-owned newspaper exclusively aimed at Coloured readers. Its sensationalist style ensured it a degree of commercial success until the introduction of television in the mid-1970s progressively undermined its profitability.

111. Derek Carelse, interviewed, 13 October 1998.

112. Rashid Seria, interviewed, 11 October 1998; Moegsien Williams, interviewed, 15 July 1998.

113. Moegsien Williams, interviewed, 15 July 1998.

114. Rashid Seria, interviewed, 11 October 1998; Moegsien Williams, interviewed, 15 July 1998.

115. In the 1990s, a greater attempt was made to report news from the African townships. *South's* nonpolitical news remained overwhelmingly focused on the Coloured community, though.

116. Moegsien Williams, interviewed, 15 July 1998.

117. *South* was acutely aware of the looming funding crisis. See the series of three articles on foreign funding in *South*, 7–21 March 1991.

118. See Adhikari, "*South*," in Switzer and Adhikari, *Resistance Press*, 355–57, 360–61, for details.

119. SNC, Memo to *South* Board of Directors Finance Sub-committee, 15 November 1993; Rashid Seria, interviewed, 16 January 1998. SNC, Minutes of *South* Bosberaad with Directors and Hod's, 7 May 1994.

120. SNC, Advertising Report, 7 May 1994.

121. C. Giffard, A. de Beer, and E. Steyn, "New Media for the New South Africa," in F. Eribo and W. Jong-Ebot, eds., *Press Freedom and Communication in Africa* (Trenton, NJ: Africa World Press, 1997), 85.

122. Abel, *Politics by Other Means*, 302.

123. SNC, Minutes of Bosberaad, 7 May 1994.

124. *South*, 4 July 1991.

125. Ibid., 12 September 1991.

126. Ibid., 13 June 1991.

127. See ibid., 4 July 1991, 7 November 1991, 2 May 1992, 14 November 1992, 20 February 1993, 3 September 1993, and 9 December 1994 for a few examples.

128. Ibid., 14 August 1993.

129. Ibid., 27 February 1992.

130. For a detailed account of the closure of *South*, see Adhikari, "*South*," in Switzer and Adhikari, *Resistance Press*, 361–67.

131. See ibid., 367–69, for a discussion of *South's* successes.

132. Moegsien Williams, interviewed, 15 July 1998.

133. *South*, 13 June 1991. Spine Road, one of the main thoroughfares in Mitchell's Plain, was a favored place for activists to erect barricades of burning tires and where numerous clashes between youths and police took place.

134. Their commitment to nonracism, a different issue, is not being questioned.

135. *South*, 13 June 1991.

Chapter 6: New Responses to Old Dilemmas

1. H. Willemse, "Die Beeldvorming van Piet Uithalder in die *APO* (1909–1922)," *Stilet* 5, no. 2 (1993): 63–76.

2. See ibid., "Beeldvorming," 65. Coloured rejectionism was not entirely dead yet, as demonstrated by the Duncan chapter cited earlier.

3. In fact, at one point, Willemse claimed that Straatpraatjes was *the* first known example of such resistance expressed in the Afrikaans language. See H. Willemse, "'Ik is Onbekend, ma Ik is Een van de Ras so Moet My nie Veracht nie': Die Beeldvorming van Piet Uithalder in die *APO* 1909–1922," paper presented at the fifth congress of the Afrikaanse Letterkunde-Vereeniging, University of Stellenbosch, 10 October 1992, 3.

4. For an earlier and more detailed version of this argument, see M. Adhikari, "'Wanner Gaat ons tog en Eksampel Neem Uit die Wit Man s'Boek': Resistance, Protest and Accommodation in Piet Uithalder's 'Straatpraatjes' Column, 1909–1922," *Stilet* 8, no. 2 (1996): 86–102.

5. For more detail on this dialect, consult R. Pheiffer, "Straatpraatjes— 'n Vroeë Voorbeeld van Alternatiewe Afrikaans," in M. Adhikari, ed., *Straatpraatjes: Language, Politics and Popular Culture in Cape Town, 1909–1922* (Pretoria: van Schaik, 1997), 141–62.

6. *APO*, 24 May 1909, 23 October 1909, and 26 February 1912.

7. See Adhikari, *Straatpraatjes*, 20–128., for a selection of illustrated and annotated Straatpraatjes columns.

8. Straatpraatjes was, for example, used to level accusations of the embezzlement of APO funds at John Tobin, its former vice president, and to finger Charles Hull, Transvaal treasurer and Member of the Legislative Assembly for Georgetown, as a "pass-white." Adhikari, *Straatpraatjes*, 63, 67, 81.

9. For details, see M. Adhikari, "Hope, Fear, Shame, Frustration: Continuity and Change in the Expression of Coloured Identity in White Supremacist South Africa, 1910–1994" (Ph.D. diss., University of Cape Town, 2002), 303–4.

10. H. Willemse, "'Ons het Lang Genoeg Gekruip Net Soes Gedierte na die Wit Man': Enkele Aspekte van Piet Uithalder se 'Straatpraatjes' Rubriek, (*APO*), 'n Eerste Verkenning," unpublished paper presented at the conference "Taal en Identiteit," Leiden University, June 1992.

11. *APO*, 24 May 1909 and 19 June 1909.

12. *APO*, 19 June 1909 and 11 March 1911. The quotations are translated from vernacular Afrikaans.

13. Adhikari, *Straatpraatjes*, 182–85.

14. C. van der Merwe, *Breaking Barriers: Stereotypes and the Changing of Values in Afrikaans Writing, 1875–1990* (Amsterdam: Rodopi, 1994), 22–34; V. February, *Mind Your Colour: The "Coloured" Stereotype in South African Literature* (London: Kegan Paul, 1981), chap. 1; J. Gerwel, *Literatuur en Apartheid: Konsepsies van "Gekleurdes" in die Afrikaanse Roman* (Kasselsvlei, SA: Kampen, 1983).

15. *APO*, 3 July 1909 and 3 June 1911. They were "particular," among other things, about their behavior and with whom they socialized.

16. For some examples, see *APO*, 24 May 1909, 26 February 1910, and 12 August 1911.

17. *APO*, 20 November 1909, 2 July 1910, 16 July 1910, 3 June 1911, and 17 June 1911.

18. Pheiffer, "Vroeë Voorbeeld," 158–59.

19. Adhikari, *Straatpraatjes*, 176–81.

20. Willemse, "Beeldvorming," 63–76. See also Willemse, "Ik is Onbekend," 163–75.

21. Willemse, "Beeldvorming," 63–64.

22. Ibid., 66–70, 71.

23. *APO*, 24 May 1909.

24. See *APO*, 24 May 1909, 19 June 1909, 17 June 1911, and 10 October 1919 for examples.

25. Refer to *APO*, 5 June 1909, 4 December 1909, 12 February 1910, 11 March 1911, 17 June 1911, and 18 November 1911 for further examples.

26. *APO*, 28 August 1909, 12 February 1910, 13 July 1912, 22 March 1913, and 21 September 1919. The term "kaffer/kaffir," which refers to the indigenous Bantu-speaking peoples of South Africa, was, however, not nearly as pejorative in the early twentieth century as it was later to become.

27. *APO*, 3 August 1910 and 18 November 1911.

28. *APO*, 15 January 1910, 29 January 1910, 12 February 1910, and 26 February 1910.

29. Willemse, "Beeldvorming," 63–64.

30. *APO*, 19 June 1909 and 17 June 1911. Translated from vernacular Afrikaans.

31. M. Adhikari, *Straatpraatjes*, 7–8.

32. S. Trapido, "The Origin and Development of the African Political Organization," *Institute of Commonwealth Studies Collected Seminar Papers on Southern Africa*, University of London 1 (1969–70), 97, 103; G. Lewis, *Between the Wire and the Wall: A History of South African "Coloured" Politics* (Cape Town: David Philip, 1987), 27–63; *APO*, 14 January 1911; *South African News*, 9 August 1905.

33. *APO*, 8 March 1913. Translated from vernacular Afrikaans. Transvalers were called greybellies because *vaal* is the Afrikaans word for gray.

34. *APO*, 13 January, 1912 and 11 February 1922. Translated from vernacular Afrikaans.

35. *APO*, 12 November 1919 and 17 April 1920. Translated from vernacular Afrikaans.

36. *APO*, 15 August 1919. Translated from vernacular Afrikaans.

37. Willemse, "Beeldvorming," 65, 70, 71.

38. D. Crummey, *Banditry, Rebellion and Social Protest in Africa* (London: James Currey, 1986), 10.

39. Ebrahim Rassool, interviewed by Shaheen Ariefdien, September 2003.

40. Emille Jansen, interviewed by Shaheen Ariefdien, September 2003; e-mail communication with Shaheen Ariefdien, 2 July 2004.

41. Rasool interview.

42. Some aspects of Coloured identity in the new South Africa are dealt with in W. James, D. Caliguire, and K. Cullinan, eds., *Now That We Are Free* (Boulder, CO: Lynne Rienner, 1996), and Z. Erasmus, *Coloured by History, Shaped by Place: New Perspectives on Coloured Identities in Cape Town* (Cape Town: Kwela Books, 2001).

43. According to the 1996 census report, Coloureds formed a majority of 54.2 percent in the Western Cape and 51.8 percent in the Northern Cape.

44. M. Adhikari, "Coloureds," in C. Saunders, advisory ed., *Illustrated Dictionary of South African History* (Sandton, SA: Ibis Books, 1994), 79.

45. This led to an abortive attempt to form a party of reformed gangsters by Pastor Albern Martins, himself a reformed gangster. It would appear that Martins has since relapsed, as he was recently arrested and charged with illegal possession of abalone and trading in cocaine. *Cape Times*, 14 January 2005.

46. This name is provocative because it mimics the name of the Afrikaner Weerstandbeweging, the most notorious of the white, ultra-right-wing, paramilitary organizations.

47. Apartheid legislation was not completely consistent in its specification of racial categories. Compare, for example, the three broad racial categories of the Population Registration Act with the four categories of the Group Areas Act.

48. *Argus*, 2 April 2003.

49. *Business Report*, 26 February 2004; S. van der Berg and M. Louw, "Changing Patterns of South African Income Distribution: Toward Time Series Estimates of Distribution and Poverty," working paper, Department of Economics and Bureau for Economic Research, Stellenbosch University, 2003.

50. D. McDonald, "The Bell Tolls for Thee: Cost Recovery, Cut-offs, and the Affordability of Municipal Services in South Africa," in D. McDonald and J. Pape, eds., *Cost Recovery and the Crisis of Service Delivery in South Africa* (Cape Town: HSRC, 2002), 167, 171.

51. J. Thomson, "A Murderous Legacy: Coloured Homicide Trends in South Africa," and T. Leggett, "Still Marginal: Crime in the Coloured Community," both in *S.A. Crime Quarterly* 7 (March 2004). See also *Cape Times*, 27 May 2004.

52. For recent examples, see *Cape Times*, 2 May 2004 and 11 February 2005.

53. My observation, based on personal experience and extensive reading of the press, is that Coloured racial hostility toward Africans and the ANC government appears to have abated somewhat between the general election of 2004 and the time of writing in May 2005 despite continued racially based political wrangling at the provincial party level, such as Democratic Alliance attempts to exploit Coloured insecurity and the mobilization of an Africanist challenge to Ebrahim Rasool's leadership of the ANC in the Western Cape.

54. See, for example, *Cape Times*, 25 August 1995, 28 March 1996, and 4 December 1996; *Mail and Guardian*, 1 December 2000.

55. Anonymous, "Retracing the Path of Memory," manuscript, African Studies Library, University of Cape Town, 1996; *Cape Times*, 9 October 1996, 16 October 1996, 17 October 1996, 21 October 1996, and 2 December 1996.

56. Erasmus, *Coloured by History*, 13–28. For a detailed evaluation of Erasmus's book, see M. Adhikari, "Coloured Identity and Creolization in Cape Town," *Social Dynamics* 29, no.1 (2003): 158–70.

57. Personal communication from Associate Professor Nigel Penn, Department of Historical Studies, University of Cape Town, who attended the conference as an observer, 16 July 2004.

Select Bibliography

Pamphlets and Contemporary Publications

A Declaration to the People of South Africa from the Non-European Unity Movement. Cape Town: NEUM, 1951.

Desmore, A. *With the Second Cape Corps through Central Africa.* Cape Town: Citadel, 1920.

Hendricks, D., and C. Viljoen. *Student Teacher's History Course: For the Use in Coloured Training Colleges.* Paarl, SA: Huguenot Drukkery, 1936.

Jordaan, K. *"The Origin and Development of Segregation in South Africa—By W. P. van Schoor—A Critique."* *Discussion* 1, no. 3 (1951).

———. "Jan van Riebeeck: His Place in South African History." *Discussion* 1, no. 5 (1952).

Kies, B. *Background of Segregation.* Cape Town: Anti-CAD, 1943.

———. *The Basis of Unity.* Cape Town: Non-European Unity Committee, 1945.

———. *The Contribution of the Non-European Peoples to World Civilization.* Cape Town: Teachers' League of South Africa, 1953.

Maurice, E. *The Colour Bar in Education.* Cape Town: Teachers' League of South Africa, 1957.

Tabata, I. *The Building of Unity.* Cape Town: Non-European Unity Committee, 1945.

———. *The Awakening of a People.* London: Spokesman Books, 1974.

van Schoor, W. *The Origin and Development of Segregation in South Africa.* Cumberwood, SA: APDUSA, 1986.

Ziervogel, C. *The Coloured People and the Race Problem.* Ceres, SA: Weber, 1936.

———. *Brown South Africa.* Cape Town: Maskew Miller, 1938.

———. *Who Are the Coloured People?* Cape Town: The African Bookman, 1944.

Theses, Seminar and Conference Papers, and Unpublished Manuscripts

Adhikari, M. "Hope, Fear, Shame, Frustration: Continuity and Change in the Expression of Coloured Identity in White Supremacist South Africa, 1910–1994." Ph.D. diss., University of Cape Town, 2002.

Bickford-Smith, V. "Commerce, Class and Ethnicity in Cape Town, 1875–1902." Ph.D. diss., Cambridge University, 1988.

Drew, A. "Social Mobilization and Racial Capitalism in South Africa." Ph.D. diss., University of California, 1991.

du Pre, R. "Confrontation, Co-optation and Collaboration: The Response and Reaction of the Labour Party to Government Policy, 1965–1984." Ph.D. diss., Rhodes University, 1994.

du Preez, R. "The Role and Policies of the Labour Party of South Africa, 1975–1978." Master's thesis, University of South Africa, 1987.

Hommel, M. "The Organization and Evolution of Coloured Political Movements in South Africa." Ph.D. diss., York University, 1978.

JanMohamed, A. "The Literary and Political Functions of Marginality in the Colonial Situation." African Studies Center Working Papers no. 52. Boston University, 1982.

Kayser, R. "The Struggle for Land and Liberty in South Africa: The Revolutionary Path of the Non-European Unity Movement of South Africa, 1933–1970." Bachelor's honors thesis, University of Cape Town, 1997.

———. "Land and Liberty: The Non-European Unity Movement and the Agrarian Question, 1933–1975." Master's thesis, University of Cape Town, 2002.

Lawrence, P. "Class, Colour Consciousness and the Search for Identity at the Kimberley Diamond Diggings, 1867–1893." Master's thesis, University of Cape Town, 1994.

Lewis, G. "The Reaction of the Cape 'Coloureds' to Segregation." Ph.D. diss., Queens University, 1984.

Maurice, E. "The Development of Policy in Regard to the Education of Coloured Pupils at the Cape, 1880–1940." Ph.D. diss., University of Cape Town, 1966.

Messina, E. "Swartbewustheid in die Wes-Kaap, 1970–1984." Ph.D. diss., University of the Western Cape, 1995.

Muzondidya, J. "Sitting on the Fence or Walking a Tightrope? A Political History of the Coloured Community of Zimbabwe, 1945–1980." Ph.D. diss., University of Cape Town, 2001.

Rhoda, J. H. "A Contribution toward the Study of Education among the Cape Coloured People." Bachelor's of education thesis, University of Cape Town, 1929.

Shifrin, T. "New Deal for Coloured People? A Study of National Party Policies towards the Coloured People." Bachelor's honors thesis, University of Cape Town, 1962.

Stone, G. "An Ethnographic and Socio-Semantic Analysis of Lexis among Working-Class, Afrikaans-Speaking, Coloured Adolescents and Young Adult Males in the Cape Peninsula, 1963–1990." Master's thesis, University of Cape Town, 1991.

van der Ross, R. "A Political and Social History of the Cape Coloured People, 1880–1970." 4 vols. Manuscript, University of Cape Town Manuscripts and Archives Division, 1973.

Viljoen, S. "Non-racialism Remains a Fiction: From Richard Rive's *Buckingham Palace, District Six*, to K. Sello Duiker's *The Quiet Violence of Dreams.*" Paper presented at the "Burden of Race" conference, University of the Witwatersrand, July 2001.

Villa-Vicencio, H. "Colour, Citizenship and Constitutionalism: An Oral History of Political Identity among Middle Class Coloured People with Special Reference to the Formation of the Coloured Advisory Council in 1943 and the Removal of the Male Franchise in 1956." Master's thesis, University of Cape Town, 1995.

Willemse, H. "'Ons Het Lang Genoeg Gekruip Net soes Gedierte Na die Wit Man': Enkele Aspekte van Piet Uithalder se 'Straatpraatjes' Rubriek, (APO), 'n eerste verkenning." Paper presented at the conference "Taal en Identiteit." Leiden University, June 1992.

———. "'Ik is Onbekend, ma Ik is Een van de Ras so Moet My nie Veracht nie': Die Beeldvorming van Piet Uithalder in die APO 1909–1922." Paper presented at the fifth congress of the Afrikaanse Letterkundevereeniging. University of Stellenbosch, October 1992.

Articles and Chapters in Books

Adhikari, M. "Responses to Marginality: Twentieth Century Coloured Politics." *South African Historical Journal* 20 (1988).

———. "The Sons of Ham: Slavery and the Making of Coloured Identity." *South African Historical Journal* 27 (1992).

———. "God, Jan van Riebeeck and the Coloured People: The Anatomy of a South African Joke." *Southern African Discourse* 4 (1992).

———. "Coloureds." In C. Saunders, advisory ed., *An Illustrated Dictionary of South African History.* Johannesburg: Ibis Books, 1994.

———. "'A Drink-Sodden Race of Bestial Degenerates': Attitudes toward Race and Class in the *Educational Journal*, 1913–1940." In E. van Heyningen, ed., *Studies in the History of Cape Town*, vol. 7. Cape Town: UCT Press, 1994.

———. "James Arnold La Guma." In E. Verwey, ed., *New Dictionary of South African Biography*. Pretoria: HSRC Publishers, 1995.

———. "Blinded by Anger: Coloured Experience under Apartheid." *South African Historical Journal* 35 (1996).

———. "'Wanner Gaat Ons Tog en Eksampel Neem Uit die Wit Man s'boek': Resistance, Protest and Accommodation in Piet Uithalder's 'Straatpraatjes' Column, 1909–1922." *Stilet* 8, no. 2 (1996).

———. "Coloured Identity and the Politics of Language: The Sociopolitical Context of Piet Uithalder's 'Straatpraatjes' Column." In Adhikari, *Straatpraatjes*.

———. "'The Product of Civilization in Its Most Repellent Manifestation': Ambiguities in the Racial Perceptions of the *APO*, 1909–1923." *Journal of African History* 38, no. 2 (1997).

———. "Voice of the Coloured Elite: *APO*, 1909–1923." In L. Switzer, ed., *South Africa's Alternative Press: Voices of Protest and Resistance, 1880s–1960s*. Cambridge: Cambridge University Press, 1997.

———. "Abdullah Abdurahman, 1872–1940." In *They Shaped Our Century: The Most Influential South Africans of the Twentieth Century*. Cape Town: Human and Rousseau, 1999.

———. "'You Have the Right to Know': *South*, 1987–1994." In Switzer and Adhikari, *South Africa's Resistance Press*.

Akhalwaya, A. "The Role of the Alternative Press." *Nieman Reports* 42 (1988).

Alexander, N. "Non-collaboration in the Western Cape, 1943–1963." In W. James Simons and M. Simons, eds., *The Angry Divide: Social and Economic History of the Western Cape*. Cape Town: David Philip, 1989.

Bhahba, H. "The Other Question: Difference, Discrimination and the Discourse of Colonialism." In F. Barker, P. Hulme, M. Iverson, and D. Loxley, eds., *Literature, Politics and Theory: Papers from the Essex Conference, 1976–1984*. London: Methuen, 1986.

Bickford-Smith, V. "The Origins and Early History of District Six to 1910." In S. Jeppie and C. Soudien, eds., *The Struggle for District Six: Past and Present*. Cape Town: Buchu Books, 1990.

Caliguire, D. "Voices from the Communities." In W. James, D. Caliguire and K. Cullinan, eds., *Now That We Are Free*.

Chisolm, L. "Making the Pedagogical More Political, and the Political More Pedagogical: Educational Traditions and Legacies of the Non-

European Unity Movement, 1943–1985." In W. Flanagan, C. Hemson, J. Muller, and N. Taylor, comps., *Vintage Kenton: A Kenton Education Association Commemoration*. Cape Town: Maskew Miller Longman, 1994.

Coetzee, J. "Blood, Taint, Flaw, Degeneration: The Novels of Sarah Gertrude Millin." In J. Coetzee, ed., *White Writing: On the Culture of Letters in South Africa*. Sandton, SA: Radix, 1988.

———. "Man's Fate in the Novels of Alex La Guma." In D. Attwell, ed., *Doubling the Point: Essays and Interviews*. London: Harvard University Press, 1992.

Cornwell, G. "James Matthews' 'Protest Songs': The Problem of Evaluation." In M. Chapman, ed., *Soweto Poetry*. Johannesburg: McGraw-Hill, 1982.

———. "Justin Alexander La Guma." In Verwey, ed., *Dictionary of South African Biography*.

Duncan, N. "'Listen Here, Just Because YOU Think I'm a Coloured . . .' Responses to the Construction of Difference in Racist Discourses." In N. Duncan, P. D. Gqola, M. Hofmeyr, T. Schefer, F. Malunga, and M. Mashige, eds., *Discourses on Difference, Discourses on Oppression*. Cape Town: Centre for Advanced Studies of African Society, 2002.

Erasmus, Z. "Introduction: Re-imagining Coloured Identities in Post-apartheid South Africa." In Erasmus, *Coloured by History*.

Evans, W. "From the Land of Canaan to the Land of Guinea: The Strange Odyssey of the 'Sons of Ham.'" *American Historical Review* 85, no. 1 (1980).

Field, S. "Fragile Identities: Memory, Emotion and Coloured Residents of Windermere." In Erasmus, *Coloured by History*.

———. "Remembering Experience, Interpreting Memory: Life Stories from Windermere." *African Studies* 60, no. 1 (2001).

Giliomee, H. "The Non-racial Franchise and Afrikaner and Coloured Identities, 1910–1994." *African Affairs* 94, no. 375 (1995).

Hendricks, C. "'Ominous' Liaisons: Tracing the Interface between 'Race' and 'Sex' at the Cape." In Erasmus, *Coloured by History*.

Jaffer, K. "'Being Coloured Is a State of Mind' or the Complexities of Identity, Selfhood and Freedom in the Writing of James Matthews." In Willemse, *More Than Brothers*.

Jeppie, S. "Popular Culture and Carnival in Cape Town: The 1940s and 1950s." In Jeppie and Soudien, *The Struggle for District Six*.

Johnson, S. "Resistance in Print I: *Grassroots* and Alternative Publishing." In K. Tomaselli and P. Louw, eds., *The Alternative Press in South Africa*. Bellville, SA: Anthropos, 1991.

Kapp, P. "Richard van der Ross." In *They Shaped Our Century*.

Lewis, D. "Writing Hybrid Selves: Richard Rive and Zoë Wicomb." In Erasmus, *Coloured by History*.

"Living through a Chunk of the Century: Peter Clarke and James Matthews in Conversation with Kayzuran Jaffer and Hein Willemse, 2 May 1999." In Willemse, *More Than Brothers*.

Louw, P. "Resistance in Print II: Developments in the Cape: *Saamstaan*, *Grassroots* and *South*." In Tomaselli and Louw, *Alternative Press*.

Matthews, J. "An Autumn Afternoon: An Excerpt from an Unpublished Novel." *Realities* Cape Town: BLAC, 1985.

———. "The Pictures Swirling in My Mind." In Willemse, *More Than Brothers*.

Messina, E. "Kleurlinge is Ook Swart: Swartbewustheid in die Wes-Kaap tot 1977." *Kronos* 22 (1995).

Mzamane, M. "Cultivating a People's Voice in the Criticism of South African Literature." *Staffrider* 9, no. 3 (1991).

Nasson, B. "The Unity Movement: Its Legacy in Historical Consciousness." *Radical History Review* 46–47 (1990).

Odendaal, A. "Developments in Popular History in the Western Cape in the 1980s." *Radical History Review* 46–47 (1990).

Pheiffer, R. "Straatpraatjes—'n Vroë Voorbeeld van Alternatiewe Afrikaans." In Adhikari, *Straatpraatjes*.

Pinnock, D. "Popularize, Organize, Educate and Mobilize: Culture and Communication in the 1980s." In Tomaselli and Louw, *Alternative Press*.

Ponelis, F. "Codes in Contradiction: The Socio-linguistics of Straatpraatjes." In Adhikari, *Straatpraatjes*.

Ratele, K. "'Mixed' Relations." In K. Ratele and N. Duncan, eds., *Social Psychology: Identities and Relationships*. Cape Town: University of Cape Town Press, 2003.

Roberge, P. "The Formation of Afrikaans." In R. Mestrie, ed., *Language and Social History: Studies in South African Socio-linguistics*. Cape Town: David Philip, 1995.

Serote, M. "Panel on Contemporary South African Poetry." *Issue* 6, no. 1 (1976).

Shifrin, T. "Abdullah Abdurahman." In W. de Kock, ed., *Dictionary of South African Biography*, vol. 1. Cape Town: Nasionale Boekhandel, 1968.

Smith, A. "The Hotnot Syndrome: Myth-Making in South African School Textbooks." *Social Dynamics* 9, no. 2 (1983).

Soudien, C. "Social Conditions, Cultural and Political Life in Working Class Cape Town, 1950 to 1990." In Willemse, *More Than Brothers*.

Stone, G. "Identity among Lower-Class Coloured People." In M. Whisson and H. van der Merwe, eds., *Coloured Citizenship in South Africa.* Cape Town: Abe Bailey Institute of Inter-racial Studies, 1972.

Switzer, L. "Review of Adhikari, M., *Teachers' League.*" *Journal of African History* 36, no. 2 (1995).

Trapido, S. "The Origin and Development of the African Political Organization." *Institute of Commonwealth Studies Collected Seminar Papers on Southern Africa,* University of London 1 (1969–70).

Trapido, S. "'The Friends of the Natives': Merchants, Peasants and the Political and Ideological Structure of Liberalism in the Cape." In S. Marks and A. Atmore, eds., *Economy and Society in Pre-industrial South Africa.* London: Longman, 1980.

Unterhalter, B. "Changing Attitudes to 'Passing for White' in an Urban Coloured Community." *Social Dynamics* 1, no. 1 (1975).

van Kessel, I. "*Grassroots:* From Washing Lines to Utopia." In Switzer and Adhikari, *Resistance Press.*

Wade, M. "Art and Morality in Alex La Guma's *A Walk in the Night.*" In K. Parker, ed., *The South African Novel in English: Essays in Criticism and Society.* New York: African Publishing, 1978.

Wicomb, Z. "Shame and Identity: The Case of the Coloured in South Africa." In D. Attridge and R. Jolly, eds., *Writing South Africa: Literature, Apartheid and Democracy, 1970–1995.* Cambridge: Cambridge University Press, 1998.

Willemse, H. "Die Beeldvorming van Piet Uithalder in die *APO,* (1909–1922)." *Stilet* 5, no. 2 (1993).

———. "'Ik Is Onbekend, Ma Ik is Een van de Ras so Moet My nie Veracht nie': Die Beeldvorming van Piet Uithalder." In Adhikari, *Straatpraatjes.*

———. "More Than Brothers: Peter Clarke and James Matthews at Seventy." In Willemse, *More Than Brothers.*

Witz, L. "The 'Write Your Own History' Project." *Radical History Review* 46–47 (1990).

Worden, N. "Adjusting to Emancipation: Freed Slaves and Farmers in Mid-nineteenth Century Southwestern Cape." In James and Simons, *The Angry Divide.*

Books

Abel, R. *Politics by Other Means: Law in the Struggle against Apartheid, 1980–1994.* New York: Routledge, 1995.

Abrahams, C. *Alex La Guma.* Boston: Twayne, 1985.

Adhikari, M. *"Let Us Live for Our Children": The Teachers' League of South Africa, 1913–1940.* Cape Town: UCT Press, 1993.

———, ed. *Jimmy La Guma: A Biography by Alex La Guma.* Cape Town: Friends of the South African Library, 1997.

———, ed. *Straatpraatjes: Language, Politics and Popular Culture in Cape Town, 1909–1922.* Pretoria: van Schaik, 1997.

———. *"Against the Current": A Biography of Harold Cressy, 1889–1916.* Cape Town: Harold Cressy High School, 2000.

———, ed. *Dr. Abdurahman: A Biographical Memoir by J. H. Raynard.* Cape Town; Friends of the South African Libarary, 2002.

Alexander, N. (No Sizwe). *One Azania, One Nation: The National Question in South Africa.* London: Zed Press, 1979.

Balutansky, K. *Alex La Guma: The Representation of a Political Conflict.* Washington, DC: Three Continents Press, 1989.

Bhana, S. *Gandhi's Legacy: The Natal Indian Congress, 1894–1994.* Pietermaritzburg, SA: Natal University Press, 1997.

Bickford-Smith, V. *Ethnic Pride and Racial Prejudice in Victorian Cape Town, 1875–1902.* Cambridge: Cambridge University Press, 1995.

Bickford-Smith, V., E. van Heyningen, and N. Worden. *Cape Town in the Twentieth Century: An Illustrated Social History.* Cape Town: David Philip, 1999.

Bosman, D., I. van der Merwe, and L. Hiemstra, eds. *Tweetalige Woordeboek: Afrikaans-Engels/Engels-Afrikaans.* Cape Town: Tafelberg, 1967.

Botha, D. *Die Opkoms van Ons Derde Stand.* Cape Town: Human and Rousseau, 1960.

Branford, J., and W. Branford, eds. *A Dictionary of South African English.* Cape Town: Oxford University Press, 1991.

Cell, J. *The Highest Stage of White Supremacy: The Origins of Segregation in South Africa and the American South.* Cambridge: Cambridge University Press, 1982.

Chandramohan, B. *Trans-ethnicity in Modern South Africa: The Writings of Alex La Guma.* Lampeter, UK: Mellen Research University Press, 1992.

Cobley, A. *Class and Consciousness: The Black Petty Bourgeiosie in South Africa, 1924 to 1950.* Westport, CT: Greenwood Press, 1990.

Crummey, D. *Banditry, Rebellion and Social Protest in Africa.* London: James Currey, 1986.

Cruse, H. *Die Opheffing van die Kleurlingbevolking: Deel I; Aanvangsjare, 1652–1795.* Stellenbosch, SA: Christen Studentevereniging, 1947.

Crwys-Williams, J. *The Penguin Dictionary of South African Quotations.* Sandton, SA: Penguin, 1999.

Davenport, T., and C. Saunders. *South Africa: A Modern History.* London: Macmillan, 2000.

Davies, R., D. O'Meara, and S. Dlamini, comps. *The Struggle for South Africa: A Reference Guide.* London: Zed Books, 1984.

Dickie-Clark, H. *The Marginal Situation: A Sociological Study of a Coloured Group.* New York: Routledge and Kegan Paul, 1996.

Dover, C. *Half-Caste.* London: Secker and Warburg, 1937.

Doxey, G. *The Industrial Colour Bar in South Africa.* Cape Town: Oxford University Press, 1961.

Drew, A. *South Africa's Radical Tradition: A Documentary History,* vol. 2. Cape Town: Buchu Books, Mayebuye Books, and UCT Press, 1997.

———. *Discordant Comrades: Identities and Loyalties on the South African Left.* Aldershot, UK: Ashgate, 2000.

Dubow, S. *Illicit Union: Scientific Racism in Modern South Africa.* Johannesburg: Witwatersrand University Press, 1995.

Dundas, A. *Cracking Jokes: Studies of Sick Humour Cycles and Stereotypes.* New York: Ten Speed Press, 1987.

du Pre, R. *The Making of Racial Conflict in South Africa.* Johannesburg: Skotaville, 1990.

———. *Separate but Unequal: The "Coloured" People of South Africa—A Political History.* Johannesburg: Jonathan Ball, 1994.

Edgar, R. ed. *An African American in South Africa: The Travel Notes of Ralphe Bunche.* Johannesburg: Witwatersrand University Press, 1992.

Erasmus, Z. *Coloured by History, Shaped by Place: New Perspectives on Coloured Identities in Cape Town.* Cape Town, South Africa: Kwela Books, 2001.

February, V. *Mind Your Colour: The "Coloured" Stereotype in South African Literature.* London: Kegan Paul, 1981.

Goldin, I. *Making Race: The Politics and Economics of Coloured Identity in South Africa.* Cape Town: Maskew Miller Longman, 1987.

Gordon, J. *Under the Harrow: Lives of White South Africans Today.* London: Heinemann, 1988.

Grobbelaar P., ed. *Readers' Digest Afrikaans-Engelse Woordeboek.* Cape Town: Readers' Digest Association of South Africa, 1987.

Harlan, L. *Booker T. Washington: The Making of a Black Leader.* New York: Oxford University Press, 1972.

Higgs, C. *The Ghost of Equality: The Public Lives of D. D. T. Jabavu of South Africa, 1885–1959.* Athens: Ohio University Press, 1997.

Hommel, M. *Capricorn Blues: The Struggle for Human Rights in South Africa.* Toronto: Culturama, 1981.

————, ed. *Contributions of Non-European Peoples to World Civilization.* Johannesburg: Skotaville, 1989.

Horrell, M. *Legislation and Race Relations: A Summary of the Main South African Laws Which Affect Race Relations.* Johannesburg: South African Institute of Race Relations, 1971.

Hugo, P. *Quislings or Realists? A Documentary Study of Coloured Politics in South Africa.* Johannesburg: Ravan Press, 1978.

Hutt, W. *The Economics of the Colour Bar: A Study of the Economic Origins and Consequences of Racial Segregation in South Africa.* London: Andre Deutch, 1964.

Jackson, G. *Breaking Story: The South African Press.* Boulder, CO: Westview Press, 1993.

Jaffe, H. (Mnguni). *Three Hundred Years.* Cape Town: New Era Fellowship, 1952.

————. *European Colonial Despotism: A History of Oppression and Resistance in South Africa.* London: Kamak House, 1994.

Jahoda, G. *Images of Savages: Ancient Roots of Modern Prejudice in Western Culture.* London: Routledge, 1999.

James, W., D. Caliguire, and K. Cullinan, eds. *Now That We Are Free: Coloured Communities in a Democratic South Africa.* Boulder, CO: Lynne Rienner, 1996.

JanMohamed, A. *Manichean Aesthetics: The Politics of Literature in Colonial Africa.* Amherst: University of Massachusetts Press, 1983.

La Guma, A. *A Walk in the Night and Other Stories.* London: Heinemann, 1967.

————. *And a Threefold Cord.* London: Kliptown Books, 1988.

————. *The Stone Country.* London: Heinemann, 1974.

————. *In the Fog of the Season's End.* London: Heinemann, 1972.

————. *Time of the Butcherbird.* London: Heinemann, 1979.

Lelyveld, J. *Move Your Shadow: South Africa Black and White.* London: Michael Joseph, 1985.

Lewis, G. *Between the Wire and the Wall: A History of South African "Coloured" Politics.* Cape Town: David Philip, 1987.

MacMillan, W. *The Cape Colour Question: A Historical Survey.* Cape Town: Balkema, 1968.

Manuel, G. *Kampvegters.* Cape Town: Nasou, 1967.

Marable, M. *W. E. B. Du Bois: Black Radical Democrat.* Boston: Twayne, 1986.

Marais, J. *The Cape Coloured People, 1652–1937.* Johannesburg: Witwatersrand University Press, 1968.

Marks, S. *The Ambiguities of Dependence in South Africa: Class, Nationalism and State in Twentieth Century Natal.* Johannesburg: Ravan Press, 1986.

Martin, D. C. *Coon Carnival: New Year in Cape Town, Past and Present.* Cape Town: David Philip, 1999.

Marx, A. *Lessons of Struggle: South African Internal Opposition, 1960–1990.* New York: Oxford University Press, 1992.

Matthews, J., ed. *Black Voices Shout! An Anthology of Poetry.* Cape Town: BLAC, 1974.

———, ed. *Black Voices Shout! An Anthology of Poetry.* Austin, TX: Troubadour Books, 1975.

———. *Pass Me a Meatball, Jones: A Gathering of Feelings.* Cape Town: BLAC, 1977.

———. *No Time for Dreams.* Cape Town: BLAC, 1981.

———. *The Park and Other Stories.* Johannesburg: Ravan Press, 1983.

———. *The Party Is Over.* Cape Town: Kwela, 1997.

———. *Poems from a Prison Cell.* Cape Town: Realities, 2001.

Matthews, J., and G. Thomas. *Cry Rage!* Johannesburg: Spro-cas Publications, 1972.

McLennan, B. *Apartheid: The Lighter Side.* Cape Town: Chameleon Press, 1990.

Meier, A. *Negro Thought in America.* Ann Arbor: Michigan University Press, 1966.

Millin, S. *God's Stepchildren.* Cape Town: A. D. Donker, 1924.

———. *The South Africans.* London: Constable, 1926.

Nasson, B. *Abraham Esau's War: A Black South African War in the Cape, 1899–1902.* Cambridge: Cambridge University Press, 1991.

Nederveen Pieterse, J. *White on Black: Images of Africa and Blacks in Western Popular Culture.* New Haven, CT: Yale University Press, 1992.

Nkosi, L. *Tasks and Masks: Themes and Styles of African Literature.* London: Longman, 1981.

———. *Home and Exile and Other Selections.* New York: Longman, 1983.

Odendaal A., and R. Field. *Liberation Chabalala: The World of Alex La Guma.* Bellville, SA: Mayebuye Books, 1993.

Patterson, S. *Colour and Culture in South Africa: A Study of the Status of Cape Coloured People in the Union of South Africa.* London: Routledge and Kegan Paul, 1953.

Rive, R. *Writing Black.* Cape Town: David Philip, 1981.

Silva, P., managing ed. *A Dictionary of South African English on Historical Principles.* Oxford: Oxford University Press, 1996.

Simons H., and R. Simons. *Class and Colour in South Africa, 1850–1950.* London: Penguin, 1969.

Stepan, N. *The Idea of Race in Science: Great Britain, 1800–1960.* London: Macmillan, 1982.

Switzer, L., and M. Adhikari, eds. *South Africa's Resistance Press: Alternative Voices in the Last Generation under Apartheid.* Athens: Ohio University Press, 2000.

Thompson, L. *The Cape Coloured Franchise.* Johannesburg: South African Institute of Race Relations, 1949.

——. *The Unification of South Africa, 1902–1910.* London: Oxford University Press, 1960.

van der Ross, R. *Myths and Attitudes: An Inside Look at the Coloured People.* Cape Town: Tafelberg, 1979.

——. *The Rise and Decline of Apartheid: A Study of Political Movements among the Coloured People of South Africa, 1880–1985.* Cape Town: Tafelberg, 1986.

——. *"Say It Out Loud": The APO Presidential Addresses and Other Major Political Speeches, 1906–1940, of Dr. Abdullah Abdurahman.* Bellville, SA: University of the Western Cape Institute for Historical Research, 1990.

Venter, A. *Coloured: A Profile of Two Million South Africans.* Cape Town: Human and Rousseau, 1974.

Watson, G. *Passing for White.* London: Tavistock, 1970.

Weinberg, M., ed. *W. E. B. duBois: A Reader.* New York: Harper and Row, 1970.

Willemse, H., ed. *More Than Brothers: Peter Clarke and James Matthews at Seventy.* Cape Town: Kwela Books, 2000.

Worden, N. *Slavery in Dutch South Africa.* Cambridge: Cambridge University Press, 1985.

Worden, N., E. van Heyningen, and V. Bickford-Smith. *Cape Town: The Making of a City.* Cape Town: David Philip, 1998.

Young, R. *Colonial Desire: Hybridity in Theory, Culture and Race.* London: Routledge, 1995.

Yousaf, N. *Alex La Guma: Politics and Resistance.* Portsmouth, UK: Heinemann, 2001.

Index

poor quality of, 33, 63, 64, 65
popular perceptions of, 15, 22, 25, 26,
   29, 33, 38, 39
progressionist approaches to, 36–45,
   49, 90–91
radical approaches to, 37, 43, 45–49,
   108–9
social constructionist interpretations
   and, 35–36
synopsis of, 1–6
traditionalist approaches to, 36
van der Ross on, 53–57, 63–65
Zievogel on, 41–45, 46, 63–65
See also Coloured identity; Coloured
   people
Coloured identity
   agency in creation of, xiii–xiv, 25, 36
   ambiguities and contradictions in,
      xiv, 12, 17, 36, 63, 66, 72–73, 74,
      79, 80–81, 85, 86, 88–89, 90, 93,
      96, 106, 110–11, 123–26, 130,
      143–44, 163, 169–70, 172–73
   assimilationism and, xii–xiv, 3, 4,
      8–10, 11–12, 16, 18, 21, 39, 44, 49,
      68, 69, 70, 72, 73–76, 77, 78, 80, 82,
      85, 86, 88, 89, 92–93, 94, 96, 182
   colonialism and, 22, 25, 27–29,
      38–39, 168
   continuity and change in expression
      of, xii–xiii, 1, 6–8, 17, 32, 162, 175,
      189n. 3
   controversy around, xi, 5, 63, 155,
      175
   imposed by whites, regarded as, xi, 6,
      34–36, 46–53, 57–63, 64, 126
   intermediate status in racial hierarchy,
      xii, xiii, 3, 10–14, 15, 18, 19, 21,
      25, 72, 79, 80, 86, 92–93, 96, 170,
      176, 181
   marginality and, xii, xiii, 13, 17–19,
      29–30, 33, 36, 63, 65, 68, 71, 72,
      74–76, 79, 80, 86, 96, 97, 172, 176,
      181
   negative connotations attached to,
      xii, xiii, 1, 12–17, 21–23 (*see also*
      Coloured people: racially attributed
      traits of; racially inferior, perceived
      as; stereotyping of)
   origins of, xiii, 2–3, 8, 25, 61–62,
      190n. 3

in postapartheid period, xii–xiii, 6, 7,
   18, 20, 22, 30, 31–32, 162, 175–87
product of miscegenation, regarded
   as, xi, xii, 2, 13–15, 20, 22, 23,
   24–25, 31, 34, 36–45, 48, 49, 50,
   53–57, 62, 64, 65, 169, 197n. 88
rainbow nationalism and, 184, 185,
   204n. 98
as residual category, 2, 14
shame, sense of, attached to, xi, xii,
   15, 22–23
See also Coloured history; Coloured
   people; Coloured rejectionism
Coloured labor preference policy, 179
Coloured people
   Africans, attitudes toward and rela-
      tionship with, xi, xiii, 2, 6, 7,
      11–12, 15, 16–20, 24, 30, 44, 47,
      50–52, 61, 72–73, 75, 76, 80–81,
      92–95, 107, 109, 110, 120–22,
      124–27, 135–46, 152–56, 159,
      162–63, 169, 174, 176, 178–82,
      185, 186, 229n. 53
   alcoholic abuse and, 26, 27, 161, 168,
      181, 197n. 95
   apartheid and, 4, 5, 9, 17, 19–21, 35,
      51, 53, 54–55, 58, 62, 64, 113,
      123, 133, 168–69, 178
   brown, characterized as, 2, 10–11,
      12, 15, 26, 27, 42, 92, 124, 126,
      127, 132–33, 169, 185, 221n. 48
   Bushman/*Boesman* racial slur
      against, 24, 28, 126, 144, 199n. 14
   civil rights, erosion of, 3–4, 70–72, 171
   class attitudes and differences within,
      xii, xiv, 8, 15–17, 29, 60–61, 67–70,
      72, 78–80, 81–85, 96, 123, 128–29,
      135, 137, 155, 157, 160, 163–64,
      166–67, 178–81, 198n. 113
   demography of, 2, 17, 18, 177
   economic discrimination against,
      3–4, 179, 180–81
   education and, 3–4, 63, 71, 75, 76, 80,
      81–83, 93–94, 108, 168, 204n. 4
   franchise and, 3–5, 18, 52, 55, 71, 78,
      104, 176, 207n. 53
   goffel stereotype and, 23, 196n. 76
   Hottentot/*Hotnot* racial slur against,
      28, 29, 61, 107, 126, 159, 169,
      198n. 107, 199n. 114

Trotskyist tradition of the South African Left, 22, 45–49, 51, 64, 98–104, 114, 115–16. *See also* Coloured history: radical approaches to; Fourth International Organization of South Africa; Jordaan, Kenneth; Non-European Unity Movement

Tsotsi, Wycliffe, 103
Tugwana, Gabu, 158

Uithalder, Piet, 163–74. *See also* Straatpraatjes
Umkhonto we Sizwe, 156
Union Council of Coloured Affairs, 55, 198n. 103, 218n. 9
Union of Black Journalists, 136
Union of South Africa, creation of, 3, 7, 70–71, 162
United Afrikaner League, 5, 56, 68, 167, 172
United Democratic Front, 6, 58, 132, 135, 146, 148, 150, 153, 155, 158, 159, 160, 175, 177, 183, 192n. 20, 220n. 68

van den Berg, Servaas, 180
van der Merwe stereotype, 30
van der Ross, David, 93
van der Ross, Richard, 53–57, 63, 64, 65, 155
van der Stel, Simon, 111, 214n. 53
van Kessel, Ineke, 146, 154
van Niekerk, Maria, 23
van Riebeeck, Jan, 19–31, 39, 43, 47, 48, 51, 64, 197n. 91
as "father" of Coloured people, 20, 21, 22, 31, 51, 64, 197n. 91
as symbol of white supremacism, 19–20, 29, 30–31
van Riebeeck Tercentenary Festival, 47, 104
van Schoor, Willem, 45–46, 47, 115
van Wyk Louw, N. P., 11
Vereeniging, Treaty of (1902), 66, 71
Viljoen, Christo, 39–41
Viljoen, Shaun, 100
Vollenhoven, Sylvia, 160

Wade, Michael, 121
Wage Act (1925), 4

A Walk in the Night (La Guma), 98, 116–30
Abrahams, Cecil on, 121, 123
academic appraisals of, 121–22
Balutansky, Kathleen, on, 121, 122, 123
Chandramohan, Balasubrian, on, 121, 122
Coetzee, J. M., on, 121
Coloured identity in, 122–24, 126–29
District Six and, 116, 117, 118–20
JanMohamed, Abdul, on, 121, 122
language usage and Coloured identity in, 128–29
manicheanism and, 121–22, 127, 129
plot, synopsis of, 116–17
publishing history of, 117
racial themes in, 120–21, 122–24, 126–29
title, meanings of, 122–23
Wade, Michael, on, 121
Youssaf, Nahem on, 121
See also La Guma, Alex
Washington, Booker T., 74–76, 89, 206n. 36, 210n. 97
Watermeyer Commission, 88
Weekly Mail, 149, 158, 223n. 90
Wicomb, Zoë, 22–23
Willemse, Hein, 138, 143, 162–64, 167–74
analysis of Straatpraatjes, 167–69
critique of, 169–74
Williams, Mrs. (in *Grassroots* cartoon strip), 153–54
Williams, Moegsien, 149, 150, 151, 156, 160
Wilson, Anthony, 180
Workers Party of South Africa, 48
World War I, 77–78, 171, 172, 207n. 54
World War II, 113, 212n. 12
Wrankmore, Rev. Bernard, 141, 220n. 46

X, Khoisan, 185

Young Communist League, 118
Youssaf, Nahem, 121

Zievogel, Christian, 11, 41–45, 49, 63, 64, 65
Zonnebloem Training College, 39, 41